Personal
Ministry
Handbook

Personal Ministry Handbook

Larry Richards

BAKER BOOK HOUSE
Grand Rapids, Michigan 49506

ISBN: 0-8010-7736-2

Printed in the United States of America

Contents

Introduction

Christian ministry is essentially interpersonal. Whether the ministry is that of a television personality or of friends visiting over a cup of coffee, the personal dimension is critical. The person receiving ministry must trust the other; the person ministering must have a deep sensitivity and love for the one with whom he or she is dealing.

This *Personal Ministry Handbook* draws together many Scripture passages and principles that give you and me guidance for our personal ministry to others. These passages are organized in two sections.

"Principles for Personal Ministry" (part 1) focuses on the basics of one-to-one ministry. It looks first of all at our relationship with the Lord. Our relationship with Jesus and our growth in him are the keys to that personal integrity that leads others to trust us. In part 1 you will also find Scripture passages that show how to build ministering relationships with others, communicate Christ effectively, and disciple others.

Our relationships with others are likely to lead us into situations in which we feel unready and unequipped for ministry. And often the problems of others do call for the help of trained counselors. However, "Resources for Personal Ministry" (part 2) gives insight into ministry in specific circumstances. In part 2 you will find articles, arranged alphabetically, that give insights into a problem, hints on how to help, and Scripture verses that apply to the situation. Solving the problem may require more help than you can provide. But you can still be God's agent of healing, and through your loving concern the Lord may do more than you can imagine to meet the deepest needs of your friends.

This *Personal Ministry Handbook* is a resource book. How is it used? First of all, for personal growth. Each chapter begins with a discussion of the facet of personal ministry it explores. Relevant Bible verses are then grouped by categories.

Second, this book can be used as a resource when a friend's suffering or a neighbor's indifference makes you wonder how you can reach out to help. Turn to the articles about specific topics and look prayerfully through the Scriptures listed. This may give just the insight you need to minister sensitively and successfully.

Third, this book can be used for training in personal ministry. A leader's guide (Appendix A) tells how to structure training sessions which can help believers respond to God's call that we minister to others.

All personal ministry, of course, ultimately depends for its effectiveness on the sovereign grace of God. You and I are channels through which his love can and will flow.

PART ONE

Principles
for Personal Ministry

1

Know the Lord

In our personal ministry to others we exercise a priestly function. On the one hand we represent the person to the Lord by
our prayers and concern. On the other hand, we represent God
to the person whose life we touch. Our lives and our words
are channels through which God communicates himself and
his truth to others. What a wonderful and awesome privilege!
And what a significant responsibility.

Equipping for Ministry

Deuteronomy 6:4–9 unveils the secret that helps us understand how you and I can be equipped to minister.

> Hear, O Israel: The LORD our God, the LORD is one. Love
> the LORD your God with all your heart and with all your soul
> and with all your strength. These commandments that I give
> you today are to be upon your hearts. Impress them on your
> children. Talk about them when you sit at home and when
> you walk along the road, when you lie down and when you
> get up. Tie them as symbols on your hands and bind them
> on your foreheads. Write them on the doorframes of your
> houses and on your gates.

The passage begins by affirming the existence of God as the Lord: "The LORD *is* one." The Hebrew word *Jahweh* is translated "Lord" in English. This is the personal name of God. It reveals his essential identity and means "the One who is always present." You and I are to know God and to acknowledge him as one who is always with us — to meet every need, to enable and to support.

This God has revealed himself to us, and we are called to respond to him. We are to love him, increasingly making him the center of our lives as we give heart and soul and strength to his service.

We show our love for God by taking "these commandments that [he] give[s] [us] today" into our hearts. We bond his Word to our personalities and weave it into our lives. The word *today* is important. None of us knows God or his Word completely. For each of us, knowing God involves a process of growth. What is vital is that in each today you and I respond to what we do know of the Lord.

How wonderful this is as we think of our calling to ministry. We don't have to know everything to be able to help others. We need not have taken everything in the Bible into our hearts and lives. All we need to do is to be responsive to what God is teaching us now. We live by the Word we understand today, sure that tomorrow will bring us more understanding and more growth.

Establishing a Framework for Ministry

There is more in Deuteronomy 6:4–9 concerning ministry. The phrase *impress them on your children* reminds us that ministry of God's Word is very personal and intimate. Whenever we talk to others about the Lord and his Word, we need to treat them in the close, warm, and loving way that characterizes family relationships.

Finally, Deuteronomy 6:4–9 encourages God's people to weave ministry to others into daily life. Ministry is to take place not just in church buildings or classrooms. We are also to talk about God and his words "when [we] sit at home and when [we] walk along the road, when [we] lie down and when [we] get up."

Thus this one passage in the Old Testament quickly establishes a framework for a personal ministry of the Word of God. You and I are to focus on him as the object of our growing love. You and I grow as we remain sensitive to what God is teaching us each day and as we take each insight to heart. As growing persons we are now able to minister to others, and we are to carry out our ministry by building family-like, loving relationships with them. Finally, our ministry is most effective when it involves talking about God and his words in the context of daily life — in our sitting and walking and relaxing with others.

Meditating on the Qualities and Works of God

How do we come to know better this God "who is always with us"? We come to know him through his revelation of himself in history and in the words of Scripture. So let's begin our preparation for personal ministry by remembering and meditating on some of the things God has told us about himself in his trustworthy Word.

Consider God the source of all. The Bible unveils God as Creator and initiator of all good things.

"In the beginning, O Lord, you laid the foundations of the earth,
and the heavens are the work of your hands.
They will perish, but you remain;
they will all wear out like a garment.
You will roll them up like a robe;
like a garment they will be changed.
But you remain the same,
and your years will never end." [Heb. 1:10–12]

"To whom will you compare me?
    Or who is my equal?" says the Holy One.
Lift your eyes and look to the heavens:
    Who created all these?
He who brings out the starry host one by one,
    and calls them each by name.
Because of his great power and mighty strength,
    not one of them is missing. [Isa. 40:25–26]

"This is what the LORD says —
    Israel's King and Redeemer, the LORD Almighty:
I am the first and I am the last;
    apart from me there is no God." [Isa. 44:6]

Blessed is he whose help is the God of Jacob,
    whose hope is in the LORD his God,
the maker of heaven and earth,
    the sea, and everything in them —
    the LORD, who remains faithful forever.
He upholds the cause of the oppressed
    and gives food to the hungry.
The LORD sets prisoners free,
    the LORD gives sight to the blind,
the LORD lifts up those who are bowed down,
    the LORD loves the righteous. . . .

The LORD reigns forever,
    your God, O Zion, for all generations.

Praise the LORD. [Ps. 146:5–8, 10]

"Praise be to you, O LORD,
    God of our father Israel,
    from everlasting to everlasting.
Yours, O LORD, is the greatness and the power
    and the glory and the majesty and the splendor,
    for everything in heaven and earth is yours.
Yours, O LORD, is the kingdom;
    you are exalted as head over all.
Wealth and honor come from you;
    you are the ruler of all things.
In your hands are strength and power
    to exalt and give strength to all." [1 Chron. 29:10–12]

"You are worthy, our Lord and God,
 to receive glory and honor and power,
for you created all things,
 and by your will they were created
 and have their being." [Rev. 4:11]

"Blessed be your glorious name, and may it be exalted above all blessing and praise. You alone are the LORD. You made the heavens, even the highest heavens, and all their starry host, the earth and all that is on it, the seas and all that is in them. You give life to everything, and the multitudes of heaven worship you." [Neh. 9:5–6]

Consider God's uniqueness. He is eternal, unchangeable, all-powerful, ever-present, all-knowing, and holy, and yet rich in love, grace, mercy, and patience.

Before the mountains were born
 or you brought forth the earth and the world,
 from everlasting to everlasting you are God. [Ps. 90:2]

For this is what the high and lofty One says —
 he who lives forever, whose name is holy:
"I live in a high and holy place,
 but also with him who is contrite and lowly in spirit. . . ."
 [Isa. 57:15]

Because God wanted to make the unchanging nature of his purpose very clear to the heirs of what was promised, he confirmed it with an oath. [Heb. 6:17]

Every good and perfect gift is from above, coming down from the Father of the heavenly lights, who does not change like shifting shadows. [James 1:17]

"O LORD, God of our fathers, are you not the God who is in heaven? You rule over all the kingdoms of the nations. Power and might are in your hand, and no one can withstand you." [2 Chron. 20:6]

Great is our Lord and mighty in power;
 his understanding has no limit. [Ps. 147:5]

Do you not know?
  Have you not heard?
The LORD is the everlasting God,
  the Creator of the ends of the earth.
He will not grow tired or weary,
  and his understanding no one can fathom. [Isa. 40:28]

  "I make known the end from the beginning,
    from ancient times, what is still to come.
  I say: My purpose will stand,
    and I will do all that I please." [Isa. 46:10]

Nothing in all creation is hidden from God's sight. Everything is uncovered and laid bare before the eyes of him to whom we must give account. [Heb. 4:13]

  "O LORD, God of Israel, there is no God like you in heaven above or on earth below — you who keep your covenant of love with your servants who continue wholeheartedly in your way." [1 Kings 8:23]

The LORD is compassionate and gracious,
  slow to anger, abounding in love.
He will not always accuse,
  nor will he harbor his anger forever;
he does not treat us as our sins deserve
  or repay us according to our iniquities.
For as high as the heavens are above the earth,
  so great is his love for those who fear him.... [Ps. 103:8–11]

But because of his great love for us, God, who is rich in mercy, made us alive with Christ even when we were dead in transgressions — it is by grace you have been saved. [Eph. 2:4–5]

Consider God's faithfulness and moral perfections. Although he is holy and the moral judge of the universe, God is committed to love and redeem his creation.

  The LORD is gracious and compassionate,
    slow to anger and rich in love.
  The LORD is good to all;
    he has compassion on all he has made.

All you have made will praise you, O LORD;
  your saints will extol you.
They will tell of the glory of your kingdom. . . . [Ps. 145:8–11]

The LORD is faithful to all his promises
  and loving toward all he has made.
The LORD upholds all those who fall
  and lifts up all who are bowed down.
The eyes of all look to you,
  and you give them their food at the proper time.
You open your hand
  and satisfy the desires of every living thing. [Ps. 145:13–16]

. . . the Lord knows how to rescue godly men from trials and to hold the unrighteous for the day of judgment, while continuing their punishment. This is especially true of those who follow the corrupt desire of the sinful nature and despise authority. [2 Peter 2:9–10]

"The fear of the LORD is the beginning of wisdom,
  and knowledge of the Holy One is understanding.
For through me your days will be many,
  and years will be added to your life.
If you are wise, your wisdom will reward you. . . ." [Prov.
  9:10–12]

Consider God's historic acts in behalf of his people.

"You saw the suffering of our forefathers in Egypt; you heard their cry at the Red Sea. You sent miraculous signs and wonders against Pharaoh, against all his officials and all the people of his land, for you knew how arrogantly the Egyptians treated them. You made a name for yourself, which remains to this day. You divided the sea before them, so that they passed through it on dry ground, but you hurled their pursuers into the depths, like a stone into mighty waters. By day you led them with a pillar of cloud, and by night with a pillar of fire to give them light on the way they were to take." [Neh. 9:9–12]

The LORD said, "I have indeed seen the misery of my people in Egypt. I have heard them crying out because of their slave drivers, and I am concerned about their suffering. So I have come down to rescue them from the hand of the Egyptians and to bring them up out of that land into a good and spacious land, a land flowing with milk and honey...." [Exod. 3:7–8]

> Great is the LORD and most worthy of praise;
>   his greatness no one can fathom.
> One generation will commend your works to another;
>   they will tell of your mighty acts.
> They will speak of the glorious splendor of your majesty,
>   and I will meditate on your wonderful works.
> They will tell of the power of your awesome works,
>   and I will proclaim your great deeds. [Ps. 145:3–6]

Consider God's revelation of himself in Jesus, the fullest and most beautiful unveiling of his character and person.

For the law was given through Moses; grace and truth came through Jesus Christ. No one has ever seen God, but God the One and Only, who is at the Father's side, has made him known. [John 1:17–18]

... but in these last days [God] has spoken to us by his Son, whom he appointed heir of all things, and through whom he made the universe. The Son is the radiance of God's glory and the exact representation of his being, sustaining all things by his powerful word. [Heb. 1:2–3]

> Who, being in very nature God,
>   did not consider equality with God something to be grasped,
> but made himself nothing,
>   taking the very nature of a servant,
>   being made in human likeness.
> And being found in appearance as a man,
>   he humbled himself
>   and became obedient to death —
>   even death on a cross!
> Therefore God exalted him to the highest place
>   and gave him the name that is above every name,

that at the name of Jesus every knee should bow,
in heaven and on earth and under the earth,
and every tongue confess that Jesus Christ is Lord,
to the glory of God the Father. [Phil. 2:6–11]

He is the image of the invisible God, the firstborn over all creation. For by him all things were created: things in heaven and on earth, visible and invisible, whether thrones or powers or rulers or authorities; all things were created by him and for him. He is before all things, and in him all things hold together. And he is the head of the body, the church; he is the beginning and the firstborn from among the dead, so that in everything he might have the supremacy. For God was pleased to have all his fullness dwell in him, and through him to reconcile to himself all things, whether things on earth or things in heaven, by making peace through his blood, shed on the cross. [Col. 1:15–20]

The Word became flesh and made his dwelling among us. We have seen his glory, the glory of the One and Only, who came from the Father, full of grace and truth. [John 1:14]

Consider what God in Jesus has done for you and me, and how his actions have enriched our lives.

He provided redemption for his people;
he ordained his covenant forever —
holy and awesome is his name.

The fear of the LORD is the beginning of wisdom;
all who follow his precepts have good understanding.
To him belongs eternal praise. [Ps. 111:9–10]

Many, O LORD my God,
are the wonders you have done.
The things you planned for us
no one can recount to you;
were I to speak and tell of them,
they would be too many to declare. [Ps. 40:5]

Praise be to the God and Father of our Lord Jesus Christ! In his great mercy he has given us new birth into a living

hope through the resurrection of Jesus Christ from the dead,
and into an inheritance that can never perish, spoil or fade —
kept in heaven for you, who through faith are shielded by
God's power until the coming of the salvation that is ready to
be revealed in the last time. [1 Peter 1:3–5]

For he chose us in him before the creation of the world to be
holy and blameless in his sight. In love he predestined us to
be adopted as his sons through Jesus Christ, in accordance
with his pleasure and will — to the praise of his glorious grace,
which he has freely given us in the One he loves. In him we
have redemption through his blood, the forgiveness of sins,
in accordance with the riches of God's grace that he lavished
on us with all wisdom and understanding. And he made known
to us the mystery of his will according to his good pleasure,
which he purposed in Christ, to be put into effect when the
times will have reached their fulfillment — to bring all things
in heaven and on earth together under one head, even Christ.
   In him we were also chosen, having been predestined according to the plan of him who works out everything in con-
formity with the purpose of his will, in order that we, who
were the first to hope in Christ, might be for the praise of his
glory. And you also were included in Christ when you heard
the word of truth, the gospel of your salvation. Having believed, you were marked in him with a seal, the promised Holy
Spirit, who is a deposit guaranteeing our inheritance. . . . [Eph.
1:4–14]

*Consider now how to respond to a God who is like our God, so rich in
his perfections, so glorious in his love.*

   Acknowledge and take to heart this day that the LORD is
God in heaven above and on the earth below. There is no
other. Keep his decrees and commands, which I am giving
you today, so that it may go well with you and your children
after you and that you may live long in the land the LORD
your God gives you for all time. [Deut. 4:39–40]

Ascribe to the LORD the glory due his name;
   worship the LORD in the splendor of his holiness. [Ps. 29:2]

I will proclaim the name of the LORD.
Oh, praise the greatness of our God!
He is the Rock, his works are perfect,
and all his ways are just.
A faithful God who does no wrong,
upright and just is he. [Deut. 32:3–4]

Love the LORD your God with all your heart and with all your
soul and with all your strength. These commandments that
I give you today are to be upon your hearts. Impress them on
your children. Talk about them when you sit at home and
when you walk along the road, when you lie down and when
you get up. [Deut. 6:5–7]

Shout for joy to the LORD, all the earth.
Worship the LORD with gladness;
come before him with joyful songs.
Know that the LORD is God.
It is he who made us, and we are his;
we are his people, the sheep of his pasture.
Enter his gates with thanksgiving
and his courts with praise;
give thanks to him and praise his name.
For the LORD is good and his love endures forever;
his faithfulness continues through all generations. [Ps. 100]

2

Keep Growing

Personal ministries grow out of deepening personal relationships. The first and most vital personal relationship on which effective ministry is based is our relationship with the Lord.

This principle is clearly established in Deuteronomy 6:4–9, which we looked at in chapter 1. The passage begins with a call to acknowledge God as LORD; as the One who is always present. We are to respond to this God with growing love. We are to focus heart and soul and strength on him.

It is not your years as a Christian, it is not the extent of your knowledge, it is not the thoroughness of your training. What qualifies you to minister to others is the intimacy of your relationship with God through Jesus Christ and your continuing growth in the Lord.

Only after focusing on relationship with God does Moses move on to say, "Impress [God's words] on your children" (Deut. 6:7). Ministry follows and grows out of relationship.

Metaphors About Growth

The Bible contains many images of growth. We Christians are to be like newborn babes, desiring the Word's pure milk "that by it [we] may grow up in [our] salvation" (1 Peter 2:2). Jesus uses the image of seed and soil, showing us that God's message, sown in our lives, is to grow and produce a crop (Matt. 13:3–9). Paul picks up the same imagery: Christian leaders are farm laborers who plant and water. But believers are God's field. The laborers are unimportant in themselves: the truly significant person is God, "who makes things grow" (1 Cor. 3:5–7).

When we think about growth it's important to ask, Growth toward what? Growth is not, and cannot be, random change. Growth implies a direction, a goal, a pattern toward which change moves. In fact, all growth is patterned by the very nature of the growing thing.

If you or I pick up an acorn, we know that if it is planted and grows, it will grow into an oak tree. It won't become a pine. It won't become a rock. It won't become a deer or a bear. The very pattern of the oak is impressed on the genetic matter in the acorn, and for the acorn growth means progress toward becoming an oak tree.

It's like this with you and me. Peter reminds us that "you have been born again, not of perishable seed, but of imperishable, through the living and enduring word of God" (1 Peter 1:23). J. B. Phillips renders it, "God has given you his own indestructible heredity."

Because God plants his own nature in us when we trust Christ, our growth too is patterned. It moves toward a goal defined by the spiritual "genetic matter" God has provided. And that goal is Christ-likeness. As Paul proclaims, we "reflect the Lord's glory," for we "are being transformed into his likeness with ever-increasing glory, which comes from the Lord, who is the Spirit" (2 Cor. 3:18).

We are growing now. We are growing in Jesus' likeness. We will not reach in this life the perfection we will know when Jesus returns. But even today we can become more and more like our Lord.

Disciplines of Growth

God has shown us in the Scripture certain disciplines that are important aids to personal spiritual growth. The Holy Spirit is the agent of our transformation, and growth in Christ-like-ness is a supernatural experience which does not depend on our actions or abilities. Yet God calls us in Scripture to "make every effort to add to [our] faith goodness; and to goodness, knowledge; and to knowledge, self-control; and to self-control, perseverance; and to perseverance, godliness; and to godli-ness, brotherly kindness; and to brotherly kindness, love" (2 Peter 1:5–7). We are to be active in our pursuit of godliness. We are to be involved in our own growth.

Paul exhorts his readers to accept responsibility for per-sonal spiritual growth. He reminds them "that in a race all the runners run, but only one gets the prize[.] Everyone who com-petes in the games goes into strict training. They do it to get a crown that will not last; but we do it to get a crown that will last forever. Therefore I do not run like a man running aim-lessly; I do not fight like a man beating the air" (1 Cor. 9:24–26). Growth in Christ is so important, and ministry to others such a priority, that the apostle committed himself to the disci-plines which promote growth in relationship with God and growth in Christ-likeness. As Peter adds, "For if you possess these qualities [faith, goodness, knowledge, self-control, etc.] in increasing measure, they will keep you from being ineffec-tive and unproductive in your knowledge of our Lord Jesus Christ" (2 Peter 1:8).

Preparation for personal ministry, then, calls first for us to focus on who God is, seeking to know him better. But prepa-ration also calls us to a personal commitment to growth in grace. Only as we grow steadily in the Lord will we move toward that Christ-likeness to which we are called and become effective and productive in personal ministry with others.

How do we grow steadily in the Lord? What disciplines and commitments does growth in Christ-likeness call for? In the rest of this chapter you will find pertinent principles and pas-sages from God's Word.

Commit yourself to fear the Lord. The phrase *the fear of the Lord*, found so often in the Old Testament, doesn't suggest terror. It means that we hold God in reverential awe. We "fear the

Lord" by acknowledging his involvement in all the events of our lives and by acting in full awareness that he is present with us at all times.

Acknowledge and take to heart this day that the LORD is God in heaven above and on the earth below. There is no other. Keep his decrees and commands, which I am giving you today, so that it may go well with you and your children after you and that you may live long in the land the LORD your God gives you for all time. [Deut. 4:39–40]

Teach me your way, O LORD,
and I will walk in your truth;
give me an undivided heart,
that I may fear your name. [Ps. 86:11]

"The fear of the LORD is the beginning of wisdom,
and knowledge of the Holy One is understanding." [Prov. 9:10]

Blessed is the man who fears the LORD,
who finds great delight in his commands....

He will have no fear of bad news;
his heart is steadfast, trusting in the LORD.
His heart is secure, he will have no fear;
in the end he will look in triumph on his foes. [Ps. 112:1, 7–8]

Fear the LORD your God, serve him only.... [Deut. 6:13]

Commit yourself to study God's Word. We can grow in the Lord only as we know him better. In Scripture God's thoughts, will, and ways are unveiled. Regular study of the Word of God is a discipline which is basic to spiritual growth.

The law of the LORD is perfect,
reviving the soul.
The statutes of the LORD are trustworthy,
making wise the simple.
The precepts of the LORD are right,
giving joy to the heart.

> The commands of the LORD are radiant,
>   giving light to the eyes.
> The fear of the LORD is pure,
>   enduring forever.
> The ordinances of the LORD are sure
>   and altogether righteous. . . .
> By them is your servant warned;
>   in keeping them there is great reward. [Ps. 19:7–9, 11]

> The unfolding of your words gives light;
>   it gives understanding to the simple. [Ps. 119:130]

All Scripture is God-breathed and is useful for teaching, rebuking, correcting and training in righteousness, so that the man of God may be thoroughly equipped for every good work. [2 Tim. 3:16–17]

Do not let this book of the Law depart from your mouth; meditate on it day and night, so that you may be careful to do everything written in it. [Josh. 1:8]

Do your best to present yourself to God as one approved, a workman who does not need to be ashamed and who correctly handles the word of truth. [2 Tim. 2:15]

Commit yourself to respond to known truth. The Word of God is to be heard in faith and acted on. It is only as you and I commit ourselves to live obediently by God's Word to us that growth is possible.

> How can a young man keep his way pure?
>   By living according to your word.
> I seek you with all my heart;
>   do not let me stray from your commands.
> I have hidden your word in my heart
>   that I might not sin against you. [Ps. 119:9–11]

Do not merely listen to the word, and so deceive yourselves. Do what it says. Anyone who listens to the word but does not do what it says is like a man who looks at his face in a mirror and, after looking at himself, goes away and immediately forgets what he looks like. But the man who looks intently into the perfect law that gives freedom, and continues to do this, not forgetting what he has heard, but doing it — he will be blessed in what he does. [James 1:22–25]

Jesus replied, "If anyone loves me, he will obey my teaching. My Father will love him, and we will come to him and make our home with him. He who does not love me will not obey my teaching." [John 14:23–24]

"Therefore everyone who hears these words of mine and puts them into practice is like a wise man who built his house on the rock. The rain came down, the streams rose, and the winds blew and beat against that house; yet it did not fall, because it had its foundation on the rock. But everyone who hears these words of mine and does not put them into practice is like a foolish man who built his house on sand. The rain came down, the streams rose, and the winds blew and beat against that house, and it fell with a great crash." [Matt. 7:24–27]

> "Today, if you hear his voice,
>   do not harden your hearts
>   as you did in the rebellion."

Who were they who heard and rebelled? Were they not all those Moses led out of Egypt? And with whom was he angry for forty years? Was it not with those who sinned, whose bodies fell in the desert? And to whom did God swear that they would never enter his rest if not to those who disobeyed? So we see that they were not able to enter, because of their unbelief. [Heb. 3:15–19]

Commit yourself to confess and deal with sin. Every person stumbles at times. Growth toward Christ-likeness is all too often interrupted by sins and failures. If we are to keep on growing, we need to deal with our sins by bringing them to the Lord, trusting in his promise of forgiveness and cleansing.

The LORD said to Moses, "Say to the Israelites: 'When a man or woman wrongs another in any way and so is unfaithful to the LORD, that person is guilty and must confess the sin he has committed. He must make full restitution for his wrong,

add one fifth to it and give it all to the person he has
wronged.' " [Num. 5:5–7]

If we claim to be without sin, we deceive ourselves and the
truth is not in us. If we confess our sins, he is faithful and
just and will forgive us our sins and purify us from all unrighteousness. If we claim we have not sinned, we make him
out to be a liar and his word has no place in our lives.

My dear children, I write this to you so that you will not
sin. But if anybody does sin, we have one who speaks to the
Father in our defense — Jesus Christ, the Righteous One. He
is the atoning sacrifice for our sins, and not only for ours but
also for the sins of the whole world. [1 John 1:8–2:2]

> Blessed is he
>> whose transgressions are forgiven,
>> whose sins are covered.
> Blessed is the man
>> whose sin the LORD does not count against him
>> and in whose spirit is no deceit.

> When I kept silent,
>> my bones wasted away
>> through my groaning all day long.
> For day and night
>> your hand was heavy upon me;
> my strength was sapped
>> as in the heat of summer.   *Selah*
> Then I acknowledged my sin to you
>> and did not cover up my iniquity.
> I said, "I will confess
>> my transgressions to the LORD" —
> and you forgave
>> the guilt of my sin.   *Selah*

> Therefore let everyone who is godly pray to you
>> while you may be found;
> surely when the mighty waters rise,
>> they will not reach him.
> You are my hiding place;
>> you will protect me from trouble
>> and surround me with songs of
>> deliverance.   *Selah* [Ps. 32:1–7]

Have mercy on me, O God,
  according to your unfailing love;
according to your great compassion
  blot out my transgressions.
Wash away all my iniquity
  and cleanse me from my sin.

For I know my transgressions,
  and my sin is always before me.
Against you, you only, have I sinned
  and done what is evil in your sight,
so that you are proved right when you speak
  and justified when you judge....
Hide your face from my sins
  and blot out all my iniquity.

Create in me a pure heart, O God,
  and renew a steadfast spirit within me....
Then I will teach transgressors your ways.... [Ps. 51:1-4,
  9-10, 13]

Commit yourself to prayer. That personal relationship with God which promotes growth involves speaking to the Lord as well as hearing and responding to his Word. In prayer we share all that is happening in our lives with the Lord as well as express our requests. Many passages in Scripture guide our prayer life and invite us to develop an intimate prayer relationship with our God. Included among them are the simple prayer that Jesus taught his disciples and many wonderful prayer promises.

"This, then, is how you should pray:

  " 'Our Father in heaven,
  hallowed be your name,
  your kingdom come,
  your will be done
    on earth as it is in heaven.
  Give us today our daily bread.
  Forgive us our debts,
    as we also have forgiven our debtors.
  And lead us not into temptation,
    but deliver us from the evil one.' " [Matt. 6:9-13]

"Ask and it will be given to you; seek and you will find; knock and the door will be opened to you. For everyone who asks receives; he who seeks finds; and to him who knocks, the door will be opened." [Matt. 7:7–8]

If any of you lacks wisdom, he should ask God, who gives generously to all without finding fault, and it will be given to him. [James 1:5]

> In the morning, O LORD, you hear my voice;
>   in the morning I lay my requests before you
>   and wait in expectation. [Ps. 5:3]

"I tell you the truth, my Father will give you whatever you ask in my name. Until now you have not asked for anything in my name. Ask and you will receive, and your joy will be complete." [John 16:23–24]

In the same way, the Spirit helps us in our weakness. We do not know what we ought to pray for, but the Spirit himself intercedes for us with groans that words cannot express. And he who searches our hearts knows the mind of the Spirit, because the Spirit intercedes for the saints in accordance with God's will. [Rom. 8:26–27]

Let us then approach the throne of grace with confidence, so that we may receive mercy and find grace to help us in our time of need. [Heb. 4:16]

Commit yourself to praise. Praise and worship are vital elements of our personal relationship with the Lord. Praising God deepens our appreciation of who he is, strengthens our trust, and stimulates personal spiritual growth.

> Therefore, since we are receiving a kingdom that cannot be shaken, let us be thankful, and so worship God acceptably with reverence and awe. . . . [Heb. 12:28]

> Through Jesus, therefore, let us continually offer to God a sacrifice of praise — the fruit of lips that confess his name. [Heb. 13:15]

> I will exalt you, my God the King;
>   I will praise your name for ever and ever.
> Every day I will praise you
>   and extol your name for ever and ever. [Ps. 145:1–2]

I will praise you, O LORD, with all my heart;
   before the "gods" I will sing your praise.
I will bow down toward your holy temple
   and will praise your name
   for your love and your faithfulness,
for you have exalted above all things
   your name and your word. [Ps. 138:1–2]

If I had cherished sin in my heart,
   the Lord would not have listened;
but God has surely listened
   and heard my voice in prayer.
Praise be to God,
who has not rejected my prayer
or withheld his love from me! [Ps. 66:18–20]

Commit yourself to a moral and holy life. Steady growth in the Lord demands a decision to turn from all forms of wickedness and to turn to righteousness.

Therefore, prepare your minds for action; be self-controlled; set your hope fully on the grace to be given you when Jesus Christ is revealed. As obedient children, do not conform to the evil desires you had when you lived in ignorance. But just as he who called you is holy, so be holy in all you do; for it is written: "Be holy, because I am holy." [1 Peter 1:13–16]

For God did not call us to be impure, but to live a holy life. Therefore, he who rejects this instruction does not reject man but God, who gives you his Holy Spirit. [1 Thess. 4:7–8]

It is God's will that you should be sanctified: that you should avoid sexual immorality; that each of you should learn to control his own body in a way that is holy and honorable, not in passionate lust like the heathen, who do not know God. ... [1 Thess. 4:3–5]

For the grace of God that brings salvation has appeared to all men. It teaches us to say "No" to ungodliness and worldly passions, and to live self-controlled, upright and godly lives in this present age, while we wait for the blessed hope — the glorious appearing of our great God and Savior, Jesus Christ, who gave himself for us to redeem us from all wickedness and to purify for himself a people that are his very own.... [Titus 2:11–14]

Commit yourself to doing what is right and good. Holiness is not just refraining from wrong; it is also expressed actively in good deeds. This commitment also stimulates our growth as Christians.

"Whoever would love life
    and see good days
must keep his tongue from evil
    and his lips from deceitful speech.
He must turn from evil and do good;
    he must seek peace and pursue it.
For the eyes of the Lord are on the righteous
    and his ears are attentive to their prayer,
but the face of the Lord is against those who do evil." [1 Peter
    3:10–12]

And as for you, brothers, never tire of doing what is right. [2 Thess. 3:13]

"Maintain justice
    and do what is right,
for my salvation is close at hand
    and my righteousness will soon be revealed.
Blessed is the man who does this,
    the man who holds it fast...." [Isa. 56:1–2]

With what shall I come before the LORD
    and bow down before the exalted God?
Shall I come before him with burnt offerings,
    with calves a year old?
Will the LORD be pleased with thousands of rams,
    with ten thousand rivers of oil?...
He has showed you, O man, what is good.
    And what does the LORD require of you?
To act justly and to love mercy
    and to walk humbly with your God. [Mic. 6:6–8]

Let us not become weary in doing good, for at the proper time we will reap a harvest if we do not give up. Therefore, as we have opportunity, let us do good to all people, especially to those who belong to the family of believers. [Gal. 6:9–10]

Commit yourself to community. God has placed us in relationships with others in the body of Christ. The web of warm and loving relationships which are to characterize Jesus' church are the context in which our growth toward Christ-likeness takes place.

"A new command I give you: Love one another. As I have loved you, so you must love one another. By this all men will know that you are my disciples, if you love one another." [John 13:34–35]

Be completely humble and gentle; be patient, bearing with one another in love. Make every effort to keep the unity of the Spirit through the bond of peace. There is one body and one Spirit — just as you were called to one hope when you were called — one Lord, one faith, one baptism; one God and Father of all, who is over all and through all and in all. . . . Instead, speaking the truth in love, we will in all things grow up into him who is the Head, that is, Christ. From him the whole body, joined and held together by every supporting ligament, grows and builds itself up in love, as each part does its work. [Eph. 4:2–5, 15–16]

Let us not give up meeting together, as some are in the habit of doing, but let us encourage one another — and all the more as you see the Day approaching. [Heb. 10:25]

May the God who gives endurance and encouragement give you a spirit of unity among yourselves as you follow Christ Jesus, so that with one heart and mouth you may glorify the God and Father of our Lord Jesus Christ.

Accept one another, then, just as Christ accepted you, in order to bring praise to God. [Rom. 15:5–7]

But encourage one another daily, as long as it is called Today, so that none of you may be hardened by sin's deceitfulness. We have come to share in Christ if we hold firmly till the end the confidence we had at first. [Heb. 3:13–14]

Commit yourself to use your spiritual gifts to minister to others. The Holy Spirit supernaturally enables each of us to make our own contribution to others' lives and growth. As we come to know, love, and serve others, these supernatural gifts operate and God works good for others through you and me. We may not know our spiritual gift. But we can be sure that as we love and serve our fellows, God's Spirit will do his work through us.

Each one should use whatever gift he has received to serve others, faithfully administering God's grace in its various forms. If anyone speaks, he should do it as one speaking the very words of God. If anyone serves, he should do it with the strength God provides, so that in all things God may be praised through Jesus Christ. [1 Peter 4:10–11]

Just as each of us has one body with many members, and these members do not all have the same function, so in Christ we who are many form one body, and each member belongs to all the others. We have different gifts, according to the grace given us. If a man's gift is prophesying, let him use it in proportion to his faith. If it is serving, let him serve; if it is teaching, let him teach; if it is encouraging, let him encourage; if it is contributing to the needs of others, let him give generously; if it is leadership, let him govern diligently; if it is showing mercy, let him do it cheerfully. [Rom. 12:4–8]

Commit yourself to serve Christ fully. Dedication to Jesus and to his will is foundational to our growth. After all, Jesus is Savior. More than that: Jesus is Lord.

And now, O Israel, what does the LORD your God ask of you but to fear the LORD your God, to walk in all his ways, to love him, to serve the LORD your God with all your heart and with all your soul. . . . [Deut. 10:12]

And he died for all, that those who live should no longer live for themselves but for him who died for them and was raised again. [2 Cor. 5:15]

Therefore, my dear brothers, stand firm. Let nothing move you. Always give yourselves fully to the work of the Lord, because you know that your labor in the Lord is not in vain. [1 Cor. 15:58]

So we make it our goal to please him, whether we are at home in the body or away from it. For we must all appear before the judgment seat of Christ, that each one may receive what is due him for the things done while in the body, whether good or bad. [2 Cor. 5:9–10]

Therefore, I urge you, brothers, in view of God's mercy, to offer your bodies as living sacrifices, holy and pleasing to God — this is your spiritual act of worship. Do not conform any longer to the pattern of this world, but be transformed by the renewing of your mind. Then you will be able to test and approve what God's will is — his good, pleasing and perfect will. [Rom. 12:1–2]

Whatever you do, work at it with all your heart, as working for the Lord, not for men, since you know that you will receive an inheritance from the Lord as a reward. It is the Lord Christ you are serving. [Col. 3:23–24]

Serve wholeheartedly. . . . [Eph. 6:7]

Commit yourself to abide in Christ. To abide means to remain close to, to stay in intimate personal relationship with. In a real sense, every growth-encouraging commitment we are called on to make is summed up in this unique biblical expression. Because faith has brought us into intimate union with Jesus, we can draw on all that Jesus is to enable us to grow, to serve, and to minister to others.

"I am the true vine, and my Father is the gardener. . . . Remain [abide] in me, and I will remain in you. No branch can bear fruit by itself; it must remain in the vine. Neither can you bear fruit unless you remain in me."
"I am the vine; you are the branches. If a man remains in me and I in him, he will bear much fruit; apart from me you can do nothing." [John 15:1, 4–5]

"As the Father has loved me, so have I loved you. Now remain in my love. If you obey my commands, you will remain in my love, just as I have obeyed my Father's commands and remain in his love. I have told you this so that my joy may be in you and that your joy may be complete. My command is this: Love each other as I have loved you. Greater love has no one than this, that he lay down his life for his friends. You are my friends if you do what I command." [John 15:9–14]

I have been crucified with Christ and I no longer live, but Christ lives in me. The life I live in the body, I live by faith in the Son of God, who loved me and gave himself for me. [Gal. 2:20]

Now if we died with Christ, we believe that we will also live with him. . . . Do not offer the parts of your body to sin, as instruments of wickedness, but rather offer yourselves to God, as those who have been brought from death to life; and offer the parts of your body to him as instruments of righteousness. [Rom. 6:8, 13]

3

Depend
on the Lord

We all have times when we are overcome by a sense of our own inadequacy: "How can I possibly minister to others?" "But I don't have the ability" (or the wisdom, or the knowledge).

This sense of inadequacy is understandable. Even the greatest of saints have had similar feelings. For instance, when Moses was called from his shepherding and told that his old dream of delivering his fellow Israelites was to be realized, he objected. "Moses said to the LORD, 'O Lord, I have never been eloquent, neither in the past nor since you have spoken to your servant. I am slow of speech and tongue' " (Exod. 4:10). The awareness of his limitations seemed overwhelming to Moses, even though he knew that God was the one who called him to his ministry.

God's answer is instructive. "The LORD said to him, 'Who gave man his mouth? Who makes him deaf or mute? Who gives him sight or makes him blind? Is it not I, the LORD? Now go; I will help you speak and will teach you what to say' " (Exod. 4:11–12).

God did not contradict Moses' self-evaluation. Moses wasn't eloquent. He was slow of speech. But Moses had been wrong in focusing on his limitation rather than on the Lord. God, who called him to ministry, was well able to help Moses speak and to teach him what to say. Fulfilling Moses' call to minister did not depend on him but on the Lord. It was not Moses' abilities which would bring success, but God's empowering.

It is the same for you and me today. We're not wrong to recognize our limitations. In fact, we're wise to acknowledge them. Jeremiah expresses God's word on the matter when he writes,

> "Cursed is the one who trusts in man,
>   who depends on flesh for his strength
>   and whose heart turns away from the LORD." [Jer. 17:5]

Depending on our own native ability and human resources is not only unwise but also wrong. Depending on ourselves means turning away from the Lord and from reliance on him. The same thought is expressed in Proverbs 3:

> Trust in the LORD with all your heart
>   and lean not on your own understanding;
> in all your ways acknowledge him,
>   and he will make your paths straight. [Prov. 3:5–6]

But awareness of our limitations is in fact the key to freedom in ministry to others, not something which leads us to draw back. When we are truly aware of our limitations, we realize that we must trust the Lord fully and rely on him to make anything we do effective.

Only God, working through our lives, is able to accomplish anything significant in the life of another person. So we are to acknowledge our inadequacy and then turn in complete dependence and trust to the Lord. He alone is able. He alone can accomplish through us what he intends when he calls us to minister to others.

What we need is to shift our focus from ourselves and others to the Lord. As we look into God's wonderful Word, our concentration shifts from ourselves to him. What we discover helps us to depend fully on the Lord.

When we depend on the Lord, we are enabled to serve.

Rely on God's greatness and power. It helps us to depend on the Lord fully to remember just who he is and how unlimited are his abilities. Surely this God is able to work through us despite our limitations and make us effective ministers of his love.

"Praise be to you, O LORD,
　　God of our father Israel,
　　from everlasting to everlasting.
Yours, O LORD, is the greatness and the power
　　and the glory and the majesty and the splendor,
　　for everything in heaven and earth is yours.
Yours, O LORD, is the kingdom;
　　you are exalted as head over all.
Wealth and honor come from you;
　　you are the ruler of all things.
In your hands are strength and power
　　to exalt and give strength to all." [1 Chron. 29:10–12]

Lift your eyes and look to the heavens:
　　Who created all these?
He who brings out the starry host one by one,
　　and calls them each by name.
Because of his great power and mighty strength,
　　not one of them is missing. [Isa. 40:26]

"Remember the former things, those of long ago;
　　I am God, and there is no other;
　　I am God, and there is none like me.
I make known the end from the beginning,
　　from ancient times, what is still to come.
I say: My purpose will stand,
　　and I will do all that I please." [Isa. 46:9–10]

"Dominion and awe belong to God;
　　he establishes order in the heights of heaven.
Can his forces be numbered?
　　Upon whom does his light not rise?" [Job 25:2–3]

I have set the LORD always before me.
　　Because he is at my right hand,
　　I will not be shaken. [Ps. 16:8]

His divine power has given us everything we need for life
and godliness through our knowledge of him. . . . [2 Peter 1:3]

David said to the Philistine, "You come against me with
sword and spear and javelin, but I come against you in the
name of the LORD Almighty. . . ." [1 Sam. 17:45]

Rely on God as loving Father. God has revealed himself in Jesus
as our Father, who loves us with a Father's love. Remembering
that God is truly our Father now gives us confidence in his
continuing, active care. To know God as Father helps us to
realize that he will never abandon us and will always come to
our aid.

"Which of you fathers, if your son asks for a fish, will give
him a snake instead? Or if he asks for an egg, will give him
a scorpion? If you then, though you are evil, know how to give
good gifts to your children, how much more will your Father
in heaven give the Holy Spirit to those who ask him!" [Luke
11:11–13]

"Therefore I tell you, do not worry about your life, what you
will eat or drink; or about your body, what you will wear. Is
not life more important than food, and the body more important than clothes? Look at the birds of the air; they do not
sow or reap or store away in barns, and yet your heavenly
Father feeds them. Are you not much more valuable than
they?" [Matt. 6:25–26]

"Do not be afraid, little flock, for your Father has been
pleased to give you the kingdom. Sell your possessions and
give to the poor. Provide purses for yourselves that will not
wear out, a treasure in heaven that will not be exhausted,
where no thief comes near and no moth destroys. For where
your treasure is, there your heart will be also." [Luke 12:32–34]

Rely on God's commitment to his own. We know that in Jesus we
have a special, personal, and permanent relationship with God.
Assurance of our salvation brings with it the confidence that
God will keep every commitment he has made to his own. We
can rely on him, because God is fully committed to us.

"My sheep listen to my voice; I know them, and they follow me. I give them eternal life, and they shall never perish; no one can snatch them out of my hand. My Father, who has given them to me, is greater than all; no one can snatch them out of my Father's hand. I and the Father are one." [John 10:27–30]

Once you were alienated from God and were enemies in your minds because of your evil behavior. But now he has reconciled you by Christ's physical body through death to present you holy in his sight, without blemish and free from accusation. . . . [Col. 1:21–22]

"Because he loves me," says the LORD, "I will rescue him;
  I will protect him, for he acknowledges my name.
He will call upon me, and I will answer him;
  I will be with him in trouble,
  I will deliver him and honor him.
With long life will I satisfy him
  and show him my salvation." [Ps. 91:14–16]

Because God wanted to make the unchanging nature of his purpose very clear to the heirs of what was promised, he confirmed it with an oath. God did this so that, by two unchangeable things in which it is impossible for God to lie, we who have fled to take hold of the hope offered to us may be greatly encouraged. We have this hope as an anchor for the soul, firm and secure. It enters the inner sanctuary behind the curtain, where Jesus, who went before us, has entered on our behalf. [Heb. 6:17–20]

"O LORD, God of Israel, there is no God like you in heaven above or on earth below — you who keep your covenant of love with your servants who continue wholeheartedly in your way." [1 Kings 8:23]

Yet I am not ashamed, because I know whom I have believed, and am convinced that he is able to guard what I have entrusted to him for that day. [2 Tim. 1:12]

Rely on God's presence. God is not limited in any way in his ability to help us. In fact, God is always present with us to aid and to empower in the moments of our need.

"Stand firm and you will see the deliverance the LORD will bring you today. The Egyptians you see today you will never see again. The LORD will fight for you; you need only to be still." [Exod. 14:13–14]

He has watched over your journey through this vast desert. These forty years the LORD your God has been with you, and you have not lacked anything. [Deut. 2:7]

"But Lord," Gideon asked, "how can I save Israel? My clan is the weakest in Manasseh, and I am the least in my family." The LORD answered, "I will be with you. . . ." [Judg. 6:15–16]

Rely on God's trustworthy character. We can depend fully on the Lord because he is ever faithful to his commitments. Meditating on God's character helps us to depend completely on him.

"God is not a man, that he should lie,
   nor a son of man, that he should change his mind.
Does he speak and then not act?
   Does he promise and not fulfill?
I have received a command to bless;
   he has blessed, and I cannot change it." [Num. 23:19–20]

The LORD is good to all;
   he has compassion on all he has made.
All you have made will praise you, O LORD;
   your saints will extol you. . . .
Your kingdom is an everlasting kingdom,
   and your dominion endures through all generations.

The LORD is faithful to all his promises
   and loving toward all he has made. . . .
The LORD is righteous in all his ways
   and loving toward all he has made.
The LORD is near to all who call on him,
   to all who call on him in truth. [Ps. 145:9–10, 13, 17–18]

Rely on God's guidance. You and I can appeal to God for guidance and be confident that he will show us what to do. Usually

God's guidance is given for each next step. Thus God keeps us relying on him daily. How good to know that he will show us his way.

> For the LORD gives wisdom,
>> and from his mouth come knowledge and understanding.
>> [Prov. 2:6]

I will instruct you and teach you in the way you should go;
> I will counsel you and watch over you.
Do not be like the horse or the mule,
> which have no understanding
but must be controlled by bit and bridle. . . . [Ps. 32:8–9]

>> Show me your ways, O LORD,
>>> teach me your paths;
>> guide me in your truth and teach me,
>>> for you are God my Savior,
>>> and my hope is in you all day long. [Ps. 25:4–5]

>> I will praise the LORD, who counsels me;
>>> even at night my heart instructs me.
>> I have set the LORD always before me.
>>> Because he is at my right hand,
>>> I will not be shaken. [Ps. 16:7–8]

"But when he, the Spirit of truth, comes, he will guide you into all truth. He will not speak on his own; he will speak only what he hears, and he will tell you what is yet to come." [John 16:13]

"I am the LORD your God,
> who teaches you what is best for you,
> who directs you in the way you should go." [Isa. 48:17]

Rely on God's sovereign control of events. Our God is in control of all things. Because God is sovereign, we can face any situation or difficulty with confidence.

>> The lot is cast into the lap,
>>> but its every decision is from the LORD. [Prov. 16:33]

Then Asa called to the LORD his God and said, "LORD, there is no one like you to help the powerless against the mighty. Help me, O LORD our God, for we rely on you, and in your name we have come against this vast army. O LORD, you are our God; do not let man prevail against you."

The LORD struck down the Cushites before Asa and Judah. [2 Chron. 14:11–12]

Rely on God's aid to those who do right. In ministry we do not depend on ourselves but on the Lord. Yet you and I can look at our own lives and see the righteousness that God has been working in our lives. The evidence of his work in us is a basis for confidence that God, who has helped us, will help us still. Scripture often emphasizes that God is committed to help those who do right. As we live righteous lives, we can depend on him to work in and through us too.

"Whoever would love life
    and see good days
must keep his tongue from evil
    and his lips from deceitful speech.
He must turn from evil and do good;
    he must seek peace and pursue it.
For the eyes of the Lord are on the righteous
    and his ears are attentive to their prayer,
    but the face of the Lord is against those who do evil."
        [1 Peter 3:10–12]

"The LORD has dealt with me according to my righteousness;
    according to the cleanness of my hands he has rewarded
    me.
For I have kept the ways of the LORD;
    I have not done evil by turning from my God.
All his laws are before me;
    I have not turned away from his decrees.
I have been blameless before him
    and have kept myself from sin.
The LORD has rewarded me according to my righteousness,
    according to my cleanness in his sight." [2 Sam. 22:21–25]

Blessed is the man
  who does not walk in the counsel of the wicked
or stand in the way of sinners
  or sit in the seat of mockers.
But his delight is in the law of the LORD,
  and on his law he meditates day and night.
He is like a tree planted by streams of water,
  which yields its fruit in season
and whose leaf does not wither.
  Whatever he does prospers. [Ps. 1:1–3]

Rely on the Holy Spirit, who is with you. The Holy Spirit in our lives is the source of unimaginable power. What we cannot do, God the Spirit can enable us to do. Because of God's gift of his Spirit, we can be effective in our ministry to others. Because God's Spirit is in us, we can reach out to others with confidence.

"But you will receive power when the Holy Spirit comes on you; and you will be my witnesses in Jerusalem, and in all Judea and Samaria, and to the ends of the earth." [Acts 1:8]

For God did not give us a spirit of timidity, but a spirit of power, of love and of self-discipline. [2 Tim. 1:7]

"When you are brought before synagogues, rulers and authorities, do not worry about how you will defend yourselves or what you will say, for the Holy Spirit will teach you at that time what you should say." [Luke 12:11–12]

"And I will ask the Father, and he will give you another Counselor to be with you forever — the Spirit of truth. The world cannot accept him, because it neither sees him nor knows him. But you know him, for he lives with you and will be in you." [John 14:16–17]

You, however, are controlled not by the sinful nature but by the Spirit, if the Spirit of God lives in you. And if anyone does not have the Spirit of Christ, he does not belong to Christ. But if Christ is in you, your body is dead because of sin, yet your spirit is alive because of righteousness. And if the Spirit of him who raised Jesus from the dead is living in you, he who raised Christ from the dead will also give life to your mortal bodies through his Spirit, who lives in you. [Rom. 8:9–11]

Now it is God who makes both us and you stand firm in Christ. He anointed us, set his seal of ownership on us, and put his Spirit in our hearts as a deposit, guaranteeing what is to come. [2 Cor. 1:21–22]

Rely not on yourself, but on the Lord. A humble attitude is basic to an experience of divine enablement. When we recognize our own deep need, we turn to the Lord. So a deep sense of our need promotes a healthy dependence on the Lord.

To the faithful you show yourself faithful,
    to the blameless you show yourself blameless,
to the pure you show yourself pure,
    but to the crooked you show yourself shrewd.
You save the humble
    but bring low those whose eyes are haughty. [Ps. 18:25–27]

"Show me, O LORD, my life's end
    and the number of my days;
    let me know how fleeting is my life.
You have made my days a mere handbreadth;
    the span of my years is as nothing before you.
    Each man's life is but a breath.

Selah

Man is a mere phantom as he goes to and fro:
    He bustles about, but only in vain;
    he heaps up wealth, not knowing who will get it.
But now, Lord, what do I look for?
    My hope is in you." [Ps. 39:4–7]

Stop trusting in man,
    who has but a breath in his nostrils.
Of what account is he? [Isa. 2:22]

Humble yourselves, therefore, under God's mighty hand, that he may lift you up in due time. [1 Peter 5:6]

Rely on God's wisdom and submit to his will. Submission isn't always easy, especially when we are in difficult circumstances. Yet it's important for us to acknowledge God as Lord and to be willing to submit to his will. To help us, we have the example of Jesus and many reminders in Scripture.

Submit yourselves, then, to God. [James 4:7]

When they hurled their insults at [Jesus], he did not retaliate; when he suffered, he made no threats. Instead, he entrusted himself to him who judges justly. [1 Peter 2:23]

... I have learned to be content whatever the circumstances. I know what it is to be in need, and I know what it is to have plenty. I have learned the secret of being content in any and every situation, whether well fed or hungry, whether living in plenty or in want. I can do everything through him who gives me strength. [Phil. 4:11–13]

Do everything without complaining or arguing, so that you may become blameless and pure, children of God without fault in a crooked and depraved generation, in which you shine like stars in the universe as you hold out the word of life. ... [Phil. 2:14–16]

The LORD Almighty is the one you are to regard as holy,
    he is the one you are to fear,
    he is the one you are to dread,
and he will be a sanctuary. ... [Isa. 8:13–14]

Rely on the Lord so much that you put your faith into action. Dependence on God is always translated into action. We show that we depend on Jesus when we do what we can to minister to those with whom God brings us in contact.

After I looked things over, I stood up and said to the nobles, the officials and the rest of the people, "Don't be afraid of them. Remember the Lord, who is great and awesome, and fight for your brothers, your sons and your daughters, your wives and your homes." [Neh. 4:14]

48   **Principles for Personal Ministry**

Therefore, prepare your minds for action; be self-controlled; set your hope fully on the grace to be given you when Jesus Christ is revealed. [1 Peter 1:13]

I answered them by saying, "The God of heaven will give us success. We his servants will start rebuilding." [Neh. 2:20]

Whatever you have learned or received or heard from me, or seen in me — put it into practice. And the God of peace will be with you. [Phil. 4:9]

Yet when you relied on the LORD, he delivered them into your hand. For the eyes of the LORD range throughout the earth to strengthen those whose hearts are fully committed to him." [2 Chron. 16:8–9]

May the God of peace, who through the blood of the eternal covenant brought back from the dead our Lord Jesus, that great Shepherd of the sheep, equip you with everything good for doing his will, and may he work in us what is pleasing to him, through Jesus Christ, to whom be glory for ever and ever. Amen. [Heb. 13:20–21]

> Teach me your way, O LORD,
>   and I will walk in your truth;
> give me an undivided heart,
>   that I may fear your name. [Ps. 86:11]

4

Build Personal Relationships

Ministry is a relational affair. Effective ministry grows out of a believer's personal relationship with God. And effective ministry calls for a healthy personal relationship with those to whom we minister.

In the first three chapters of this book we've looked at passages which help us understand how to deepen our personal relationship with the Lord. We've seen passages which help us as we seek to know the Lord better, to grow steadily in the Lord, and to depend fully on the Lord. This exploration reflects the framework for ministry expressed in Deuteronomy 6:4–9. Effective ministry can take place only when you and I acknowledge the Lord as the one who is always present, grow in our love for him, and express that love in responsiveness to his Word.

After calling us to acknowledge, love, and obey the Lord, Moses goes on to say, "Impress them [the commands we ourselves have taken into our hearts] on your children. Talk about them when you sit at home and when you walk along the road, when you lie down and when you get up" (Deut. 6:7).

As I noted before, this passage gives us insight into both the climate for personal ministry and the best context for personal ministry.

That climate is established by the reference to "your children." In Old Testament times, nurture in faith was viewed essentially as a family affair. Mom and Dad, in the intimacy of family life, were to share their own faith and experience with the Lord with their children.

We'd be wrong if we argued that this passage means that the family is the only place to minister to children. But we would be just as wrong if we overlooked that family relationships — intimate and loving — best demonstrate the climate in which ministry of the Word of God is to take place.

We see this in the New Testament as well. There the church is viewed as a family, with its members often identified as brothers and sisters. There too, when the apostle Paul describes his own relationships with those to whom he ministered, the imagery of the family is adopted. In 1 Thessalonians Paul writes of being "gentle among you, like a mother caring for her little children" (2:7). The bonding of the apostle and the new believers was so great that Paul writes, "We loved you so much that we were delighted to share with you not only the gospel of God but our lives as well, because you had become so dear to us" (2:8).

A little later in the same passage Paul changes the image slightly, but still retains the family model. "For you know that we dealt with each of you as a father deals with his own [adolescent] children, encouraging, comforting and urging you to live lives worthy of God" (2:11–12).

When the Old Testament or the New Testament writers describe ministering relationships, they turn again and again to metaphors about family love. In this kind of love we find the key to effectiveness in our ministry with others. If we are to be used by God to touch the lives of others, we need to build intimate, family-type relationships with them! In a climate of deep caring, of love, of bonding together, we can effectively share the Word and the love of God with others.

As we learn to love in God's way, we do build those ministering relationships with others which open the way to effective personal ministry.

Love is basic to ministering relationships. No interpersonal theme is emphasized as much in the New Testament. Here are a few of the passages that call us to love others deeply and fully.

If anyone says, "I love God," yet hates his brother, he is a liar. For anyone who does not love his brother, whom he has seen, cannot love God, whom he has not seen. And he has given us this command: Whoever loves God must also love his brother. [1 John 4:20–21]

Whoever loves his brother lives in the light, and there is nothing in him to make him stumble. But whoever hates his brother is in the darkness and walks around in the darkness; he does not know where he is going, because the darkness has blinded him. [1 John 2:10–11]

Love is patient, love is kind. It does not envy, it does not boast, it is not proud. It is not rude, it is not self-seeking, it is not easily angered, it keeps no record of wrongs. Love does not delight in evil but rejoices with the truth. It always protects, always trusts, always hopes, always perseveres. [1 Cor. 13:4–7]

Be imitators of God, therefore, as dearly loved children, and live a life of love, just as Christ loved us and gave himself up for us as a fragrant offering and sacrifice to God. [Eph. 5:1–2]

"A new command I give you: Love one another. As I have loved you, so you must love one another. By this all men will know that you are my disciples, if you love one another." [John 13:34–35]

"But I tell you who hear me: Love your enemies, do good to those who hate you, bless those who curse you, pray for those who mistreat you. . . .
"If you love those who love you, what credit is that to you? Even 'sinners' love those who love them. . . . But love your enemies, do good to them, and lend to them without expecting to get anything back. Then your reward will be great, and you will be sons of the Most High, because he is kind to the

ungrateful and wicked. Be merciful, just as your Father is merciful." [Luke 6:27–28, 32, 35–36]

Love is to be expressed in forgiveness. We build and maintain ministering relationships by recognizing the frailty of others and being ready to restore intimacy by extending and receiving forgiveness.

Above all, love each other deeply, because love covers over a multitude of sins. [1 Peter 4:8]

Brothers, if someone is caught in a sin, you who are spiritual should restore him gently. But watch yourself, or you also may be tempted. Carry each other's burdens, and in this way you will fulfill the law of Christ. [Gal. 6:1–2]

Do not say, "I'll do to him as he has done to me;
    I'll pay that man back for what he did." [Prov. 24:29]

"If your brother sins, rebuke him, and if he repents, forgive him. If he sins against you seven times in a day, and seven times comes back to you and says, 'I repent,' forgive him." [Luke 17:3–4]

And do not grieve the Holy Spirit of God, with whom you were sealed for the day of redemption. Get rid of all bitterness, rage and anger, brawling and slander, along with every form of malice. Be kind and compassionate to one another, forgiving each other, just as in Christ God forgave you. [Eph. 4:30–32]

"For if you forgive men when they sin against you, your heavenly Father will also forgive you." [Matt. 6:14]

Love is expressed in seeking to meet others' needs. Reaching out to support and help in practical, caring ways is an important aspect of Christian love and of ministering relationships.

And do not forget to do good and to share with others, for with such sacrifices God is pleased. [Heb. 13:16]

This is how we know what love is: Jesus Christ laid down his life for us. And we ought to lay down our lives for our brothers. If anyone has material possessions and sees his brother in need but has no pity on him, how can the love of God be in him? Dear children, let us not love with words or tongue but with actions and in truth. [1 John 3:16–18]

> A generous man will himself be blessed,
>   for he shares his food with the poor. [Prov. 22:9]

> Do not withhold good from those who deserve it,
>   when it is in your power to act.
> Do not say to your neighbor,
>   "Come back later; I'll give it tomorrow" –
> when you now have it with you. [Prov. 3:27–28]

Religion that God our Father accepts as pure and faultless is this: to look after orphans and widows in their distress and to keep oneself from being polluted by the world. [James 1:27]

Love is expressed in the unity and harmony which are to mark relationships in Christ's church. The Bible describes attitudes and actions which create harmony in interpersonal relationships and encourage effective personal ministry.

> Finally, all of you, live in harmony with one another; be sympathetic, love as brothers, be compassionate and humble. Do not repay evil with evil or insult with insult, but with blessing, because to this you were called so that you may inherit a blessing. [1 Peter 3:8–9]

> If you have any encouragement from being united with Christ, if any comfort from his love, if any fellowship with the Spirit, if any tenderness and compassion, then make my joy complete by being like-minded, having the same love, being one in spirit and purpose. Do nothing out of selfish ambition or vain conceit, but in humility consider others better than yourselves. Each of you should look not only to your own interests, but also to the interests of others. [Phil. 2:1–4]

> I appeal to you, brothers, in the name of our Lord Jesus Christ, that all of you agree with one another so that there may be no divisions among you and that you may be perfectly united in mind and thought. [1 Cor. 1:10]

If it is possible, as far as it depends on you, live at peace with everyone. [Rom. 12:18]

Love is expressed by a nonjudgmental attitude toward others. We are to love and accept others and are not to pass judgment on areas in which they differ from us.

"Do not judge, or you too will be judged. For in the same way you judge others, you will be judged, and with the measure you use, it will be measured to you." [Matt. 7:1–2]

Brothers, do not slander one another. Anyone who speaks against his brother or judges him speaks against the law and judges it. When you judge the law, you are not keeping it, but sitting in judgment on it. There is only one Lawgiver and Judge, the one who is able to save and destroy. But you — who are you to judge your neighbor? [James 4:11–12]

Therefore let us stop passing judgment on one another. Instead, make up your mind not to put any stumbling block or obstacle in your brother's way. [Rom. 14:13]

I care very little if I am judged by you or by any human court; indeed, I do not even judge myself. My conscience is clear, but that does not make me innocent. It is the Lord who judges me. Therefore judge nothing before the appointed time; wait till the Lord comes. He will bring to light what is hidden in darkness and will expose the motives of men's hearts. At that time each will receive his praise from God. [1 Cor. 4:3–5]

Accept him whose faith is weak, without passing judgment on disputable matters.... Who are you to judge someone else's servant? To his own master he stands or falls. And he will stand, for the Lord is able to make him stand....

For this very reason, Christ died and returned to life so that he might be the Lord of both the dead and the living. You, then, why do you judge your brother? Or why do you look down on your brother? For we will all stand before God's judgment seat. [Rom. 14:1, 4, 9–10]

Love is expressed by accepting and caring for all. Each of us will naturally be drawn to some and feel less immediate affection for others. But we Christians are called to love as Jesus loved. We are to reach out to the unlovely as well as to the attractive. We are to abandon favoritism in favor of a warm, loving concern for all.

> But the LORD said to Samuel, "Do not consider his appearance or his height, for I have rejected him. The LORD does not look at the things man looks at. Man looks at the outward appearance, but the LORD looks at the heart." [1 Sam. 16:7]

> If you really keep the royal law found in Scripture, "Love your neighbor as yourself," you are doing right. But if you show favoritism, you sin and are convicted by the law as lawbreakers. [James 2:8–9]

> [Do] not take pride in one man over against another. For who makes you different from anyone else? What do you have that you did not receive? And if you did receive it, why do you boast as though you did not? [1 Cor. 4:6–7]

> My brothers, as believers in our glorious Lord Jesus Christ, don't show favoritism. Suppose a man comes into your meeting wearing a gold ring and fine clothes, and a poor man in shabby clothes also comes in. If you show special attention to the man wearing fine clothes and say, "Here's a good seat for you," but say to the poor man, "You stand there" or "Sit on the floor by my feet," have you not discriminated among yourselves and become judges with evil thoughts? [James 2:1–4]

Love is to be expressed by identifying with others. Persons who see us as being like them, rather than unlike them, can more easily accept the ministry we offer them. We are all the same in our humanity and in our need for God's love and grace. Christian love means that we recognize how much others are like us, set aside any pride, and relate to our fellows humbly and honestly.

> To the weak I became weak, to win the weak. I have become all things to all men so that by all possible means I might

save some. I do all this for the sake of the gospel, that I may share in its blessings. [1 Cor. 9:22–23]

Since the children have flesh and blood, [Jesus] too shared in their humanity so that by his death he might destroy him who holds the power of death — that is, the devil — and free those who all their lives were held in slavery by their fear of death. For surely it is not angels he helps, but Abraham's descendants. [Heb. 2:14–16]

Praise be to the God and Father of our Lord Jesus Christ, the Father of compassion and the God of all comfort, who comforts us in all our troubles, so that we can comfort those in any trouble with the comfort we ourselves have received from God. For just as the sufferings of Christ flow over into our lives, so also through Christ our comfort overflows. If we are distressed, it is for your comfort and salvation; if we are comforted, it is for your comfort, which produces in you patient endurance of the same sufferings we suffer. And our hope for you is firm, because we know that just as you share in our sufferings, so also you share in our comfort. [2 Cor. 1:3–7]

Love is expressed in honesty and openness in our relationships with others. Honesty in relationships means more than not telling lies. It means a willingness to communicate our true feelings; a willingness to let another person really know us. When we have an honest relationship with another person, that person is far more likely to be open to our ministry.

We have spoken freely to you, Corinthians, and opened wide our hearts to you. We are not withholding our affection from you, but you are withholding yours from us. As a fair exchange — I speak as to my children — open wide your hearts also. [2 Cor. 6:11–13]

Therefore each of you must put off falsehood and speak truthfully to his neighbor, for we are all members of one body. [Eph. 4:25]

Therefore, rid yourselves of all malice and all deceit, hypocrisy, envy, and slander of every kind. [1 Peter 2:1]

> An honest answer
> is like a kiss on the lips. [Prov. 24:26]

Do not lie to each other, since you have taken off your old self with its practices and have put on the new self, which is being renewed in knowledge in the image of its Creator. [Col. 3:9–10]

> He who rebukes a man will in the end gain more favor
> than he who has a flattering tongue. [Prov. 28:23]

We are not trying to please men but God, who tests our hearts. You know we never used flattery, nor did we put on a mask to cover up greed — God is our witness. We were not looking for praise from men, not from you or anyone else. [1 Thess. 2:4–6]

Instead, speaking the truth in love, we will in all things grow. ... [Eph. 4:15]

Love is expressed by encouraging and serving others. When another person knows that we have his or her best interests at heart, a climate for personal ministry will develop. A servant's attitude leads to responsiveness and love.

> See to it, brothers, that none of you has a sinful, unbelieving heart that turns away from the living God. But encourage one another daily, as long as it is called Today, so that none of you may be hardened by sin's deceitfulness. [Heb. 3:12–13]

Nobody should seek his own good, but the good of others. [1 Cor. 10:24]

But do not use your freedom to indulge the sinful nature; rather, serve one another in love. [Gal. 5:13]

And let us consider how we may spur one another on toward love and good deeds. Let us not give up meeting together, as some are in the habit of doing, but let us encourage one another — and all the more as you see the Day approaching. [Heb. 10:24–25]

Therefore encourage one another and build each other up, just as in fact you are doing. [1 Thess. 5:11]

[The elders] replied, "If today you will be a servant to these people and serve them and give them a favorable answer, they will always be your servants." [1 Kings 12:7]

I long to see you so that I may impart to you some spiritual gift to make you strong — that is, that you and I may be mutually encouraged by each other's faith. [Rom. 1:11–12]

There are different kinds of gifts, but the same Spirit. There are different kinds of service, but the same Lord. There are different kinds of working, but the same God works all of them in all men. [1 Cor. 12:4–6]

Love is expressed by confronting sin in our fellow Christians and by following the Bible's teaching on church discipline. Discipline is to be exercised only when a person is regularly practicing what the Bible identifies as sin. But the discipline is an act of love, which leads to restoration to fellowship and ministering relationships.

If anyone does not obey our instruction in this letter, take special note of him. Do not associate with him, in order that he may feel ashamed. Yet do not regard him as an enemy, but warn him as a brother. [2 Thess. 3:14–15]

"If your brother sins against you, go and show him his fault, just between the two of you. If he listens to you, you have won your brother over. But if he will not listen, take one or two others along, so that 'every matter may be established by the testimony of two or three witnesses.' If he refuses to listen to them, tell it to the church; and if he refuses to listen even to the church, treat him as you would a pagan or a tax collector." [Matt. 18:15–17]

I urge you, brothers, to watch out for those who cause divisions and put obstacles in your way that are contrary to the teaching you have learned. Keep away from them. For such people are not serving our Lord Christ, but their own appetites. [Rom. 16:17–18]

God will judge those outside. "Expel the wicked man from among you." [1 Cor. 5:13]

If anyone has caused grief, he has not so much grieved me as he has grieved all of you, to some extent — not to put it too severely. The punishment inflicted on him by the majority is sufficient for him. Now instead, you ought to forgive and comfort him, so that he will not be overwhelmed by excessive sorrow. I urge you, therefore, to reaffirm your love for him. [2 Cor. 2:5–8]

Love is expressed by controlling our talk about others. Maintaining a positive attitude toward others and speaking in positive ways about them help to create a climate for personal ministries and express love significantly.

We all stumble in many ways. If anyone is never at fault in what he says, he is a perfect man, able to keep his whole body in check. [James 3:2]

Don't grumble against each other, brothers, or you will be judged. [James 5:9]

Do not let any unwholesome talk come out of your mouths, but only what is helpful for building others up according to their needs, that it may benefit those who listen. And do not grieve the Holy Spirit of God, with whom you were sealed for the day of redemption. Get rid of all bitterness, rage and anger, brawling and slander, along with every form of malice. Be kind and compassionate to one another, forgiving each other, just as in Christ God forgave you. [Eph. 4:29–32]

Set a guard over my mouth, O LORD;
keep watch over the door of my lips. [Ps. 141:3]

My dear brothers, take note of this: Everyone should be quick to listen, slow to speak and slow to become angry, for man's anger does not bring about the righteous life that God desires. [James 1:19–20]

Love is expressed in an attitude of humility which gives priority to the concerns and the needs of others. The person who is truly humble is not perceived as a threat by others. The person who honestly cares about others soon builds relationships in which personal ministries can take place.

> Be completely humble and gentle; be patient, bearing with one another in love. Make every effort to keep the unity of the Spirit through the bond of peace. [Eph. 4:2–3]

> Do not think of yourself more highly than you ought, but rather think of yourself with sober judgment, in accordance with the measure of faith God has given you. [Rom. 12:3]

> Submit to one another out of reverence for Christ. [Eph. 5:21]

> Do nothing out of selfish amibition or vain conceit, but in humility consider others better than yourselves. Each of you should look not only to your own interests, but also to the interests of others.
> Your attitude should be the same as that of Christ Jesus. . . . [Phil. 2:3–5]

> And the Lord's servant must not quarrel; instead, he must be kind to everyone, able to teach, not resentful. Those who oppose him he must gently instruct, in the hope that God will grant them repentance leading them to a knowledge of the truth. . . . [2 Tim. 2:24–25]

> But the wisdom that comes from heaven is first of all pure; then peace-loving, considerate, submissive, full of mercy and good fruit, impartial and sincere. Peacemakers who sow in peace raise a harvest of righteousness. [James 3:17–18]

> . . . clothe yourselves with compassion, kindness, humility, gentleness and patience. Bear with each other and forgive whatever grievances you may have against one another. Forgive as the Lord forgave you. [Col. 3:12–13]

Love is to be expressed to non-Christians as well as to fellow believers. As we live a life of love for outsiders as well as for the members of the family of faith, we build a climate in which we can share the message of Christ. Although we are to be careful not to adopt the lifestyle of unbelievers, we are still called to build relationships with them in which Christ can be communicated.

But the Pharisees and the teachers of the law who belonged to their sect complained to [Jesus'] disciples, "Why do you eat and drink with tax collectors and 'sinners'?"

Jesus answered them, "It is not the healthy who need a doctor, but the sick. I have not come to call the righteous, but sinners to repentance." [Luke 5:30–32]

" 'When an alien lives with you in your land, do not mistreat him. The alien living with you must be treated as one of your native-born. Love him as yourself, for you were aliens in Egypt. I am the LORD your God.' " [Lev. 19:33–34]

I have written you in my letter not to associate with sexually immoral people — not at all meaning the people of this world who are immoral, or the greedy and swindlers, or idolaters. In that case you would have to leave this world. But now I am writing you that you must not associate with anyone who calls himself a brother but is sexually immoral or greedy, an idolater or a slanderer, a drunkard or a swindler. With such a man do not even eat.

What business is it of mine to judge those outside the church? Are you not to judge those inside? God will judge those outside. [1 Cor. 5:9–13]

Jesus told them another parable: "The kingdom of heaven is like a man who sowed good seed in his field. But while everyone was sleeping, his enemy came and sowed weeds among the wheat, and went away. When the wheat sprouted and formed heads, then the weeds also appeared.

"The owner's servants came to him and said, . . . 'Do you want us to go and pull them up?'

" 'No,' he answered, 'because while you are pulling the weeds, you may root up the wheat with them. Let both grow together until the harvest.' " [Matt. 13:24–30]

"You have heard that it was said, 'Love your neighbor and hate your enemy.' But I tell you: Love your enemies and pray for those who persecute you, that you may be sons of your

Father in heaven. He causes his sun to rise on the evil and the good, and sends rain on the righteous and the unrighteous. If you love those who love you, what reward will you get? Are not even the tax collectors doing that? And if you greet only your brothers, what are you doing more than others? Do not even pagans do that? Be perfect, therefore, as your heavenly Father is perfect. [Matt. 5:43–48]

5

Comfort
the Suffering

Each of us undergoes times of suffering. A loved one dies. We're gripped by a lingering sickness. We lose the job we depended on to provide for our family. An engagement or a marriage is broken.

We can understand the pain. But all too often, when we're with others who are suffering, we simply don't know what to say. Comforting the suffering is one of the most difficult, yet most important, of personal ministries.

Job's Experience

The Old Testament tells the story of Job, a good man, who was suddenly crushed by a series of tragedies. In the space of a day he lost his children, and all his great wealth. Shortly after Job himself suffered a painful illness. When Job's friends came to comfort him, they were so shocked at his condition that they could only sit with him, silent, for days.

When finally they did begin to talk, it was clear that Job was in the grip of a common despair. He couldn't understand why God should permit him to suffer so. Job knew that he had lived a good life, seeking to honor God and show kindness to others. Why then should this happen to him?

Job's friends had only one answer. They assumed that God must be punishing Job. And so the remedy they suggested was that Job confess his sin and appeal to God for mercy.

Job, tormented by his tragedies and his inability to understand the why, would not accept their diagnosis. He knew he had not done anything to deserve such punishment. But he had no alternative explanation.

The Book of Job reports the endless, circular argument, as Job's friends desert their mission of comfort and instead seek to force Job to accept their interpretation of his suffering. The pathos of the book is revealed as we see that Job agrees with their theology — God *is* one who punishes sin and the sinner — but can find no explanation for his own suffering other than that it is a punishment he knows he does not deserve.

The issue is finally resolved as a young observer named Elihu speaks up. Job and his comforters are wrong. Job is wrong to claim purity before God; the comforters are wrong in charging Job with some hidden sin neither they nor Job are aware of. And both are wrong to suppose that a mere human being can explain God's actions or penetrate his motives. As for the notion that suffering is always punishment for sin, that is wrong too, for God may well use suffering to instruct a person and lead him or her to draw closer to the Lord.

In the end God speaks, not to explain Job's suffering, but to show himself to be great and beyond human understanding. Job bows then, acknowledging God's sovereignty and right to do as he chooses. God invites Job to pray for his comforters, that they might be forgiven for their sins of presumption and judgmentalism. Then God heals Job and restores to him all that he had lost.

Lessons for the Comforter

What can we learn from the story of Job?
We learn first that comforters are not called to explain why

to the sufferer. Particularly, we are not to explain another's experience in terms of divine punishment. We do not know God's reasons for what he does in the life of another person. What we do know is that God is good and loving, and even pain is intended to work together with "all things" in an individual's life "for the good" (Rom. 8:28). We can affirm the goodness and the love of God, something a person in the grip of suffering needs to remember and hold on to. We cannot add to the sufferer's burden by charging him or her with unknown sins or insisting that the pain is somehow his or her fault because of a lack of faith.

We learn that a person who is suffering may hurt most from mental stress. The uncertainty, the doubts, the fears associated with suffering may be the most difficult thing of all to bear. A ministry of comforting can and should focus on the feelings of the sufferer and help the person find a restored confidence in God. That confidence comes not by knowing the why, but by remembering that God continues to love, continues to be committed, to his own.

We learn too that answers are not what is most important to a sufferer. Elihu did not say, "This is why Job is suffering." All Elihu did was to point out that the tragedies need not be seen as punishment for sin. When God appeared, he offered Job no explanation for his action, but simply called on his servant to commit himself to a sovereign Lord. It is not answers that are needed, but simply another person who cares, and who in caring helps to reassure that God continues to care too.

Some of the verses in this chapter help you explore your own attitude as you seek to relate to sufferers in a healing way. Other verses are listed as resources: words from God that you can share with those who hurt, to strengthen them and to remind them of God's unending love.

We comfort others best when we identify with them. Paul speaks of his own suffering as something which in fact qualified him to comfort. Only because we know from our own pain what others may experience, and from God's grace how our Lord can comfort, can we reach out to help. Sharing in the suffering of others doesn't mean talking endlessly about our troubles. It simply means letting others know that we truly do understand their pain and are subject to the same weaknesses.

Praise be to the God and Father of our Lord Jesus Christ, the Father of compassion and the God of all comfort, who comforts us in all our troubles, so that we can comfort those in any trouble with the comfort we ourselves have received from God. [2 Cor. 1:3–4]

Everyone should be quick to listen, slow to speak. . . . [James 1:19]

He who answers before listening —
that is his folly and his shame. [Prov. 18:13]

We have spoken freely to you, Corinthians, and opened wide our hearts to you. We are not withholding our affection from you. . . . [2 Cor. 6:11–12]

Blessed is he who has regard for the weak;
the LORD delivers him in times of trouble. . . .
The LORD will sustain him on his sickbed
and restore him from his bed of illness. [Ps. 41:1, 3]

To the weak I became weak, to win the weak. I have become all things to all men so that by all possible means I might save some. [1 Cor. 9:22]

"A despairing man should have the devotion of his friends,
even though he forsakes the fear of the Almighty." [Job 6:14]

"But my mouth would encourage you;
comfort from my lips would bring you relief." [Job 16:5]

[The Lord] has sent me to bind up the brokenhearted,
to proclaim freedom for the captives
and release from darkness for the prisoners,
to proclaim the year of the LORD's favor
and the day of vengeance of our God,
to comfort all who mourn
and provide for those who grieve. . . . [Isa. 61:1–3]

We comfort others best when we accept rather than reject their feelings. Suffering typically has a dramatic impact on feelings. A normally cheerful person may grow despondent; an optimistic person bitter. Feelings of guilt and anger may swirl as the sufferer seeks to deal with his or her experience. How good to know that feelings can and will change. In comforting others we need to accept their feelings and avoid showing shock or disappointment. God understands those feelings and will help his child work through the painful feelings to an experience of his peace. The Bible shows how godly people often experienced what we think of as "negative" feelings, expressed them, and ultimately found peace through relationship with the Lord.

"I have no peace, no quietness;
    I have no rest, but only turmoil." [Job 3:26]

"When I lie down I think, 'How long before I get up?'
    The night drags on, and I toss till dawn." [Job 7:4]

How long, O LORD? Will you forget me forever?
    How long will you hide your face from me?
How long must I wrestle with my thoughts
    and every day have sorrow in my heart? [Ps. 13:1–2]

For I am poor and needy,
    and my heart is wounded within me.
I fade away like an evening shadow;
    I am shaken off like a locust.
My knees give way from fasting;
    my body is thin and gaunt.
I am an object of scorn to my accusers;
    when they see me, they shake their heads. [Ps. 109:22–25]

[Jesus] took Peter and the two sons of Zebedee along with him, and he began to be sorrowful and troubled. Then he said to them, "My soul is overwhelmed with sorrow to the point of death. Stay here and keep watch with me." [Matt. 26:37–38]

"The waves of death swirled about me;
    the torrents of destruction overwhelmed me. . . .
"In my distress I called to the LORD. . . ." [2 Sam. 22:5, 7]

*We comfort best when we remember and share our conviction that God
is compassionate.* The mystery of suffering, like the mystery of
evil, is great. Yet we Christians know a God who has revealed
himself in Jesus to be a God of overwhelming love. The love
and compassion of God are realities: realities which the suffering can affirm and hold to even when they are suffering
something they cannot understand.

Since [the crowd] had nothing to eat, Jesus called his disciples
to him and said, "I have compassion for these people; they
have already been with me three days and have nothing to
eat. If I send them home hungry, they will collapse on the
way. . . ." [Mark 8:1–3]

> The LORD is gracious and righteous;
>   our God is full of compassion.
> The LORD protects the simplehearted;
>   when I was in great need, he saved me.
> Be at rest once more, O my soul,
>   for the LORD has been good to you. [Ps. 116:5–7]

For the LORD your God is a merciful God; he will not abandon
or destroy you or forget the covenant with your forefathers,
which he confirmed to them by oath. [Deut. 4:31]

> "For a brief moment I abandoned you,
>   but with deep compassion I will bring you back.
> In a surge of anger
>   I hid my face from you for a moment,
> but with everlasting kindness
>   I will have compassion on you,"
>   says the LORD your Redeemer. [Isa. 54:7–8]

> "For he wounds, but he also binds up;
>   he injures, but his hands also heal." [Job 5:18]

> One thing God has spoken,
>   two things have I heard:
> that you, O God, are strong,
>   and that you, O Lord, are loving. [Ps. 62:11–12]

May your unfailing love be my comfort,
   according to your promise to your servant. [Ps. 119:76]

"Though the mountains be shaken
   and the hills be removed,
yet my unfailing love for you will not be shaken
   nor my covenant of peace be removed,"
   says the LORD, who has compassion on you. [Isa. 54:10]

We comfort best by remembering that God is both able and willing to restore the sufferer. We may need to wait on God's timing. And that wait may seem painfully long. But we remain confident. God is able. And God is willing. He will heal and restore in his good time.

"I have seen his ways, but I will heal him;
   I will guide him and restore comfort to him,
   creating praise on the lips of the mourners. . . ." [Isa. 57:18–19]

   Remember your word to your servant,
      for you have given me hope.
   My comfort in my suffering is this:
      your promise preserves my life. [Ps. 119:49–50]

And when they heard that the LORD was concerned about them and had seen their misery, they bowed down and worshiped. [Exod. 4:31]

"See now that I myself am He!
   There is no god besides me.
I put to death and I bring to life,
   I have wounded and I will heal,
   and no one can deliver out of my hand." [Deut. 32:39]

      Heal me, O LORD, and I will be healed;
         save me and I will be saved,
         for you are the one I praise. [Jer. 17:14]

"Surely this is our God;
   we trusted in him, and he saved us.
This is the LORD, we trusted in him;
   let us rejoice and be glad in his salvation." [Isa. 25:9]

We comfort others best when we affirm the presence of God, even in times of deepest suffering. And we can show something of God's own love by giving the gift of our presence.

For I am convinced that neither death nor life, neither angels nor demons, neither the present nor the future, nor any powers, neither height nor depth, nor anything else in all creation, will be able to separate us from the love of God that is in Christ Jesus our Lord. [Rom. 8:38–39]

"Do not be afraid, for I am with you. . . ." [Isa. 43:5]

"He reached down from on high and took hold of me;
    he drew me out of deep waters.
He rescued me from my powerful enemy.
    from my foes, who were too strong for me.
They confronted me in the day of my disaster,
    but the LORD was my support." [2 Sam. 22:17–19]

"For I am the LORD, your God,
    who takes hold of your right hand
and who says to you, Do not fear;
    I will help you." [Isa. 41:13]

He tends his flock like a shepherd:
    He gathers the lambs in his arms
and carries them close to his heart;
    he gently leads those that have young. [Isa. 40:11]

Do you not know?
    Have you not heard?
The LORD is the everlasting God,
    the Creator of the ends of the earth.
He will not grow tired or weary,
    and his understanding no one can fathom.
He gives strength to the weary
    and increases the power of the weak.
Even youths grow tired and weary,
    and young men stumble and fall;
but those who hope in the LORD
    will renew their strength.
They will soar on wings like eagles;
    they will run and not grow weary,
    they will walk and not be faint. [Isa. 40:28–31]

The LORD is my shepherd, I shall not be in want.
  He makes me lie down in green pastures,
he leads me beside quiet waters,
  he restores my soul.
He guides me in paths of righteousness
  for his name's sake.
Even though I walk
  through the valley of the shadow of death,
I will fear no evil,
  for you are with me. ... [Ps. 23:1–4]

Though I walk in the midst of trouble,
  you preserve my life;
  ... with your right hand you save me. [Ps. 138:7]

We comfort best when we remember that Jesus shared our human condition and suffered too. God is not withdrawn, far away, unable to understand or to sympathize. There is nothing we experience that Jesus did not experience too; there is no suffering of ours that surpasses the suffering of our Lord. When we remember his suffering, we realize that Jesus fully understands, and we come to him freely, with confidence, for the grace and help we need.

Since the children have flesh and blood, he too shared in their humanity so that by his death he might destroy him who holds the power of death — that is, the devil — and free those who all their lives were held in slavery by their fear of death. [Heb. 2:14–15]

Because he himself suffered when he was tempted, he is able to help those who are being tempted. [Heb. 2:18]

During the days of Jesus' life on earth, he offered up prayers and petitions with loud cries and tears to the one who could save him from death, and he was heard because of his reverent submission. Although he was a son, he learned obedience from what he suffered and, once made perfect, he became the source of eternal salvation for all who obey him. ... [Heb. 5:7–9]

"Come to me, all you who are weary and burdened, and I will give you rest. Take my yoke upon you and learn from me, for I am gentle and humble in heart, and you will find rest for your souls. For my yoke is easy and my burden is light." [Matt. 11:28–30]

For we do not have a high priest who is unable to sympathize with our weaknesses, but we have one who has been tempted in every way, just as we are — yet was without sin. Let us then approach the throne of grace with confidence, so that we may receive mercy and find grace to help us in our time of need. [Heb. 4:15–16]

We comfort others best as we remember that there is always hope for good to come in the future. An attitude of positive expectation, rooted in the trustworthiness of God, is something we can display and share.

Brothers, as an example of patience in the face of suffering, take the prophets who spoke in the name of the Lord. As you know, we consider blessed those who have persevered. You have heard of Job's perseverance and have seen what the Lord finally brought about. The Lord is full of compassion and mercy. [James 5:10–11]

So do not throw away your confidence; it will be richly rewarded. You need to persevere so that when you have done the will of God, you will receive what he has promised. [Heb. 10:35–36]

Let us hold unswervingly to the hope we profess, for he who promised is faithful. [Heb. 10:23]

Blessed is the man who perseveres under trial, because when he has stood the test, he will receive the crown of life that God has promised to those who love him. [James 1:12]

But do not forget this one thing, dear friends: With the Lord a day is like a thousand years, and a thousand years are like a day. The Lord is not slow in keeping his promise, as some understand slowness. [2 Peter 3:8–9]

Praise be to the God and Father of our Lord Jesus Christ! In his great mercy he has given us new birth into a living hope through the resurrection of Jesus Christ from the dead, and into an inheritance that can never perish, spoil or fade — kept in heaven for you, who through faith are shielded by God's power until the coming of the salvation that is ready to be revealed in the last time. In this you greatly rejoice, though now for a little while you may have had to suffer grief in all kinds of trials. These have come so that your faith — of greater worth than gold, which perishes even though refined by fire — may be proved genuine and may result in praise, glory and honor when Jesus Christ is revealed. Though you have not seen him, you love him; and even though you do not see him now, you believe in him and are filled with an inexpressible and glorious joy. . . . [1 Peter 1:3–8]

Therefore we do not lose heart. Though outwardly we are wasting away, yet inwardly we are being renewed day by day. [2 Cor. 4:16]

We comfort best when we rely on God and communicate by our own trust in him a sense of his trustworthiness. How rich are those passages of Scripture that invite us to rely on the Lord and remind us of how reliable our God is. Whatever our needs, we can count fully on him.

Though the fig tree does not bud
  and there are no grapes on the vines,
though the olive crop fails
  and the fields produce no food,
though there are no sheep in the pen
  and no cattle in the stalls,
yet I will rejoice in the LORD,
  I will be joyful in God my Savior.
The Sovereign LORD is my strength;
  he makes my feet like the feet of a deer,
  he enables me to go on the heights. [Hab. 3:17–19]

Three times I pleaded with the Lord to take it [Paul's "thorn in the flesh"] away from me. But he said to me, "My grace is

sufficient for you, for my power is made perfect in weakness."
Therefore I will boast all the more gladly about my weaknesses, so that Christ's power may rest on me. That is why,
for Christ's sake, I delight in weaknesses, in insults, in hardships, in persecutions, in difficulties. For when I am weak,
then I am strong. [2 Cor. 12:8–10]

> The LORD is good to those whose hope is in him,
>   to the one who seeks him;
> it is good to wait quietly
>   for the salvation of the LORD. [Lam. 3:25–26]

> You will keep in perfect peace
>   him whose mind is steadfast,
>   because he trusts in you.
> Trust in the LORD forever,
>   for the LORD, the LORD, is the Rock eternal. [Isa. 26:3–4]

> Even to your old age and gray hairs
>   I am he, I am he who will sustain you.
> I have made you and I will carry you;
>   I will sustain you and I will rescue you. [Isa. 46:4]

> Yet I am always with you;
>   you hold me by my right hand.
> You guide me with your counsel,
>   and afterward you will take me into glory. . . .
> My flesh and my heart may fail,
>   but God is the strength of my heart
>   and my portion forever. [Ps. 73:23–24, 26]

*We comfort best when we assure others that God does have a purpose
in their suffering.* There is a great difference between affirming
that some good purpose exists and trying to explain what that
purpose is. God's motives and purposes are beyond our grasp.
We can never say, "This is why." But we can say that what God
permits us to experience is never meaningless; we are never
the victims of mere chance.

> Therefore, since Christ suffered in his body, arm yourselves
> also with the same attitude, because he who has suffered in

his body is done with sin. As a result, he does not live the rest of his earthly life for evil human desires, but rather for the will of God. [1 Peter 4:1–2]

But if you suffer for doing good and you endure it, this is commendable before God. To this you were called, because Christ suffered for you, leaving you an example, that you should follow in his steps. [1 Peter 2:20–21]

Dear friends, do not be surprised at the painful trial you are suffering, as though something strange were happening to you. But rejoice that you participate in the sufferings of Christ, so that you may be overjoyed when his glory is revealed. [1 Peter 4:12–13]

Endure hardship as discipline; God is treating you as sons. For what son is not disciplined by his father? . . . Our fathers disciplined us for a little while as they thought best; but God disciplines us for our good, that we may share in his holiness. No discipline seems pleasant at the time, but painful. Later on, however, it produces a harvest of righteousness and peace for those who have been trained by it. [Heb. 12:7–11]

Consider it pure joy, my brothers, whenever you face trials of many kinds, because you know that the testing of your faith develops perseverance. Perseverance must finish its work so that you may be mature. . . . [James 1:2–4]

And we know that in all things God works for the good of those who love him, who have been called according to his purpose. For those God foreknew he also predestined to be conformed to the likeness of his Son, that he might be the firstborn among many brothers. [Rom. 8:28–29]

Remember how the LORD your God led you all the way in the desert these forty years, to humble you and to test you in order to know what was in your heart, whether or not you would keep his commands. He humbled you, causing you to hunger and then feeding you with manna, which neither you nor your fathers had known, to teach you that man does not live on bread alone but on every word that comes from the mouth of the LORD. [Deut. 8:2–3]

We comfort others best when we pray with them and show them how to express their distress in prayer. Prayer remains the basic resource of those who suffer and the firmest support on which to rest. Believers are to freely express feelings to the Lord. Yet prayer is far more than this. We believe that God will answer our prayers.

> Is any one of you sick? He should call the elders of the church to pray over him and anoint him with oil in the name of the Lord. And the prayer offered in faith will make the sick person well; the Lord will raise him up. If he has sinned, he will be forgiven. Therefore confess your sins to each other and pray for each other so that you may be healed. [James 5:14–16]

> Humble yourselves, therefore, under God's mighty hand, that he may lift you up in due time. Cast all your anxiety on him because he cares for you. [1 Peter 5:6–7]

> Do not be anxious about anything, but in everything, by prayer and petition, with thanksgiving, present your requests to God. And the peace of God, which transcends all understanding, will guard your hearts and your minds in Christ Jesus. [Phil. 4:6–7]

> In the same way, the Spirit helps us in our weakness. We do not know what we ought to pray for, but the Spirit himself intercedes for us with groans that words cannot express. And he who searches our hearts knows the mind of the Spirit, because the Spirit intercedes for the saints in accordance with God's will. [Rom. 8:26–27]

> During the days of Jesus' life on earth, he offered up prayers and petitions with loud cries and tears to the one who could save him from death, and he was heard because of his reverent submission. [Heb. 5:7]

We comfort best when we remember that God's goodness is ultimately displayed in eternity. Not every pain is soothed here; not every illness healed. How good to know that the individual's life does not end in bodily death. The joy we are promised is not limited to our few brief years on earth.

Brothers, we do not want you to be ignorant about those who fall asleep, or to grieve like the rest of men, who have no hope. We believe that Jesus died and rose again and so we believe that God will bring with Jesus those who have fallen asleep in him. According to the Lord's own word, we tell you that we who are still alive, who are left till the coming of the Lord, will certainly not precede those who have fallen asleep. For the Lord himself will come down from heaven, with a loud command, with the voice of the archangel and with the trumpet call of God, and the dead in Christ will rise first. After that, we who are still alive and are left will be caught up together with them in the clouds to meet the Lord in the air. And so we will be with the Lord forever. [1 Thess. 4:13–17]

> The righteous perish,
> and no one ponders it in his heart;
> devout men are taken away,
> and no one understands
> that the righteous are taken away
> to be spared from evil.
> Those who walk uprightly
> enter into peace;
> they find rest as they lie in death. [Isa. 57:1–2]

> ... you will fill me with joy in your presence,
> with eternal pleasures at your right hand. [Ps. 16:11]

6

Encourage
the Distressed

One of the most beautiful words in our Bible is "encourage." The Hebrew words it translates mean "to strengthen." The basic Greek words (v. *parakaleo*, n. *paraklesis*) appear more than a hundred times in the New Testament. They have three different meanings: to invite, to exhort or encourage, and to comfort.

What then does it mean to "encourage" someone? The focus of encouragement in personal ministry is strengthening, calling forth renewed commitment. Typically in the New Testament believers are encouraged *to* some godly course of action.

We see this emphasis when Paul encouraged young believers to "live lives worthy of God" (1 Thess. 2:12) and to strengthen each other "in every good deed and word" (2 Thess. 2:17).

What a warm and wonderful ministry the ministry of encouragement is. Everyone becomes discouraged at times. We experience failures. Things don't go as we expected. We're overcome by a spiritual dry spell. At times like these each of us needs Christian brothers or sisters who will strengthen us in our resolve to continue to walk worthy of our God.

The verses in this chapter explore how we can reach out to others with a ministry of encouragement. The chapter also contains some of the most encouraging passages of Scripture, passages which will strengthen others to walk God's way.

We are each called to a ministry of encouraging others. The Bible often reminds us that our involvement in a caring way truly can strengthen Christian brothers and sisters in their commitment to our Lord.

> May our Lord Jesus Christ himself and God our Father, who loved us and by his grace gave us eternal encouragement and good hope, encourage your hearts and strengthen you in every good deed and word. [2 Thess. 2:16–17]

> We loved you so much that we were delighted to share with you not only the gospel of God but our lives as well, because you had become so dear to us. . . . For you know that we dealt with each of you as a father deals with his own children, encouraging, comforting and urging you to live lives worthy of God, who calls you into his kingdom and glory. [1 Thess. 2:8, 11–12]

> My purpose is that they may be encouraged in heart and united in love, so that they may have the full riches of complete understanding, in order that they may know the mystery of God, namely, Christ. . . . [Col. 2:2]

> When I said, "My foot is slipping,"
>   your love, O LORD, supported me.
> When anxiety was great within me,
>   your consolation brought joy to my soul. [Ps. 94:18–19]

A ministry of encouragement involves having a deep concern for others. We are to be sensitive to the pains and sympathetic to the hurts which others feel. When we are distressed for others and communicate that distress as loving concern, we build a relationship in which encouragement is most likely to be welcomed and received.

> For I wrote you out of great distress and anguish of heart and with many tears, not to grieve you but to let you know the depth of my love for you. [2 Cor. 2:4]

Keep on loving each other as brothers. . . . Remember those in prison as if you were their fellow prisoners, and those who are mistreated as if you yourselves were suffering. [Heb. 13:1, 3]

Above all, love each other deeply, because love covers over a multitude of sins. Offer hospitality to one another without grumbling. Each one should use whatever gift he has received to serve others. . . . [1 Peter 4:8–10]

Each of you should look not only to your own interests, but also to the interests of others. [Phil. 2:4]

We who are strong ought to bear with the failings of the weak and not to please ourselves. Each of us should please his neighbor for his good, to build him up. For even Christ did not please himself but, as it is written: "The insults of those who insult you have fallen on me." For everything that was written in the past was written to teach us, so that through endurance and the encouragement of the Scriptures we might have hope. [Rom. 15:1–4]

Even the strongest Christian may feel powerless at times before a particular temptation. We who have the ministry of encouragement can identify with such feelings and yet confidently affirm that God can and will enable our brother or sister to overcome the temptation. Some passages we can use to strengthen others include promises; others point to the wonderful example set by Jesus.

No temptation has seized you except what is common to man. And God is faithful; he will not let you be tempted beyond what you can bear. But when you are tempted, he will also provide a way out so that you can stand up under it. [1 Cor. 10:13]

Because [Jesus] himself suffered when he was tempted, he is able to help those who are being tempted. [Heb. 2:18]

Blessed is the man who perseveres under trial, because when he has stood the test, he will receive the crown of life that God has promised to those who love him. [James 1:12]

When tempted, no one should say, "God is tempting me." For God cannot be tempted by evil, nor does he tempt anyone; but each one is tempted when, by his own evil desire, he is dragged away and enticed. [James 1:13–14]

We can encourage and strengthen others by helping them recapture a vision of our calling as Christians and the real nature of our hope. Discouragement is often linked with a loss of perspective. We may lose heart as we suffer reverses in this world. But our hope is never to be anchored in the events of our present life.

All these people were still living by faith when they died. They did not receive the things promised; they only saw them and welcomed them from a distance. And they admitted that they were aliens and strangers on earth. People who say such things show that they are looking for a country of their own. If they had been thinking of the country they had left, they would have had opportunity to return. Instead, they were longing for a better country — a heavenly one. Therefore God is not ashamed to be called their God, for he has prepared a city for them. [Heb. 11:13–16]

Sometimes you were publicly exposed to insult and persecution; at other times you stood side by side with those who were so treated. You sympathized with those in prison and joyfully accepted the confiscation of your property, because you knew that you yourselves had better and lasting possessions. [Heb. 10:33–34]

"Show me, O LORD, my life's end
and the number of my days;
let me know how fleeting is my life.
You have made my days a mere handbreadth;
the span of my years is as nothing before you.
Each man's life is but a breath.   *Selah*
Man is a mere phantom as he goes to and fro:
He bustles about, but only in vain....
"But now, Lord, what do I look for?
My hope is in you." [Ps. 39:4–7]

Rather, as servants of God we commend ourselves in every way: in great endurance; in troubles, hardships and distresses; in beatings, imprisonments and riots; in hard work, sleepless nights and hunger; in purity, understanding, patience and kindness; in the Holy Spirit and in sincere love; in truthful speech and in the power of God; with weapons of righteousness in the right hand and in the left; through glory and dishonor, bad report and good report; genuine, yet regarded as imposters; known, yet regarded as unknown; dying, and yet we live on; beaten, and yet not killed; sorrowful, yet always rejoicing; poor, yet making many rich; having nothing, and yet possessing everything. [2 Cor. 6:4–10]

We need to remind others that God will deliver us from troubles. "Man is born to trouble" (Job 5:7), but the troubles that come on the Christian are not the result of impersonal, overwhelming fate. God himself is a guard around the believer. Those troubles which touch us are permitted by the Lord and are intended to bring us good.

Those whom I love I rebuke and discipline. So be earnest, and repent. [Rev. 3:19]

My son, do not despise the LORD's discipline
   and do not resent his rebuke,
because the LORD disciplines those he loves,
   as a father the son he delights in. [Prov. 3:11–12]

A righteous man may have many troubles,
   but the LORD delivers him from them all. . . . [Ps. 34:19]

Blessed is the man you discipline, O LORD,
   the man you teach from your law;
you grant him relief from days of trouble,
   till a pit is dug for the wicked.
For the LORD will not reject his people;
   he will never forsake his inheritance. [Ps. 94:12–14]

Satisfy us in the morning with your unfailing love,
   that we may sing for joy and be glad all our days.
Make us glad for as many days as you have afflicted us,
   for as many years as we have seen trouble.
May your deeds be shown to your servants,
   your splendor to their children. [Ps. 90:14–16]

And you have forgotten that word of encouragement that ad-
dresses you as sons:
  "My son, do not make light of the Lord's discipline,
    and do not lose heart when he rebukes you,
  because the Lord disciplines those he loves,
    and he punishes everyone he accepts as a son."
Endure hardship as discipline; God is treating you as sons.
For what son is not disciplined by his father? [Heb. 12:5–7]

Faith is the basic principle of the Christian life. We realize that God
alone is able: able to save, able to sustain, able to enable us
to walk with him. Our part is simply to rely completely on him,
trusting him as we take each daily step. Encouragement will
often involve a reminder that God can be trusted; a call to
exercise again the faith which has brought us every blessing
we experience in him. How good to know that God can be
trusted. And that faith can lift us when we fall.

  By faith Abraham, when called to go to a place he would
later receive as his inheritance, obeyed and went, even though
he did not know where he was going. By faith he made his
home in the promised land like a stranger in a foreign country; he lived in tents, as did Isaac and Jacob, who were heirs
with him of the same promise. For he was looking forward to
the city with foundations, whose architect and builder is God.
  By faith Abraham, even though he was past age — and Sarah
herself was barren — was enabled to become a father because
he considered him faithful who had made the promise. [Heb.
11:8–11]

      To you, O LORD, I lift up my soul;
        in you I trust, O my God.
      Do not let me be put to shame,
        nor let my enemies triumph over me.
      No one whose hope is in you
        will ever be put to shame. ... [Ps. 25:1–3]

He will be the sure foundation for your times,
  a rich store of salvation and wisdom and knowledge;
  the fear of the LORD is the key to this treasure. [Isa. 33:6]

Find rest, O my soul, in God alone;
    my hope comes from him.
He alone is my rock and my salvation;
    he is my fortress, I will not be shaken.
My salvation and my honor depend on God;
    he is my mighty rock, my refuge.
Trust in him at all times, O people;
    pour out your hearts to him,
    for God is our refuge.   *Selah* [Ps. 62:5–8]

But I trust in you, O LORD;
    I say, "You are my God."
My times are in your hands;
    deliver me from my enemies
    and from those who pursue me. [Ps. 31:14–15]

Often the encouragement our friends will need is the exhortation to hold on and wait with patience for God to act. It's not so much troubles which discourage us. It's when troubles seem to drag on and on, without relief. Yet the Bible speaks much of patience and endurance.

Be patient, then, brothers, until the Lord's coming. See how the farmer waits for the land to yield its valuable crop and how patient he is for the autumn and spring rains. You too, be patient and stand firm, because the Lord's coming is near. [James 5:7–8]

May the Lord direct your hearts into God's love and Christ's perseverance. [2 Thess. 3:5]

Be still before the LORD and wait patiently for him;
    do not fret when men succeed in their ways,
    when they carry out their wicked schemes.
Refrain from anger and turn from wrath;
    do not fret — it leads only to evil.
For evil men will be cut off,
    but those who hope in the LORD will inherit the land. [Ps. 37:7–9]

. . . imitate those who through faith and patience inherit what has been promised. [Heb. 6:12]

Even in the most discouraging times, we Christians can be confident. We can be confident because we know that God will make his strength available to us. We can be confident because we know that as we keep on doing what is right, God will act. An encouraging word in discouraging times expresses confidence that our brother or sister will be strong and God's end will be good.

So do not throw away your confidence; it will be richly rewarded. You need to persevere so that when you have done the will of God, you will receive what he has promised. For in just a very little while,

"He who is coming will come and will not delay.
But my righteous one will live by faith.
And if he shrinks back,
I will not be pleased with him." [Heb. 10:35–38]

The salvation of the righteous comes from the LORD;
he is their stronghold in time of trouble.
The LORD helps them and delivers them;
he delivers them from the wicked and saves them,
because they take refuge in him. [Ps. 37:39–40]

As for God, his way is perfect;
the word of the LORD is flawless.
He is a shield
for all who take refuge in him.
For who is God besides the LORD?
And who is the Rock except our God?
It is God who arms me with strength
and makes my way perfect.
He makes my feet like the feet of a deer;
he enables me to stand on the heights.
He trains my hands for battle;
my arms can bend a bow of bronze. [Ps. 18:30–34]

Moses answered the people, "Do not be afraid. Stand firm and you will see the deliverance the LORD will bring you today." [Exod. 14:13]

Love the LORD, all his saints!
The LORD preserves the faithful,
but the proud he pays back in full.
Be strong and take heart,
all you who hope in the LORD. [Ps. 31:23–24]

But the LORD is with me like a mighty warrior;
so my persecutors will stumble and not prevail. [Jer. 20:11]

... [be] confident of this, that he who began a good work
in you will carry it on to completion until the day of Christ
Jesus. [Phil. 1:6]

Discouragement and despair are often linked to a sense of failure. We
can encourage others by reminding them of those things which
God values; criteria by which he measures success. When we
find our satisfaction in the things which are important to God,
we are strengthened in our walk with the Lord.

But the fruit of the Spirit is love, joy, peace, patience, kindness, goodness, faithfulness, gentleness and self-control. [Gal.
5:22–23]

... I have learned to be content whatever the circumstances. I know what it is to be in need, and I know what it
is to have plenty. I have learned the secret of being content
in any and every situation, whether well fed or hungry, whether
living in plenty or in want. I can do everything through him
who gives me strength. [Phil. 4:11–13]

The apostles left the Sanhedrin, rejoicing because they had
been counted worthy of suffering disgrace for the Name. Day
after day, in the temple courts and from house to house, they
never stopped teaching and proclaiming the good news that
Jesus is the Christ. [Acts 5:41–42]

Therefore we do not lose heart. Though outwardly we are
wasting away, yet inwardly we are being renewed day by day.
For our light and momentary troubles are achieving for us an
eternal glory that far outweighs them all. So we fix our eyes
not on what is seen, but on what is unseen. For what is seen
is temporary, but what is unseen is eternal. [2 Cor. 4:16–18]

We pray this so that the name of our Lord Jesus may be glorified in you, and you in him. . . . [2 Thess. 1:12]

May God himself, the God of peace, sanctify you through and through. May your whole spirit, soul and body be kept blameless at the coming of our Lord Jesus Christ. The one who calls you is faithful and he will do it. [1 Thess. 5:23]

A *sense of confidence replaces our distress if we have a sense of direction and purpose in life.* For the Christian, that sense of direction is provided by a personal commitment to follow Jesus. Encouragement may mean helping another sense the satisfaction that comes as we let relationship with God establish the direction in which life can move.

"Whoever would love life
    and see good days
must keep his tongue from evil
    and his lips from deceitful speech.
He must turn from evil and do good;
    he must seek peace and pursue it.
For the eyes of the Lord are on the righteous
    and his ears are attentive to their prayer,
but the face of the Lord is against those who do evil."
[1 Peter 3:10–12]

"Come, let us return to the LORD.
He has torn us to pieces
    but he will heal us;
he has injured us
    but he will bind up our wounds. . . .
Let us acknowledge the LORD;
    let us press on to acknowledge him.
As surely as the sun rises,
    he will appear. . . ." [Hos. 6:1, 3]

How good to know that even in times of deepest distress we can appeal to God. Prayer with and for others is one way to encourage them. Reading passages that remind others of the access we have to God is another way to encourage.

But I pray to you, O LORD,
    in the time of your favor;
in your great love, O God,
    answer me with your sure salvation.
Rescue me from the mire,
    do not let me sink;
deliver me from those who hate me,
    from the deep waters. . . .
Answer me, O LORD, out of the goodness of your love. . . . [Ps.
    69:13–14, 16]

"Now therefore, O our God, the great, mighty and awesome
God, who keeps his covenant of love, do not let all this hardship seem trifling in your eyes — the hardship that has come
upon us. . . ." [Neh. 9:32]

I cry aloud to the LORD;
    I lift up my voice to the LORD for mercy.
I pour out my complaint before him;
    before him I tell my trouble. [Ps. 142:1–2]

Turn to me and be gracious to me,
    for I am lonely and afflicted.
The troubles of my heart have multiplied;
    free me from my anguish. [Ps. 25:16–17]

"In my distress I called to the LORD;
    I called out to my God.
From his temple he heard my voice;
    my cry came to his ears." [2 Sam. 22:7]

Then Jesus told his disciples a parable to show them that
they should always pray and not give up. He said: "In a certain
town there was a judge who neither feared God nor cared
about men. And there was a widow in that town who kept
coming to him with the plea, 'Grant me justice against my
adversary.'

"For some time he refused. But finally he said to himself,
'Even though I don't fear God or care about men, yet because
this widow keeps bothering me, I will see that she gets justice,
so that she won't eventually wear me out with her coming!' "

And the Lord said, "Listen to what the unjust judge says.

And will not God bring about justice for his chosen ones, who cry out to him day and night? Will he keep putting them off? I tell you, he will see that they get justice, and quickly." [Luke 18:1–8]

> In my distress I called to the LORD;
>   I cried to my God for help.
> From his temple he heard my voice. . . . [Ps. 18:6]

> I love the LORD, for he heard my voice;
>   he heard my cry for mercy.
> Because he turned his ear to me,
>   I will call on him as long as I live. [Ps. 116:1–2]

One of the causes of distress in our day, as in biblical times, is finances. Christians may encourage others by giving financial aid in emergencies. But God encourages us further by providing a word which helps us put the role of money in our lives in fresh perspective.

> "Two things I ask of you, O LORD;
>   do not refuse me before I die:
> Keep falsehood and lies far from me;
>   give me neither poverty nor riches,
>   but give me only my daily bread.
> Otherwise, I may have too much and disown you
>   and say, 'Who is the LORD?'
> Or I may become poor and steal,
>   and so dishonor the name of my God." [Prov. 30:7–9]

But godliness with contentment is great gain. For we brought nothing into the world, and we can take nothing out of it. But if we have food and clothing, we will be content with that. [1 Tim. 6:6–8]

> But the needy will not always be forgotten,
>   nor the hope of the afflicted ever perish. [Ps. 9:18]

"For this is what the LORD, the God of Israel, says: 'The jar of flour will not be used up and the jug of oil will not run dry until the day the LORD gives rain on the land.' " [1 Kings 17:14]

"So do not worry, saying, 'What shall we eat?' or 'What shall we drink?' or 'What shall we wear?' For the pagans run after all these things, and your heavenly Father knows that you need them. But seek first his kingdom and his righteousness, and all these things will be given to you as well." [Matt. 6:31–33]

Above all, however great our distress, we have great and wonderful promises given to us by God. How encouraging to others, and to us, as we share these promises with our brothers and sisters in the Lord.

> ... along unfamiliar paths I will guide them;
> I will turn the darkness into light before them
> and make the rough places smooth.
> These are the things I will do;
> I will not forsake them. [Isa. 42:16]

"For the foundations of the earth are the LORD's;
upon them he has set the world.
He will guard the feet of his saints,
but the wicked will be silenced in darkness." [1 Sam. 2:8–9]

> But now, this is what the LORD says —
> he who created you, O Jacob,
> he who formed you, O Israel:
> "Fear not, for I have redeemed you;
> I have summoned you by name; you are mine.
> When you pass through the waters,
> I will be with you;
> and when you pass through the rivers,
> they will not sweep over you." [Isa. 43:1–2]

> He who dwells in the shelter of the Most High
> will rest in the shadow of the Almighty....
> He will cover you with his feathers,
> and under his wings you will find refuge;
> his faithfulness will be your shield and rampart.
> You will not fear the terror of night,
> nor the arrow that flies by day,
> nor the pestilence that stalks in the darkness,

nor the plague that destroys at midday.
A thousand may fall at your side,
    ten thousand at your right hand,
    but it will not come near you.
You will only observe with your eyes
    and see the punishment of the wicked.
If you make the Most High your dwelling —
    even the LORD, who is my refuge —
then no harm will befall you,
    no disaster will come near your tent.
For he will command his angels concerning you
    to guard you in all your ways;
they will lift you up in their hands,
    so that you will not strike your foot against a stone. . . .
"Because he loves me," says the LORD, "I will rescue him;
    I will protect him, for he acknowledges my name.
He will call upon me, and I will answer him;
    I will be with him in trouble,
    I will deliver him and honor him.
With long life will I satisfy him
    and show him my salvation." [Ps. 91:1, 4–12, 14–16]

7

Exhort
the Uninvolved

In his second letter to Timothy, the apostle Paul notes that all Scripture is "useful for teaching, rebuking, correcting and training in righteousness, so that the man of God may be thoroughly equipped for every good work" (2 Tim. 3:16–17). It is striking that two of the uses of Scripture which Paul mentions are confrontational. Scripture is to be used in rebuking and correcting.

Most of us feel uncomfortable with confrontation. It's understandable. We want to avoid conflict. And we don't want to intrude on another's life. But there are times in every relationship when we want to confront, because we honestly want to help. Our problem at such times is often one of knowing how to exhort or rebuke another person effectively.

The Bible calls on Jesus' people to speak the truth in love (Eph. 4:15). The truth, spoken without love, alienates and creates hostility. Often our confrontation of others falls short of ministering simply because our attitude is judgmental and negative. Others sense our attitude, resent it, and refuse to hear what we have to say. But if we have taken the time to develop a loving, ministering relationship with another person, our words of rebuke or correction or exhortation may be corrective. When Paul writes in another letter of "admonishing and teaching everyone with all wisdom, so that we may present everyone perfect in Christ" (Col. 1:28), he sets forth both his motive and attitude. Paul truly cares about others and their relationship with the Lord. Paul cares enough to confront when confrontation can help.

If we adopt Paul's attitude as we exhort the uninvolved, and rid ourselves of judgmentalism and a critical spirit, you and I can be used by the Lord not only to strengthen the obedient but also to turn others back to Christ.

Speaking the truth in love is double-edged. When we speak we are called on to maintain an attitude of love. But we are also reminded that love compels us to speak the truth. We are called to care about others enough to confront and exhort when this seems necessary.

When love does call us to exhort another person, what we want to do is to express our concern and invite others to consider truths set forth in Scripture.

Paul wrote that "all Scripture" is God-breathed and useful for teaching, rebuking, correcting and training" (2 Tim. 3:16). It would be wrong for us to pick out just a few Bible verses and say, "These are for exhorting," and to say of others, "These are for encouraging." Yet there are certain recurring problems which call for confrontation. In this chapter a number of verses which express useful truths are linked with situations which do call for our involvement. Pointing out these truths in a loving and caring way can help us to "serve one another in love" (Gal. 5:13).

And we do need to remember that "the entire law is summed up in a single command: 'Love your neighbor as yourself' " (Gal. 5:14). In love, you and I are to speak out and to exhort the uninvolved.

Exhorting is an important part of our personal ministry to others. God expects us to confront when we see a brother or sister who is uninvolved or unresponsive. Both the Old and New Testaments have reminders for us.

" 'Do not hate your brother in your heart. Rebuke your neighbor frankly so you will not share in his guilt.' " [Lev. 19:17]

My brothers, if one of you should wander from the truth and someone should bring him back, remember this: Whoever turns a sinner from the error of his way will save him from death and cover over a multitude of sins. [James 5:19–20]

Do not rebuke an older man harshly, but exhort him as if he were your father. Treat younger men as brothers, older women as mothers, and younger women as sisters, with absolute purity. [1 Tim. 5:1–2]

Keep yourselves in God's love as you wait for the mercy of our Lord Jesus Christ to bring you to eternal life.
Be merciful to those who doubt; snatch others from the fire and save them; to others show mercy, mixed with fear — hating even the clothing stained by corrupted flesh. [Jude 21–23]

Scripture often warns about the deceptiveness of wealth. We live in a materialistic society. Often the desire for riches, a passion for things, draws hearts away from commitment to the Lord. It is not wrong to be rich. But it is wrong to love riches.

People who want to get rich fall into temptation and a trap and into many foolish and harmful desires that plunge men into ruin and destruction. For the love of money is a root of all kinds of evil. Some people, eager for money, have wandered from the faith and pierced themselves with many griefs. [1 Tim. 6:9–10]

But godliness with contentment is great gain. For we brought nothing into the world, and we can take nothing out of it. But if we have food and clothing, we will be content with that. [1 Tim. 6:6–8]

Keep your lives free from the love of money and be content with what you have, because God has said,

> "Never will I leave you;
> never will I forsake you." [Heb. 13:5]

No servant can serve two masters. Either he will hate the one and love the other, or he will be devoted to the one and despise the other. You cannot serve both God and Money." [Luke 16:13]

"Do not store up for yourselves treasures on earth, where moth and rust destroy, and where thieves break in and steal. But store up for yourselves treasures in heaven, where moth and rust do not destroy, and where thieves do not break in and steal. For where your treasure is, there your heart will be also." [Matt. 6:19–21]

> Do not be overawed when a man grows rich,
>> when the splendor of his house increases;
> for he will take nothing with him when he dies,
>> his splendor will not descend with him.
> Though while he lived he counted himself blessed —
>> and men praise you when you prosper —
> he will join the generation of his fathers,
>> who will never see the light of life.
> A man who has riches without understanding
>> is like the beasts that perish. [Ps. 49:16–20]

Our society is enraptured by sex and proclaims a right to promiscuity. Sexuality certainly is part of God's plan and his design. Sexual relations in marriage is a great gift, bonding two together in a unique expression of commitment. But those who are deceived by society's free and easy attitude toward sex harm themselves and others and stray from the path of godliness. How good to have a corrective word from God.

> ... may you rejoice in the wife of your youth.
> A loving doe, a graceful deer —
>> may her breasts satisfy you always,
>> may you ever be captivated by her love.
> Why be captivated, my son, by an adulteress?
>> Why embrace the bosom of another man's wife?
> For a man's ways are in full view of the LORD,
>> and he examines all his paths.
> The evil deeds of a wicked man ensnare him;
>> the cords of his sin hold him fast.
> He will die for lack of discipline. ... [Prov. 5:18–23]

The acts of the sinful nature are obvious: sexual immorality, impurity and debauchery; ... and envy; drunkenness, orgies, and the like. I warn you, as I did before, that those who live like this will not inherit the kingdom of God. [Gal. 5:19, 21]

In a similar way, Sodom and Gomorrah and the surrounding towns gave themselves up to sexual immorality and perversion. They serve as an example of those who suffer the punishment of eternal fire. [Jude 7]

It is God's will that you should be sanctified: that you should avoid sexual immorality; that each of you should learn to control his own body in a way that is holy and honorable, not in passionate lust like the heathen, who do not know God; and that in this matter no one should wrong his brother or take advantage of him. [1 Thess. 4:3–6]

And do this, understanding the present time. The hour has come for you to wake up from your slumber, because our salvation is nearer now than when we first believed. The night is nearly over; the day is almost here. So let us put aside the deeds of darkness and put on the armor of light. Let us behave decently, as in the daytime, not in orgies and drunkenness, not in sexual immorality and debauchery, not in dissension and jealousy. Rather, clothe yourselves with the Lord Jesus Christ, and do not think about how to gratify the desires of the sinful nature. [Rom. 13:11–14]

The body is not meant for sexual immorality, but for the Lord, and the Lord for the body. By his power God raised the Lord from the dead, and he will raise us also. Do you not know that your bodies are members of Christ himself? Shall I then take the members of Christ and unite them with a prostitute? Never! Do you not know that he who unites himself with a prostitute is one with her in body? For it is said, "The two will become one flesh." But he who unites himself with the Lord is one with him in spirit.

Flee from sexual immorality. All other sins a man commits are outside his body, but he who sins sexually sins against his own body. Do you not know that your body is a temple of the Holy Spirit, who is in you, whom you have received from God? You are not your own; you were bought at a price. Therefore honor God with your body. [1 Cor. 6:13–20]

Many today who know what the Bible says seem unwilling to submit to its authority. Yet one of the consistent themes of Scripture is the authority of the Word of God: an authority which calls for submission and obedience. Whenever anyone says, "I know the Bible says that, but . . ." the Scripture has a word of exhortation and rebuke.

If only you had paid attention to my commands,
    your peace would have been like a river,
    your righteousness like the waves of the sea. [Isa. 48:18]

" 'When I called, they did not listen; so when they called, I would not listen,' says the LORD Almighty. 'I scattered them with a whirlwind among all the nations, where they were strangers. The land was left so desolate behind them that no one could come or go. This is how they made the pleasant land desolate.' " [Zech. 7:13–14]

We know that we have come to know him if we obey his commands. The man who says, "I know him," but does not do what he commands is a liar, and the truth is not in him. [1 John 2:3–4]

So be careful to do what the LORD your God has commanded you; do not turn aside to the right or to the left. Walk in all the way that the LORD your God has commanded you, so that you may live and prosper and prolong your days in the land that you will possess. [Deut. 5:32–33]

The Bible warns us against being driven and controlled by the wants, the passions to have, that dominate the lives of so many. A strong element in our society suggests that we have a "right" to satisfy all our desires. Scripture suggests instead that we have a responsibility to stand in judgment on our desires. We are to determine which are right and which are wrong — and which ways of satisfying them are right and which are wrong.

What causes fights and quarrels among you? Don't they come from your desires that battle within you? You want something but don't get it. You kill and covet, but you cannot have what you want. You quarrel and fight. You do not have,

because you do not ask God. When you ask, you do not receive, because you ask with wrong motives, that you may
spend what you get on your pleasures. [James 4:1–3]

You were taught, with regard to your former way of life, to put
off your old self, which is being corrupted by its deceitful
desires; to be made new in the attitude of your minds; and
to put on the new self, created to be like God in true righteousness and holiness. [Eph. 4:22–24]

Do not love the world or anything in the world. If anyone
loves the world, the love of the Father is not in him. For
everything in the world — the cravings of sinful man, the lust
of his eyes and the boasting of what he has and does — comes
not from the Father but from the world. The world and its
desires pass away, but the man who does the will of God lives
forever. [1 John 2:15–17]

Is there any real alternative to faith in God and obedience to him?
Many think so, and like the prodigal son set out to find the
good life away from their spiritual home and Father. Yet Scripture contains many warnings against forsaking God and seeking life's meaning from some other source.

> "Your wickedness will punish you;
>   your backsliding will rebuke you.
> Consider then and realize
>   how evil and bitter it is for you
> when you forsake the LORD your God
>   and have no awe of me,"
>   declares the Lord, the LORD Almighty. [Jer. 2:19]

> Woe to those who go to great depths
>   to hide their plans from the LORD,
> who do their work in darkness and think,
>   "Who sees us? Who will know?"
> You turn things upside down,
>   as if the potter were thought to be like the clay!
> Shall what is formed say to him who formed it,
>   "He did not make me"?
> Can the pot say of the potter,
>   "He knows nothing"? [Isa. 29:15–16]

" 'The LORD is slow to anger, abounding in love and forgiving sin and rebellion. Yet he does not leave the guilty unpunished; he punishes the children for the sin of the fathers to the third and fourth generation.' " [Num. 14:18]
Note that the point of the passage is that the sins parents commit affect the lives of their children for generations. For example, a person who was abused by his parents is most likely to abuse his own boys and girls.

Each of life's choices has consequences. Good choices bring us good; wrong choices bring us evil. Too often friends or those we love make wrong choices, thinking "it can't happen to me." But the Bible warns against this kind of thinking. We live in a moral universe, governed by moral law. Wrong choices bring evil just as surely as an object that is tossed in the air will come down.

But because of your stubbornness and your unrepentant heart, you are storing up wrath against yourself for the day of God's wrath, when his righteous judgment will be revealed. [Rom. 2:5]

But the wicked are like the tossing sea,
which cannot rest,
whose waves cast up mire and mud.
"There is no peace," says my God, "for the wicked." [Isa. 57:20–21]

Jesus replied, "I tell you the truth, everyone who sins is a slave to sin." [John 8:34]

"If you remain hostile toward me and refuse to listen to me, I will multiply your afflictions seven times over, as your sins deserve." [Lev. 26:21]

The faithless will be fully repaid for their ways,
and the good man rewarded for his. [Prov. 14:14]

Do not be deceived: God cannot be mocked. A man reaps what he sows. The one who sows to please his sinful nature, from that nature will reap destruction; the one who sows to

please the Spirit, from the Spirit will reap eternal life. Let us
not become weary in doing good, for at the proper time we
will reap a harvest if we do not give up. [Gal. 6:7–9]

Remember this: Whoever sows sparingly will also reap
sparingly, and whoever sows generously will also reap generously. [2 Cor. 9:6]

Now reform your ways and your actions. . . . [Jer. 26:13]

*Moral consequences have been built into the nature of the universe and
into human nature itself.* But wrong choices place us in even
greater peril. God is himself a moral Judge: he must and will
punish sin. For those who turn to Jesus and the cleansing
power of his blood, there is forgiveness. For those who persist
in doing evil, there is only the prospect of certain judgment.

PART TWO

Resources
for Personal Ministry

Abortion

Insight

In *Roe v. Wade* (1973), the Supreme Court ruled that decisions about abortion during the first three months of pregnancy can legally be made by a woman and her doctor only. Current efforts to overturn this decision focus on winning recognition that a fetus is a living human being, entitled to protection under our Constitution.

A fetus is not merely part of the mother's body. Each cell in the human body carries a distinctive individual pattern of genes and chromosomes. The genetic code of a fetus is different from that of the mother; a fetus is an unborn child, a separate individual.

The Bible affirms that God is involved in conception, supervising this creative act (Gen. 4:1; 16:2; 30:22; Ruth 4:13). In Old Testament times unwanted newborns were sometimes left to die (Ezek. 16:5); this practice parallels voluntary abortion.

Christians who realize that God holds every human life precious will want to guard the life of the unborn and help those considering abortion to find another, better alternative.

Hints

In talking with a woman who is considering abortion, be sensitive to the pressures the woman faces. Are there financial problems? Are others urging this course? Who are they, and what are their reasons? What are her specific fears? Often a woman does not want an abortion but sees no other way out of the situation. Listen sympathetically; this is a first, important step.

When you identify a woman's reasons for considering an abortion, you can help her find other solutions. Check with your church and other local congregations. Many churches know of residences for unwed mothers; others have established adoption programs for unwanted newborns. Check for Christian counselors in your area who can provide specific suggestions for solving other problems.

As the woman's fears and uncertainties are reduced, emphasize lovingly God's concern for both her and her unborn child. The Scriptures will help you show that God is involved in conception, and that an unborn child *is* a person.

Resource Scriptures

Then God remembered Rachel; he listened to her and opened her womb. [Gen. 30:22]

... the LORD enabled [Ruth] to conceive, and she gave birth to a son. [Ruth 4:13]

"If men who are fighting hit a pregnant woman and she gives birth prematurely but there is no serious injury, the offender must be fined whatever the woman's husband demands and the court allows." [Exod. 21:22]
Note that the law establishes a fine even if there is no serious injury, because the act might have endangered human life. Application of this law to fetus and woman shows that the fetus is considered a person.

Surely I was sinful at birth,
   sinful from the time my mother conceived me. [Ps. 51:5]
Note that David speaks of himself as a distinct individual
from the time of conception.

For you created my inmost being;
   you knit me together in my mother's womb.
I praise you because I am fearfully and wonderfully made;
   your works are wonderful,
   I know that full well.
My frame was not hidden from you
   when I was made in the secret place.
When I was woven together in the depths of the earth,
   your eyes saw my unformed body. [Ps. 139:13–16]

Adoption

Insight

Most adoptions are handled through licensed agencies. A
list of these can be obtained from your state social-services
department. Adoption generally is a lengthy process, and the
number of adoptions has decreased drastically since the 1970s.
In part this reflects changes in the laws about abortion. About
half of the children who are adopted today are taken by relatives.

Some churches sponsor counseling and care of unwed
mothers. Many of these mothers place their children for adoption. Check with your pastor and Christian counseling centers
for information about such programs in your area.

The cost of adopting a child varies considerably. One point

to remember is that it is important to have a lawyer to take care of the required legal papers.

Some people hesitate to adopt because they fear that a child might have genetic defects. Others are willing to adopt children with handicaps. These children are more difficult to place than are other children; there is a need for adoptive parents who will accept children with special needs.

Studies show that even older children who are taken into stable, loving homes do well and are responsive to their parents. Most adopted children, when they are told early that they have been especially chosen by their parents, feel comfortable and secure, and grow up to live successful, normal lives.

Persons who want children, or who are concerned about unwanted boys and girls, and desire to adopt, can have a deeply rewarding, life-shaping ministry in such children's lives.

On the other hand, women with unwanted pregnancies can work with adoption agencies or Christian counselors to be sure their babies are placed in Christian homes.

Hints

Whether a couple wants to adopt or an individual is looking at adoption as an alternative to abortion, they will need information. Be a good listener; find out what you can about questions and concerns. You may want to refer your friend to a professional counselor or a government agency. Talking with someone who has adopted or has placed a child for adoption may be particularly helpful.

But do not be too quick to simply pass a concerned friend on to professional counselors or agencies, especially in the case of unwanted pregnancy. Often emotional turmoil is so great that a woman needs another individual to go with her, step by step, to make necessary contacts. You can stay close and supportive without taking responsibility for the personal decisions another individual must make.

Resource Scriptures

In love [God] predestined us to be adopted as his sons through Jesus Christ, in accordance with his pleasure and will. [Eph. 1:4–5]

> Sons are a heritage from the LORD,
>   children a reward from him. . . .
> Blessed is the man
>   whose quiver is full of them. [Ps. 127:3, 5]

Defend the cause of the weak and fatherless;
    maintain the rights of the poor and oppressed.
Rescue the weak and needy;
    deliver them from the hand of the wicked. [Ps. 82:3–4]

Religion that God our Father accepts as pure and faultless is this: to look after orphans and widows in their distress and to keep oneself from being polluted by the world. [James 1:27]

> Children's children are a crown to the aged,
>   and parents are the pride of their children. [Prov. 17:6]

Jesus said, "Let the little children come to me, and do not hinder them, for the kingdom of heaven belongs to such as these." [Matt. 19:14]

Train a child in the way he should go,
    and when he is old he will not turn from it. [Prov. 22:6]
Note that it is not so much heredity as training that shapes
    a child.

Adultery

Insight

Researchers have found that well over 50 percent of Americans have extramarital affairs. Christians are not immune to the temptation.

Warnings in the Old Testament and in the New Testament epistles show clearly that sexual entanglements have always been a problem for human beings.

Scripture is particularly clear in this moral area. Marriage is intended by God to meet the sexual needs of human beings. More importantly, human sexuality is designed to enrich the marital relationship. Rightly understood, sexual relations are a sign and a symbol of the lifetime commitment of one man and one woman to each other. Only in the context of marriage can sex be truly fulfilling, a vital element in enriching life's most special interpersonal relationship.

Hints

Scripture deals directly and openly with adultery and the adulterer. First there are warnings against the temptation. Then there are injunctions to the church to first confront and then discipline the adulterer (1 Cor. 5:1–5, 9–13). In a significant sense, Christians can show love for brothers and sisters by going to them if adultery is suspected or admitted. Give encouragement to a person who is struggling with temptation. Confront a person who is involved in an extramarital affair. And support a person who has determined to break off an illicit relationship.

Although the Bible makes it clear that adultery is a serious sin, it is also a forgivable sin. We are to welcome back into fellowship a person who has repented (2 Cor. 2:5–11).

Although adultery is generally accepted as grounds for divorce, any sin is first of all grounds for forgiveness. Only in the case of repeated infidelity, rather than an isolated incident, should divorce be considered.

Resource Scriptures

For the lips of an adulteress drip honey,
and her speech is smoother than oil;

but in the end she is bitter as gall,
   sharp as a double-edged sword. [Prov. 5:3–4]

Do not lust in your heart after her beauty
   or let her captivate you with her eyes,
for the prostitute reduces you to a loaf of bread,
   and the adulteress preys upon your very life.
Can a man scoop fire into his lap
   without his clothes being burned?
Can a man walk on hot coals
   without his feet being scorched?
So is he who sleeps with another man's wife;
   no one who touches her will go unpunished. [Prov. 6:25–29]

"You have heard that it was said, 'Do not commit adultery.'
But I tell you that anyone who looks at a woman lustfully has
already committed adultery with her in his heart." [Matt.
5:27–28]
Jesus is saying that we are not to look at or relate to other
persons as sex objects, but are to see each individual as a
person who has worth and value.

Flee from sexual immorality. All other sins a man commits
are outside his body, but he who sins sexually sins against
his own body. Do you not know that your body is a temple of
the Holy Spirit, who is in you, whom you have received from
God? You are not your own; you were bought at a price. Therefore honor God with your body. [1 Cor. 6:18–20]

But among you there must not be even a hint of sexual
immorality, or of any kind of impurity, or of greed, because
these are improper for God's holy people. [Eph. 5:3]

Marriage should be honored by all, and the marriage bed
kept pure, for God will judge the adulterer and all the sexually
immoral. [Heb. 13:4]

Aging and Retirement

Insight

By the year 2000 fifty million people, more than 18 percent of our population, are expected to be over age sixty-five. Most older persons are relatively healthy, and claim to be happier than younger people! Only about 5 percent of older adults are in nursing homes or similar facilities. Most own their own homes. More importantly, most older adults retain their intelligence and ability to learn and to help others. The "golden years" can be more satisfying than most people imagine.

But for retirement to be satisfying, a person needs to have a sense of purpose and goals. People need not only to relax, but also to keep busy.

Older adults probably have more free time than they had at any other stage of life. Volunteering to serve in community or church programs can add significance to life. Many organizations for senior citizens can suggest avenues of service.

It is crucial for a person who is moving from an active work life to plan for retirement. This includes financial planning, but should also emphasize setting personal goals and planning ahead for activities and service.

Hints

Some people are hesitant and worried about retirement. Some have planned carefully. Others are looking forward to freedom from work routines, but have made no plans at all. Asking these people questions can be particularly helpful. What activities does a friend look forward to? How does he or she plan to use the extra time? You can show enthusiasm for a friend's future without prying, and sensitive questions can help him or her think ahead to make retirement and old age fulfilling.

It's good to remember that the greatest achievements of many Bible characters came in old age. Moses led Israel to freedom after he was eighty. Caleb was about the same age when he won victories in the Promised Land. And Paul encouraged Titus to teach the "older women" to train the younger women to be good wives and mothers (1 Titus 2:3–5). A godly older man or woman often has the wisdom to guide and counsel others in God's way.

Resource Scriptures

" 'Rise in the presence of the aged, show respect for the elderly. . . .' " [Lev. 19:32]

No widow may be put on the list of widows [a ministry group in New Testament times] unless she is over sixty, has been faithful to her husband, and is well known for her good deeds. . . . [1 Tim. 5:9–10]

Even to your old age and gray hairs
I am he, I am he who will sustain you.
I have made you and I will carry you;
I will sustain you and I will rescue you. [Isa. 46:4]

But as for me, I will always have hope;
I will praise you more and more. . . .
Even when I am old and gray,
do not forsake me, O God,
till I declare your power to the next generation,
your might to all who are to come. [Ps. 71:14, 18]

The righteous will flourish like a palm tree. . . .
They will still bear fruit in old age,
they will stay fresh and green,
proclaiming, "The LORD is upright;
he is my Rock, and there is no wickedness in him." [Ps. 92:12, 14–15]

I was young and now I am old,
yet I have never seen the righteous forsaken
or their children begging bread. . . .

Turn from evil and do good;
   then you will dwell in the land forever. [Ps. 37:25, 27]

But let all who take refuge in you be glad;
   let them ever sing for joy.
Spread your protection over them,
   that those who love your name may rejoice in you. [Ps.
   5:11−12]

Alcohol Abuse

Insight

Psalm 104:15 speaks of God as one who gives "wine that gladdens the heart of man." Does the Bible view alcohol as a good thing? Wine was viewed as a blessing that heightened the pleasure of those who shared joyous social occasions.

However, the Bible plainly speaks against the excessive use of alcohol, and it also condemns drunkenness. Furthermore, in ancient times, wine was often mixed with three parts water. Some rabbis held that wine must be mixed with ten parts water; otherwise the drinker would be defiled (that is, at risk of being intoxicated and therefore not in complete control of his behavior).

Alcohol, rather than being transferred to other tissues, stays in the bloodstream until the liver detoxifies it. As the level of alcohol in the bloodstream increases, it affects a person's attitudes and judgment; he tends to act impulsively rather than responsibly. In addition, his reactions are impaired. Alcohol is a factor in more than half of the fatal auto accidents in the United States.

The long-term effects of alcohol abuse include damage to body tissues, especially the liver.

Hints

If you are in contact with an alcoholic or a member of an alcoholic's family, you can receive help by contacting Alcoholics Anonymous or other alcohol-treatment programs. Alcoholics Anonymous provides written material to help an individual recognize symptoms of alcoholism.

Members of an alcoholic's family are always affected. They also need insight and help. Many tend to react in ways that make solution of the problem more difficult. Often alcohol-treatment programs include meetings of support groups for the alcoholic's family.

Although alcohol is addictive to many, the alcoholic must be held responsible for his choice to drink. Neither pity nor excuses can help.

In a real sense alcoholism illustrates the Bible's teaching that sin enslaves. When a person yields to an evil, he becomes a slave to sin. Only a commitment to God, and yielding to him, can bring true freedom from those things which hold us captive.

Salvation does not necessarily bring instant release from alcohol addiction. The process of recovery is apt to be long. Supportive Christian friends who walk with the alcoholic through success and relapse are needed. Prayers, encouragement, and the belief that full release will come through Jesus is a gift Christians can offer to brothers and sisters breaking out of bondage to alcohol.

Resource Scriptures

Wine is a mocker and beer a brawler;
   whoever is led astray by them is not wise. [Prov. 20:1]

Do not join those who drink too much wine
   or gorge themselves on meat,
for drunkards and gluttons become poor. .... [Prov. 23:20–21]

For you have spent enough time in the past doing what pagans choose to do — living in debauchery, lust, drunkenness. . . . [1 Peter 4:3]

Do not get drunk on wine, which leads to debauchery. Instead, be filled with the Spirit. [Eph. 5:18]

Therefore do not let sin reign in your mortal body so that you obey its evil desires. Do not offer the parts of your body to sin, as instruments of wickedness, but rather offer yourselves to God, as those who have been brought from death to life; and offer the parts of your body to him as instruments of righteousness. For sin shall not be your master, because you are not under law, but under grace. [Rom. 6:12–14]

You, however, are controlled not by the sinful nature but by the Spirit, if the Spirit of God lives in you. [Rom. 8:9]

So whether you eat or drink or whatever you do, do it all for the glory of God. [1 Cor. 10:31]

Anger

Insight

Bible heroes were no strangers to anger. David was furious when he was insulted by a wealthy man whose animals his men had protected. Only the quick thinking of the man's wife, Abigail, kept David from taking bloody revenge (1 Sam. 25:33). Afterward David thanked God that his emotional reaction had not resulted in a sinful act.

But more than avoiding sinful acts is involved in a Christian approach to anger. Jesus pointed out that the Law deals with external acts: for instance, it condemns murder. But the Law says nothing about anger. Yet anger, that reaction of the inner man to real or imagined slights, is the source from which murder springs, and this too lies under the judgment of God (see Matt. 5:21–24).

The Bible does speak of God's anger. But God's anger is always righteous. And in anger, God never forgets mercy. Human beings fall short of this perfection, so anger is particularly dangerous to us. We are likely to be carried away by our emotions, unable to keep Paul's injunction: " 'In your anger do not sin' " (Eph. 4:26).

Two issues are involved in anger. First, when anger flares we must take it as a warning signal and refuse to act on an angry impulse. Second, we must realize that God is at work in our lives to make us loving rather than angry persons. We must rely on God to work his transformation in our lives.

Hints

Persons who are easily angered often claim that their anger is justified. Help them realize that their anger is at odds with godliness. Only the person who is willing to face that his angry response to situations or to other persons is rooted in the sin nature will open his life to God and seek the Lord's help.

Resource Scriptures

Anger is cruel and fury overwhelming. . . . [Prov. 27:4]

A fool gives full vent to his anger,
    but a wise man keeps himself under control. [Prov. 29:11]
Note that the word *fool* refers to a morally defective person.

An angry man stirs up dissension,
    and a hot-tempered one commits many sins. [Prov. 29:22]

The acts of the sinful nature are obvious: sexual immorality, impurity and debauchery; idolatry and witchcraft; hatred, discord, jealousy, fits of rage. . . . [Gal. 5:19–20]

Get rid of all bitterness, rage and anger, brawling and slander, along with every form of malice. Be kind and compassionate to one another, forgiving each other, just as in Christ God forgave you. [Eph. 4:31–32]

But now you must rid yourselves of all such things as these: anger, rage, malice. . . . since you have taken off your old self with its practices and have put on the new self, which is being renewed in knowledge in the image of its Creator. [Col. 3:8–10]

My dear brothers, take note of this: Everyone should be quick to listen, slow to speak and slow to become angry, for man's anger does not bring about the righteous life that God desires. Therefore, get rid of all moral filth and the evil that is so prevalent and humbly accept the word planted in you, which can save you. [James 1:19–21]

But the wisdom that comes from heaven is first of all pure; then peace-loving, considerate, submissive, full of mercy and good fruit, impartial and sincere. [James 3:17]

"In your anger do not sin": Do not let the sun go down while you are still angry, and do not give the devil a foothold. [Eph. 4:26–27]

Do not take revenge, my friends, but leave room for God's wrath, for it is written: "It is mine to avenge; I will repay," says the Lord. [Rom. 12:19]

Anxiety

Insight

Anxiety has been called a feeling of apprehension, worry, or tension. Many people in our society are gripped by what could be called neurotic anxiety. They feel apprehensive and threatened, even though nothing in their situation seems to be really wrong.

At times a person experiences what could be termed normal anxiety. This is the result of circumstances that could be a real threat — for example, his factory is laying people off, or he is going to his doctor to hear the results of a series of tests. Such anxiety is understandable and is relieved when the situation is resolved.

In our relationships with others we will meet people with both normal and neurotic anxiety. They may need the help we can give as we remind them of Jesus' love and offer other suggestions as well.

Hints

Don't make the mistake of viewing an anxious friend as a spiritual failure or of identifying anxiety as sin. Our times of anxiety can lead to great spiritual experiences and victories, for these times give us opportunities to exercise trust in God.

How can we help others grow through times of anxiety? First, we can reduce feelings of guilt that may come if a person views anxiety as spiritual failure. Second, we can help clarify his vision of God as trustworthy and powerful. Third, we can help him take action to deal with the circumstances that are causing anxiety. Finally, we can help a friend consciously commit himself to God in prayer.

Resource Scriptures

When I said, "My foot is slipping,"
    your love, O LORD, supported me.
When anxiety was great within me,
    your consolation brought joy to my soul. [Ps. 94:18–19]

"Come to me, all you who are weary and burdened, and I will give you rest." [Matt. 11:28]

"In this world you will have trouble. But take heart! I have overcome the world." [John 16:33]

I am with you and will watch over you wherever you go, and I will bring you back to this land. I will not leave you until I have done what I have promised you." [Gen. 28:15]

Some trust in chariots and some in horses,
    but we trust in the name of the LORD our God. [Ps. 20:7]

"Call upon me in the day of trouble;
    I will deliver you, and you will honor me." [Ps. 50:15]

Cast your cares on the LORD
    and he will sustain you. . . . [Ps. 55:22]

In the day of my trouble I will call to you,
    for you will answer me. [Ps. 86:7]

"For I am the LORD, your God,
    who takes hold of your right hand
and says to you, Do not fear;
    I will help you." [Isa. 41:13]

Trust in the LORD with all your heart
    and lean not on your own understanding;
in all your ways acknowledge him,
    and he will make your paths straight. [Prov. 3:5–6]

He tends his flock like a shepherd:
    He gathers the lambs in his arms
and carries them close to his heart;
    he gently leads those that have young. [Isa. 40:11]

Cast all your anxiety on him because he cares for you. [1 Peter 5:7]

Do not be anxious about anything, but in everything, by prayer and petition, with thanksgiving, present your requests to God. And the peace of God, which transcends all understanding, will guard your hearts and minds in Christ Jesus. [Phil 4:6–7]

Astrology and the Occult

Insight

Astrology is based on the idea that the position of heavenly bodies on the day of a person's birth influences his personality and his destiny. Horoscopes are supposed to warn a person of tendencies and possible dangers. The practice of astrology is at least twenty-four hundred years old. It can be traced in ancient Babylon and was popular in ancient Greece. One modern who depended greatly on astrology was Adolf Hitler.

Spiritualists and other practitioners of the occult believe that there is a supernatural world that influences our lives. They claim to contact supernatural beings or forces and gain information from them which can be used to guide choices.

Astrology and occult arts have this in common: each claims to offer guidance to people who realize they need help if they are to avoid mistakes and make choices which will help rather than hurt them.

Today there are some five thousand working astrologers in the United States. Millions of people read astrology columns in newspapers and magazines and try to apply their vague advice. Others, hoping to find help in making the decisions that shape their lives, go to spiritualists and palm readers.

The Bible strictly forbids believers to turn to any such source for guidance (Deut. 18:9–13, especially v. 10). We are to depend completely on God, who has committed himself to provide guidance for his own.

Hints

Read the passages that forbid such practices, but also go on to emphasize God's promises that he will show his people the way we should go.

Resource Scriptures

Let no one be found among you . . . who practices divination
or sorcery, interprets omens, engages in witchcraft, or casts
spells, or who is a medium or spiritist or who consults the
dead. Anyone who does these things is detestable to the
LORD. . . . You must be blameless before the LORD your God.
[Deut. 18:10–13]

"In your unfailing love you will lead
the people you have redeemed.
In your strength you will guide them
to your holy dwelling." [Exod. 15:13]

"I will help you speak and will teach you what to say." [Exod.
4:12]

Whether you turn to the right or to the left, your ears will hear
a voice behind you, saying, "This is the way; walk in it." [Isa.
30:21]

For the LORD gives wisdom,
and from his mouth come knowledge and understanding.
[Prov. 2:6]

I will instruct you and teach you in the way you should go.
. . . [Ps. 32:8]

"But . . . the Holy Spirit, whom the Father will send in my
name, will teach you all things and will remind you of everything I have said to you." [John 14:26]

"But it is the spirit in a man,
the breath of the Almighty, that gives him understanding."
[Job 32:8]

You guide me with your counsel,
and afterward you will take me into glory. [Ps. 73:24]

The secret things belong to the LORD our God, but the
things revealed belong to us and to our children forever, that
we may follow all the words of this law. [Deut. 29:29]

"I will give you words and wisdom that none of your adver-
saries will be able to resist or contradict." [Luke 21:15]

"But when he, the Spirit of truth, comes, he will guide you
into all truth." [John 16:13]

Bitterness

Insight

Others may plant the seeds of bitterness. But we cultivate those seeds and carefully tend the weeds that grow.

Most people who are bitter can give reasons to explain why they feel as they do. Others have hurt them. Life has not been fair. But every person has experiences like these. The seeds from which bitterness can grow are scattered liberally into each of our lives.

What enables one person to grow into a loving, warm, and caring individual, while another becomes bitter and angry, is the way each responds to his disappointments. We may not be able to control the unfair circumstances of our lives. But we can control the way we respond when those circumstances seem unfair.

Hints

The person who exhibits bitterness will often complain about circumstances in the past or present and claim they are the cause of his or her attitude. Agree that the things mentioned were or are painful. But don't agree that painful experiences justify bitterness.

Try to help the bitter person see that he or she is responsible for his or her own feelings and attitudes. We *choose* to be bitter; nothing can *make* us bitter.

The Christian understands that all our circumstances in life are in the hands of our loving God. Pain and disappointment are intended to strengthen us and make us more like Jesus. When we choose to praise God even for the things that hurt us most, he transforms those experiences and shapes them into good.

Resource Scriptures

And we know that in all things God works for the good of those who love him, who have been called according to his purpose. For those God foreknew he also predestined to be conformed to the likeness of his Son, that he might be the firstborn among many brothers. [Rom. 8:28–29]

Endure hardship as discipline. ... God disciplines us for our good, that we may share in his holiness. No discipline seems pleasant at the time, but painful. Later on, however, it produces a harvest of righteousness and peace for those who have been trained by it. ... See to it that no one misses the grace of God and that no bitter root grows up to cause trouble and defile many. [Heb. 12:7, 10–11, 15]

But if you harbor bitter envy and selfish ambition in your hearts, do not boast about it or deny the truth. Such "wisdom" does not come down from heaven but is earthly, unspiritual, of the devil. ...

But the wisdom that comes from heaven is first of all pure; then peace-loving, considerate, submissive. [James 3:14–17]

Trust in him at all times, O people;
    pour out your hearts to him,
    for God is our refuge. [Ps. 62:8]

One thing God has spoken,
    two things have I heard:
that you, O God, are strong,
    and that you, O Lord, are loving.
Surely you will reward each person
    according to what he has done. [Ps. 62:11–12]

You will keep in perfect peace
    him whose mind is steadfast,
    because he trusts in you.
Trust in the LORD forever,
    for the LORD, the LORD, is the Rock eternal.
                                        [Isa. 26:3–4]

May our Lord Jesus Christ himself and God our Father, who loved us and by his grace gave us eternal encouragement and good hope, encourage your hearts and strengthen you in every good deed and word. [2 Thess. 2:16–17]

> Trust in the LORD and do good;
> dwell in the land and enjoy safe pasture. [Ps. 37:3]

Borrowing

Insight

We live in a credit economy. Many people borrow so heavily that they have no discretionary funds. Interest rates remain high, further creating strain on a family's income. The Bible does not deal directly with our society's particular structure. But it does suggest principles and attitudes which can make us more responsible financially.

In the Old Testament, God's people were encouraged to lend to each other — without interest — to meet basic needs. Thus lending was a matter of social justice: those with funds gave the use of their wealth to those who were needy. Other mechanisms in Old Testament law provided for persons who needed help to support themselves.

The New Testament focuses on our basic attitude toward material possessions. Our treasures are to be spiritual, to the extent that we are not to be obsessively concerned even with basic necessities like food and clothing. Christians are called to put God's kingdom first. By doing so, we can moderate the desire for possessions, which leads so many to borrow excessively.

Hints

Many agencies provide guidance for persons who have over-extended their credit. Such services work with creditors to set up reduced payment schedules and with the borrower to establish a realistic budget. Check to see what counseling services are available, and offer that information to a family or person who needs credit counseling.

The best way to help a person heading toward credit problems may be to help him consciously choose values which will put purchases into spiritual perspective.

Resource Scriptures

"Therefore I tell you, do not worry about your life, what you will eat or drink; or about your body, what you will wear." [Matt. 6:25]

"For the pagans run after all these things, and your heavenly Father knows that you need them. But seek first his kingdom and his righteousness, and all these things will be given you as well. Therefore do not worry about tomorrow, for tomorrow will worry about itself." [Matt. 6:32–34]

"Do not store up for yourselves treasures on earth, where moth and rust destroy, and where thieves break in and steal. But store up for yourselves treasures in heaven, where moth and rust do not destroy, and where thieves do not break in and steal. For where your treasure is, there your heart will be also." [Matt. 6:19–21]

But godliness with contentment is great gain. For we brought nothing into the world, and we can take nothing out of it. But if we have food and clothing, we will be content with that. People who want to get rich fall into temptation and a trap and into many foolish and harmful desires that plunge men into ruin and destruction. [1 Tim. 6:6–9]

Straining toward what is ahead, I press on toward the goal to win the prize for which God has called me heavenward in Christ Jesus.

All of us who are mature should take such a view of things. [Phil. 3:14–15]

I have learned the secret of being content in any and every situation, whether well fed or hungry, whether living in plenty or in want. [Phil. 4:12]

Cancer

Insight

Cancer remains one of the most feared of modern diseases. Yet more than one-third of all cancer victims now are cured; for some types of cancer, as many as 90 percent of the patients are considered cured. Many more cancer patients live long lives with their disease under control.

Persons with cancer face a great deal of uncertainty. The uncertainty may even create an anxiety which hinders the body in fighting the disease.

Also, a person who has cancer may fear pain. Pain can be controlled in a number of ways, including the use of drugs. These methods are almost always effective. A related issue is that some treatments for cancer have side effects (notably nausea, fatigue, loss of hair, changes in weight). The treatments or the side effects can sometimes cause serious emotional swings.

Yet another concern is the cost of treatment, and these costs are high.

A person who has just learned that he or she has cancer will typically be angry, afraid, or confused. Other reactions may be disbelief, denial, bargaining, or despair. The person's mood may change from hope to deep discouragement. Someone who is struggling with the disease over a long period of time may be especially prone to such emotional changes, and may experience the other emotions as well.

Someone who has cancer (or those who have other serious illnesses) needs friends who will sympathize and remain supportive.

Hints

You may want to read more about cancer and how it may affect your friend emotionally as well as physically. Be prepared for times when he or she seems to be angry and rejecting.

You may need to offer practical help (e.g., transportation to doctor's appointments and treatments, cooking, child care); sometimes the greatest help is listening and "being there."

Information and support for cancer patients are available from a variety of sources. The local branch of the American Cancer Society is a good place to begin.

Your friend will surely need comforting words concerning God's continuing love and unending commitment to his children.

Resource Scriptures

"Fear not, for I have redeemed you;
I have summoned you by name; you are mine.
When you pass through the waters,
I will be with you;
and when you pass through the rivers,
they will not sweep over you.
When you walk through the fire,
you will not be burned;
the flames will not set you ablaze.
For I am the LORD, your God,
the Holy One of Israel, your Savior. ..." [Isa. 43:1–3]

"... I am the LORD, who heals you." [Exod. 15:26]

> Even though I walk
>> through the valley of the shadow of death,
> I will fear no evil,
>> for you are with me;
> your rod and your staff,
>> they comfort me. [Ps.23:4]

Yet you brought me out of the womb;
> you made me trust in you
> even at my mother's breast.
From birth I was cast upon you;
> from my mother's womb you have been my God.
Do not be far from me,
> for trouble is near,
> and there is no one to help. [Ps. 22:9–11]

"And even the very hairs of your head are all numbered. So don't be afraid; you are worth more than many sparrows." [Matt. 10:30–31]

> "But I will not take my love from him,
>> nor will I ever betray my faithfulness." [Ps. 89:33]

But from everlasting to everlasting
> the LORD's love is with those who fear him. ... [Ps. 103:17]

> The LORD is the everlasting God,
>> the Creator of the ends of the earth.
> He will not grow tired or weary,
>> and his understanding no one can fathom.
> He gives strength to the weary
>> and increases the power of the weak. [Isa. 40:28–29]

He will cover you with his feathers,
> and under his wings you will find refuge;
> his faithfulness will be your shield and rampart. [Ps. 91:4]

> If you make the Most High your dwelling —
>> even the LORD, who is my refuge —
> then no harm will befall you,
>> no disaster will come near. ... [Ps. 91:9–10]

>> For he is our God
>>> and we are the people of his pasture,
>> the flock under his care. [Ps. 95:7]

Child Abuse

Insight

"Child abuse," according to federal law, is "any physical or mental injury, sexual abuse, negligent treatment, or maltreatment of a child under the age of eighteen by a person who is responsible for the child's welfare under circumstances which indicate that the child's health or welfare is harmed or threatened." Since the federal legislation was passed, a number of state and local laws have taken effect. Social agencies also have become involved. Finding out what agencies exist in your state or locality is a first step to take when you suspect child abuse.

Indications of child abuse include shyness, crying, fear of adults, or hostile destructiveness. These as well as obvious injuries, hunger, and dirtiness may be clues that Christians will want to follow up to see if a child and family need help.

Research shows that many parents who abuse children were themselves abused in childhood. Such adults are usually immature and frustrated, and expect unrealistically adult behavior from their boys and girls. These parents, like their children, need help.

Hints

Avoid trying to deal with child abuse alone. Find out which agencies in your community are responsible for investigating cases of suspected child abuse. The first priority is to be sure the children are protected from continuing abuse. This may be done without removing the child from the home. At other times it will be necessary and important that the child be removed.

Do not threaten the parents. Also try to avoid an adversary relationship with them: many are unhappy about the way they treat their children. If it is possible, establish a support group for parents who abuse their children. Discussion groups, led by people who can help these parents to find other options in dealing with their children, have sometimes proven successful.

If God has given you a concern for abused children, try to form a prayer group with others in your church who share that concern. Consider opening your homes and serving as foster parents to abused children. Work closely with social agencies that are responsible for protecting boys and girls. Christian concern will often need to go beyond simply reporting incidents of child abuse to overworked and usually understaffed government agencies.

As you explore what God might want you to do, consider the following passages from God's Word.

Resource Scriptures

As a father has compassion on his children,
    so the LORD has compassion on those who fear him;
for he knows how we are formed,
    he remembers that we are dust. [Ps. 103:13–14]

Yet the LORD longs to be gracious to you;
    he rises to show you compassion. [Isa. 30:18]

Religion that God our Father accepts as pure and faultless is this: to look after orphans and widows in their distress and to keep oneself from being polluted by the world. [James 1:27]

Therefore, as God's chosen people, holy and dearly loved, clothe yourselves with compassion, kindness. . . . [Col. 3:12]

Then little children were brought to Jesus for him to place his hands on them and pray for them. But the disciples rebuked those who brought them.

Jesus said, "Let the little children come to me, and do not

hinder them, for the kingdom of heaven belongs to such as these." [Matt. 19:13–14]

Childlessness

Insight

One in every six married couples experiences some problem in having children. The difficulty may be in conceiving or in carrying a child to term. At least half of those who seek medical treatment because of childlessness can be helped.

The cause of the problem is found in the woman about 30 percent of the time. Causes may be as diverse as blocked fallopian tubes, scarring in the reproductive tract, hormone disorders, or damage caused by an abortion. Some 30 percent of the time the cause is found in the husband. Male problems typically are a failure to produce enough sperm or an inability of the sperm to survive long enough to reach and fertilize the wife's egg. The other 40 percent of the time both partners have problems. The notion that childlessness is a psychological problem has been shown to be false. In nearly every case the reasons are physiological and medical.

Although many childless couples can be helped medically to conceive and bear children, there are still well over a million couples who want children but are unable to have them. These couples are often deeply disturbed by their childlessness. One or both partners may feel guilt. A person may become angry at and blame his or her spouse. Couples who work through this stage may grow closer to each other, but still must determine how they will react to childlessness.

Hints

If you know a couple who are concerned about their childlessness, your role will vary with their situation. If they have not sought medical help, encourage them to see a doctor. Remember that at least half of those who have problems can be helped to have children of their own.

If you are dealing with a couple who know they cannot have children and have responded with guilt or blaming behavior, be especially sensitive to their feelings. Encourage each to express his or her feelings, and communicate your compassion — without agreeing with either the feelings of guilt or the anger. Recognize that these are typical reactions, and help the persons involved to recognize this too.

If you know a couple who have worked through the initial emotional reactions, help them think ahead and plan their future. What about adoption? What about becoming foster parents for children in special need? Will childlessness give the couple extra time to work with a local church ministry? This condition may be God's invitation to some other type of ministry which demands more time than could be given by a couple with children. God, who is sovereign over conception as over all things, intends childlessness, like children, to be a blessing. Insights can be gained from Paul, who, although he was unmarried, developed intimate relationships with many in his ministry.

Resource Scriptures

And we know that in all things God works for the good of those who love him, who have been called according to his purpose. [Rom. 8:28]

For you know that we dealt with each of you as a father deals with his own children, encouraging, comforting and urging you to live lives worthy of God, who calls you into his kingdom and glory. [1 Thess. 2:11–12]

For what is our hope, our joy, or the crown in which we will glory in the presence of our Lord Jesus when he comes? Is it not you? Indeed, you are our glory and joy. [1 Thess. 2:19–20]

To Timothy my true son in the faith.... [1 Tim. 1:2; also see Titus 1:4]

Choosing a Church

Insight

God calls all his people to draw together, building those close personal relationships which are appropriate for a people who are, in Christ, a family and a living Body. The examples given in Acts (2:42–47; 4:32–35), exhortations in the Epistles (Heb. 10:24–25), and revelations of the nature of the church (see Rom. 12; 1 Cor. 12; Eph. 4) all teach us the importance of being an active part of a local congregation.

But how do we choose a local church? What are we to look for in a congregation? We should look not so much at the agencies which a church maintains to provide services to its members as at the quality of life exhibited by the people of the congregation. Does the shared life in a congregation show those characteristics that Scripture itself emphasizes?

Hints

What specifically can we look for in a church? We need to attend long enough and participate actively enough to sense the following characteristics:

Loving, caring relationships. Jesus' new commandment is that believers love one another as he has loved us (John 13:34). Are the people in a church warm to you and to each other? Can you sense caring? Are prayers honest and real, not just for superficial and obvious needs?

Active ministry. Every believer is gifted by the Holy Spirit with an ability to contribute to the spiritual and personal growth of others. Are the people in a church actively involved in ministry? Are there many opportunities to serve, both through church programs and through ministries developed by members? Are lay leaders of the congregation ministering people, or simply officers running the organizational aspect of the church?

Active witness. Believers are called to testify to Jesus by deed and word. Does the congregation have a concern for the needy of the world? Is this concern expressed in practical, caring ways internationally and in the community? Does the congregation reach out to share the gospel of Christ clearly and actively? Is the Good News of Jesus as expressed in authoritative Scripture taught from the pulpit and in the congregation's classes?

Although there is no guarantee that any local church will be ideal, we do need to be sensitive to biblical priorities when we are choosing a church. And when we have made our choice, we need to become actively involved in the congregation, helping it to become even more an expression of all that God desires in a group of his beloved people.

Resource Scriptures

And I pray that you, being rooted and established in love, may have power, together with all the saints, to grasp how wide and long and high and deep is the love of Christ. . . . [Eph. 3:17–18]

And let us consider how we may spur one another on toward love and good deeds. Let us not give up meeting together, as

some are in the habit of doing, but let us encourage one
another. . . . [Heb. 10:24–25]

Let the word of Christ dwell in you richly as you teach and
admonish one another with all wisdom, and as you sing
psalms, hymns and spiritual songs with gratitude in your hearts
to God. [Col. 3:16]

Be imitators of God, therefore, as dearly loved children and
live a life of love, just as Christ loved us and gave himself up
for us. . . . [Eph. 5:1–2]

Confessing Sin

Insight

The apostle John insists that "if we claim to be without sin,
we deceive ourselves and the truth is not in us" (1 John 1:8).
In the same passage John encourages all believers to "walk in
the light, as he is in the light" (v. 7). In this context the word
light does not refer to sinlessness. Instead, it connotes total
honesty. We cannot have fellowship with God if we try to pretend in our relationship with him.

The exhortation is accompanied by a promise. Instead of
pretending we have not fallen short when we sin, we are to
come openly to God and to confess our sin. When we confess,
God commits himself both to forgive us and to keep on cleansing us.

What does the verb *confess* mean? The Greek word means
"to acknowledge." We are to agree with God's evaluation of
our failure to act correctly and to acknowledge our guilt to
him. When we acknowledge sin, God forgives us on the basis

of Jesus' death for us and is free to keep on working in our lives to shape us toward holiness. When we try to mask our failures and refuse to acknowledge our sin we cut ourselves off from that cleansing fellowship with God which is ours in Jesus.

Hints

It's difficult for many of us to acknowledge our sins and failures. Scripture states the case clearly: we "deceive ourselves." Yet the Holy Spirit does give inner testimony and carry out his convicting ministry. If we know a friend whose acts violate a biblical norm, we can minister by using Scripture to rebuke and correct (2 Tim. 3:16) while we emphasize the release that God's promised forgiveness brings.

Resource Scriptures

Blessed is he
    whose transgressions are forgiven,
    whose sins are covered.
Blessed is the man
    whose sin the LORD does not count against him
    and in whose spirit is no deceit.

When I kept silent,
    my bones wasted away
    through my groaning all day long.
For day and night your hand was heavy upon me. . . .
Then I acknowledged my sin to you
    and did not cover up my iniquity.
I said, "I will confess
    my transgressions to the LORD" —
and you forgave
    the guilt of my sin. [Ps. 32:1–5]

For I know my transgressions,
    and my sin is always before me.
Against you, you only, have I sinned
    and done what is evil in your sight. . . .

Create in me a pure heart, O God,
  and renew a steadfast spirit within me.
Do not cast me from your presence
  or take your Holy Spirit from me.
Restore to me the joy of your salvation,
  and grant me a willing spirit, to sustain me.

Then I will teach transgressors your ways,
  and sinners will turn back to you. [Ps. 51:3–4, 10–13]

If we confess our sins, he is faithful and just and will forgive us our sins and purify us from all unrighteousness. If we claim we have not sinned, we make him out to be a liar and his word has no place in our lives.

My dear children, I write this to you so that you will not sin. But if anybody does sin, we have one who speaks to the Father in our defense — Jesus Christ, the Righteous One. He is the atoning sacrifice for our sins, and not only for ours but also for the sins of the whole world. [1 John 1:9–2:2]

My brothers, if one of you should wander from the truth and someone should bring him back, remember this: Whoever turns a sinner from the error of his way will save him from death and cover over a multitude of sins. [James 5:19–20]

Brothers, if someone is caught in a sin, you who are spiritual should restore him gently. But watch yourself, or you also may be tempted. [Gal. 6:1]

Confessing to Others

Insight

All sin is committed against God. Yet our sins and failures often hurt others. In this sense, we also sin against them.

We know that when we sin against God we are to confess our sins to him, so that his forgiveness can restore the broken fellowship and his Holy Spirit can continue God's cleansing work within our personality. But we are not quite as clear about how to deal with others who have been hurt by a failing or an act of ours.

The Bible teaches first that just as we seek God's forgiveness, so we are to seek the forgiveness of others whom our sins and failings have offended. Although only God can forgive in the sense of sending away our sins, Christians are exhorted to forgive in the sense of being gracious to each other. Forgiveness is to be extended to restore broken fellowship between believers.

But another biblical theme is closely linked with that of forgiveness. When we sin against others we are expected to make the wrong right. The principle is most strongly expressed in the Old Testament teaching on restitution. A wrong is to be repaired by not only acknowledging one's failure, but also taking active steps to make up for the wrong done.

Hints

Encourage friends who may bear a grudge, or who know that others have a grievance against them, to take the first step. Go to the other person and acknowledge any personal fault. Ask forgiveness. But also ask what can be done to help make up for the earlier failure. Confession and an offer of restitution can heal hurts.

Resource Scriptures

"Therefore, if you are offering your gift at the altar and there remember that your brother has something against you, leave your gift there in front of the altar. First go and be reconciled to your brother; then come and offer your gift." [Matt. 5:23–24]

I plead with Euodia and I plead with Syntyche to agree with each other in the Lord. Yes, and I ask you, loyal yoke-fellow, help these women who have contended at my side in the cause of the gospel.... [Phil. 4:2–3]

"When a man or woman wrongs another in any way and so is unfaithful to the LORD, that person is guilty and must confess the sin he has committed. He must make full restitution for his wrong, add one fifth to it and give it all to the person he has wronged." [Num. 5:6–7]

"If a man steals an ox or a sheep and slaughters it or sells it, he must pay back five head of cattle for the ox and four sheep for the sheep." [Exod. 22:1]

Get rid of all bitterness, rage and anger, brawling and slander, along with every form of malice. Be kind and compassionate to one another, forgiving each other, just as in Christ God forgave you. [Eph. 4:31–32]

Therefore, as God's chosen people, holy and dearly loved, clothe yourselves with compassion, kindness, humility, gentleness and patience. Bear with each other and forgive whatever grievances you may have against one another. Forgive as the Lord forgave you. And over all these virtues put on love, which binds them all together in perfect unity. [Col. 3:12–14]

Convictions

Insight

Christians develop personal and shared convictions about issues not dealt with directly in the Bible. British Christians of an earlier era had strong convictions about keeping Sunday and maintained lists of appropriate seventh-day activities. In the 1850s archery and dancing after vespers were acceptable, but bowling and bearbaiting were not.

More recently Christians in our country have held convictions about buying and selling on Sunday, mixed swimming, attending movies, dancing, popular music, smoking, or social drinking. Groups also have convictions about what a person should or should not eat, wearing cosmetics, or playing cards. Others have convictions about military service, buying products from South Africa, and other serious issues.

A glance at this list makes several things clear. First, in each of these areas there are no direct instructions in the Bible. Second, the rationale for various convictions differs. For example, there are solid medical reasons why a person should not smoke, and Christians who are convinced that their bodies are temples of the Holy Spirit may well argue that to smoke is both foolish and sinful. On the other hand, the rationale for not bowling on Sunday is a little harder to explain. Third, at times and in different groups each listed item has been considered something of a test of spirituality.

How does Scripture deal with matters of personal conviction? It affirms the responsibility of the individual to be guided by the Lord and to be sensitive to the consciences of others. Rules that humans make are never an adequate test of spirituality, and we are to refrain from judging others. The Bible gives us clear guidance in this area.

Resource Scriptures

Therefore do not let anyone judge you by what you eat or drink. . . .

Since you died with Christ to the basic principles of this world, why, as though you still belonged to it, do you submit to its rules: "Do not handle! Do not taste! Do not touch!"? These are all destined to perish with use, because they are based on human commands and teachings. [Col. 2:16, 20–22]

Accept him whose faith is weak, without passing judgment on disputable matters. One man's faith allows him to eat everything, but another man, whose faith is weak, eats only vegetables. The man who eats everything must not look down on him who does not, and the man who does not eat everything must not condemn the man who does, for God has accepted him. Who are you to judge someone else's servant? [Rom. 14:1–4]

Each one should be fully convinced in his own mind. He who regards one day as special, does so to the Lord. He who eats meat, eats to the Lord, for he gives thanks to God; and he who abstains, does so to the Lord and gives thanks to God. . . .

For this very reason, Christ died and returned to life so that he might be the Lord of both the dead and the living. You, then, why do you judge your brother? Or why do you look down on your brother? For we will all stand before God's judgment seat. . . . So then, each of us will give an account of himself to God. [Rom. 14:5–6, 9–10, 12]

As one who is in the Lord Jesus, I am fully convinced that no food is unclean in itself. But if anyone regards something as unclean, then for him it is unclean. If your brother is distressed because of what you eat, you are no longer acting in love. Do not by your eating destroy your brother for whom Christ died. [Rom. 14:14–15]

So whatever you believe about these things keep between yourself and God. Blessed is the man who does not condemn himself by what he approves. [Rom. 14:22]

Death

Insight

Death is represented in Scripture as an enemy, just as it is experienced by human beings (1 Cor. 15:54). But death, although it is inevitable and unwelcome, has a different dimension for Christians than it does for the rest of humankind. We know from the resurrection of Jesus that death has been conquered. And we know that our death will bring us into the presence of Jesus.

Often death is portrayed in Scripture as a gift, a release from earthly troubles. Life is always to be valued, but death is no longer to be feared.

As ministering Christians we are likely to be called on to help persons with terminal illness or those whose loved ones have died. How wonderful that the Word of God has fully equipped us to comfort and encourage all.

Hints

Paul notes that death causes us to sorrow, but not as do others who lack our hope (1 Thess. 4:13). Grief is nearly always associated with death, and we should not try to short-cut the process of grieving. What we can do as grief takes hold is simply to be there, comforting with our presence. As friends are ready for another kind of comfort, we can share God's good Word with them.

Resource Scriptures

We believe that Jesus died and rose again and so we believe that God will bring with Jesus those who have fallen asleep in him. [1 Thess. 4:14]

Now we know that if the earthly tent we live in is destroyed, we have a building from God, an eternal house in heaven, not built by human hands. Meanwhile we groan, longing to be clothed with our heavenly dwelling, ... so that what is mortal may be swallowed up by life. [2 Cor. 5:1–2, 4]

[Jesus] too shared in their humanity so that by his death he might destroy him who holds the power of death — that is, the devil — and free those who all their lives were held in slavery by their fear of death. [Heb. 2:14–15]

> Even though I walk
>> through the valley of the shadow of death,
> I will fear no evil,
>> for you are with me;
> your rod and your staff,
>> they comfort me. [Ps. 23:4]

> The righteous perish,
>> and no one ponders it in his heart;
> devout men are taken away,
>> and no one understands
> that the righteous are taken away
>> to be spared from evil.
> Those who walk uprightly
>> enter into peace;
>> they find rest as they lie in death. [Isa. 57:1–2]

For the perishable must clothe itself with the imperishable, and the mortal with immortality. When the perishable has been clothed with the imperishable, and the mortal with immortality, then the saying that is written will come true: "Death has been swallowed up in victory." [1 Cor. 15:53–54]

For I am convinced that neither death nor life, neither angels nor demons, neither the present nor the future, nor any powers, neither height nor depth, nor anything else in all creation, will be able to separate us from the love of God that is in Christ Jesus our Lord. [Rom. 8:38–39]

"They will be his people, and God himself will be with them and be their God. He will wipe every tear from their eyes. There will be no more death or mourning or crying or pain, for the old order of things has passed away." [Rev. 21:3–4]

Jesus said to [Martha], "I am the resurrection and the life. He who believes in me will live, even though he dies. . . ." [John 11:25]

Depression

Insight

Most people in the United States will at some time consult a doctor because they feel depressed. Emotions linked with depression are sadness, hopelessness, and at times guilt and anger. Depression is often associated with stress or loss.

People who are depressed do not respond well to attempts to cheer them up. Understanding without pity, and awareness that depression is intensely painful, are called for.

In some cases a hormonal or chemical imbalance causes the feelings of depression. Chemical depression is often treatable by doctors, and a number of helpful, nonaddictive drugs are available. When events cause depression, time and caring friends are the best healers.

Hints

It is important not to confront or attack a person who is depressed, as such pressures tend to deepen feelings of guilt and hopelessness. Instead, show that you recognize the pain the person is experiencing and that you care about him. Many great men of faith knew depression too (see especially 1 Kings 18–19 and Job 1–2). But do go beyond acknowledging depression. Also contribute your own positive attitude: your conviction that there is hope for your friend's future. Don't be distressed if your reassurance is rejected at this time. Remain quietly confident and continue to be a friend.

You can also give practical help by suggesting simple daily goals the depressed person can work toward and achieve. Even small successes help rebuild a sense of competence that can lead to release.

Resource Scriptures

"I will give [you] comfort and joy instead of sorrow."
[Jer. 31:13]

"The LORD himself goes before you and will be with you; he
will never leave you nor forsake you. Do not be afraid; do not
be discouraged." [Deut. 31:8]

Weeping may remain for a night,
but rejoicing comes in the morning. [Ps. 30:5]

Gladness and joy will overtake them,
and sorrow and sighing will flee away. [Isa. 35:10]

May your unfailing love be my comfort,
according to your promise to your servant. [Ps. 119:76]

"A despairing man should have the devotion of his friends.
. . ." [Job 6:14]

We were under great pressure, far beyond our ability to endure, so that we despaired even of life. Indeed, in our hearts
we felt the sentence of death. But this happened that we
might not rely on ourselves but on God, who raises the dead.
He has delivered us from such a deadly peril, and he will
deliver us. On him we have set our hope that he will continue
to deliver us, as you help us by your prayers. [2 Cor. 1:8–11]

Send forth your light and your truth,
let them guide me;
let them bring me to your holy mountain,
to the place where you dwell.
Then will I go to the altar of God,
to God, my joy and my delight. . . .

Why are you downcast, O my soul?
Why so disturbed within me?
Put your hope in God,
for I will yet praise him,
my Savior and my God. [Ps. 43:3–5]

Cast your cares on the LORD
and he will sustain you;
he will never let the righteous fall. [Ps. 55:22]

When I am afraid,
  I will trust in you.
In God, whose word I praise,
  in God I trust; I will not be afraid.
  What can mortal man do to me? [Ps. 56:3–4]

"For I am the LORD, your God,
  who takes hold of your right hand
and says to you, Do not fear. . . ." [Isa. 41:13]

Dieting

Insight

More than half the women in the United States have dieted. Most have gone on to gain back the pounds lost and to diet again. A significant number of men have been caught in the same cyclical trap.

Medical evidence indicates that serious overweight does shorten life expectancy and leads to or complicates a number of diseases. The millions of dollars spent each year on diet pills and aids makes it just as clear that people feel a need for help in changing their eating habits.

Dietary problems may be blamed in part on the kinds of foods that Americans have learned to eat. Our highly processed, sugar-laden foods certainly are unhealthy. Yet many who cringe at the thought of looking in the mirror or trying to fit into new clothes are unwilling to face the need to take charge of their own eating habits. Pills, fad diets, or desperate starts and subsequent eating binges are much more the pattern.

Christians are called in Scripture to live responsible lives. We are to exercise our God-given wills to make choices that benefit rather than harm us. God's gift to us is not diet pills, but the intelligence and the courage, as we depend on him, to choose to do what is right for us.

Hints

Those who intend to go on a diet should check out their plan and their general health with a doctor. Some problems, such as low blood sugar, call for a special diet. However, once the pattern has been established, what the dieter needs most is the support of those who care for him or her. Praise for progress and encouragement to persist are the most important diet aids of all.

Resource Scriptures

> Two are better than one,
>   because they have a good return for their work:
> if one falls down,
>   his friend can help him up.
> But pity the man who falls
>   and has no one to help him up! [Eccles. 4:9–10]

For the kingdom of God is not a matter of eating and drinking, but of righteousness, peace and joy in the Holy Spirit.... [Rom. 14:17]

"Please test your servants for ten days: Give us nothing but vegetables to eat and water to drink. Then compare our appearance with that of the young men who eat the royal food, and treat your servants in accordance with what you see...."
    At the end of the ten days they looked healthier and better nourished than any of the young men who ate the royal food. [Dan. 1:12–13, 15]

> Put a knife to your throat
>   if you are given to gluttony.
> Do not crave ... delicacies. ... [Prov. 23:2–3]

> Do not join those who drink too much wine
>   or gorge themselves on meat. ... [Prov. 23:20]

Disappointments

Insight

Life holds disappointments for all of us, from the child who doesn't get a passionately desired Christmas present, to the young adult whose proposal is rejected, to the father who loses his job, to the mature person whose partner of many years is lost. Hurts are an unavoidable part of every life. Big or little, each disappointment can cause pain.

How we deal with disappointments is a key to our development and to our character. God's Word provides us a perspective which can help us deal with disappointments in a godly and a constructive way.

Hints

Be sensitive to the pain of a person who has experienced a serious disappointment. Don't rush in too soon with reassurance. Instead be a friend, and when the opportunity arises share one of the many comforting words with which Scripture is filled.

Resource Scriptures

And my God will meet all your needs according to his glorious riches in Christ Jesus. [Phil. 4:19]

Now he who supplies seed to the sower and bread for food will also supply and increase your store of seed and will enlarge the harvest of your righteousness. You will be made rich in every way so that you can be generous on every occasion. ... [2 Cor. 9:10–11]

"In this world you will have trouble. But take heart! I have overcome the world." [John 16:33]

> Trust in the LORD with all your heart
>   and lean not on your own understanding;
> in all your ways acknowledge him,
>   and he will make your paths straight. [Prov. 3:5–6]

> He tends his flock like a shepherd:
>   He gathers the lambs in his arms
> and carries them close to his heart;
>   he gently leads those that have young. [Isa. 40:11]

He fulfills the desires of those who fear him. . . . [Ps. 145:19]

> Turn my eyes away from worthless things;
>   preserve my life according to your word. [Ps. 119:37]

> For the LORD God is a sun and shield;
>   the LORD bestows favor and honor;
> no good thing does he withhold
>   from those whose walk is blameless. [Ps. 84:11]

> In his heart a man plans his course,
>   but the LORD determines his steps. [Prov. 16:9]

"You know with all your heart and soul that not one of all the good promises the LORD your God gave you has failed. Every promise has been fulfilled; not one has failed." [Josh. 23:14]

> "I am the LORD your God,
>   who teaches you what is best for you,
>   who directs you in the way you should go." [Isa. 48:17]

Dear friends, do not be surprised at the painful trial you are suffering, as though something strange were happening to you. But rejoice that you participate in the sufferings of Christ, so that you may be overjoyed when his glory is revealed. [1 Peter 4:12–13]

> Let him who walks in the dark,
>   who has no light,
> trust in the name of the LORD
>   and rely on his God. [Isa. 50:10]

"I will turn the darkness into light. ..." [Isa. 42:16]

"When you pass through the waters,
  I will be with you;
and when you pass through the rivers,
  they will not sweep over you.
When you walk through the fire,
  you will not be burned;
  the flames will not set you ablaze.
For I am the LORD, your God. ..." [Isa. 43:2–3]

Look to the LORD and his strength;
  seek his face always. [1 Chron. 16:11]

Disciplining Children

Insight

Balance in disciplining children is difficult to achieve. This is in part because discipline is often understood as punishment rather than guidance and correction. Certainly there is a role for punishment. And children seldom experience any firm guidance as a delight! Yet Scripture provides many guidelines for parents. The most significant of them are found in Hebrews, where God shows us how he disciplines his children — you and me. Christian parents will want to model their discipline of children on his.

Hints

We need to apply the Bible's guidelines to our own child-rearing. At times we'll feel strongly that friends or relatives need to apply them to theirs! But our advice is not usually welcome unless it is asked for. The best way to encourage others to ask our advice is to listen when they talk of family problems, nod, and mention similar problems we have had. Don't add the advice; let the other person sense that we really do understand. When, and only when, our friend asks what we have done, is the time to share practical ideas and biblical principles.

Resource Scriptures

Train a child in the way he should go,
   and when he is old he will not turn from it. [Prov. 22:6]

Folly is bound up in the heart of a child,
   but the rod of discipline will drive it far from him. [Prov. 22:15]
Note that "folly" means "moral evil." A child needs discipline to keep him from following sinful impulses.

   Do not withhold discipline from a child;
      if you punish him with the rod, he will not die.
   Punish him with the rod
      and save his soul from death. [Prov. 23:13–14]

The rod of correction imparts wisdom,
   but a child left to himself disgraces his mother. [Prov. 29:15]

   Discipline your son, and he will give you peace;
      he will bring delight to your soul. [Prov. 29:17]

"My son, do not make light of the Lord's discipline,
   and do not lose heart when he rebukes you,
because the Lord disciplines those he loves,
   and he punishes everyone he accepts as a son." [Heb. 12:5–6; Prov. 3:11–12]

   Endure hardship as discipline; God is treating you as sons. For what son is not disciplined by his father? If you are not disciplined (and everyone undergoes discipline), then you are illegitimate children and not true sons. Moreover, we have all had human fathers who disciplined us and we respected them for it. How much more should we submit to the Father of our spirits and live! Our fathers disciplined us for a little while as they thought best; but God disciplines us for our good, that we may share in his holiness. No discipline seems pleasant at the time, but painful. Later on, however, it produces a harvest of righteousness and peace for those who have been trained by it. [Heb. 12:7–11]

Fathers, do not embitter your children, or they will become discouraged. [Col. 3:21]

Fathers, do not exasperate your children; instead, bring them up in the training and instruction of the Lord. [Eph. 6:4]

I have been reminded of your sincere faith, which first lived in your grandmother Lois and in your mother Eunice and, I am persuaded, now lives in you also.... from infancy you have known the holy Scriptures, which are able to make you wise for salvation.... [2 Tim. 1:5; 3:15]

Whatever you have learned or received or heard from me, or seen in me — put it into practice. And the God of peace will be with you. [Phil. 4:9]

Divorce

Insight

Although the rate is dropping slightly, millions of families are still affected by the tragedy of divorce. Divorce is no stranger in the Christian community either. Many struggle with how to relate to and help others with the pain of an action that Christians agree must involve sin on the part of one partner or both.

We gain perspective and compassion, however, when we realize that God himself made provision for divorce. And Jesus sadly observed that this provision was made because of the hardness of men's hearts (Matt. 19:8). Human sinfulness will at times make remaining together more harmful than divorce. Only this tragic reality caused our loving Lord to relax his demand for lifelong commitment.

The Bible makes it clear that God does hate divorce, and that in Christ mutual forgiveness and commitment make the healing of marital hurts possible. Only when one or both partners will not take God's path to reconciliation and harmony will divorce take place.

Hints

Don't become involved in trying to determine if a divorce is "lawful." The Pharisees, who took it upon themselves to act as an ecclesiastical court, were rebuked by Jesus. What God had joined "no man" (that is, no human authority) had the right to sunder. The Old Testament guards this principle by making the giving of a bill of divorce the responsibility of the husband — it is a matter which must be determined by the couple involved (see Deut. 24:1–4). Do discourage divorce by stressing the way of mutual forgiveness. But if a couple have made the decision to divorce, do all you can to give comfort and support in the pain that most surely comes.

Resource Scriptures

The LORD is acting as the witness between you and the wife of your youth, because you have broken faith with her, though she is your partner, the wife of your marriage covenant. [Mal. 2:14]

Jesus replied, "Moses permitted you to divorce your wives because your hearts were hard. But it was not this way from the beginning. I tell you that anyone who divorces his wife, except for marital unfaithfulness, and marries another woman commits adultery." [Matt. 19:8–9]

Then Peter came to Jesus and asked, "Lord, how many times shall I forgive my brother when he sins against me? Up to seven times?"

Jesus answered, "I tell you, not seven times, but seventy-seven times." [Matt. 18:21–22]

The word *seventy-seven* indicates unlimited forgiveness.

If any brother has a wife who is not a believer and she is willing to live with him, he must not divorce her. And if a woman has a husband who is not a believer and he is willing to live with her, she must not divorce him. For the unbelieving husband has been sanctified through his wife, and the unbelieving wife has been sanctified through her believing husband. . . .

But if the unbeliever leaves, let him do so. A believing man or woman is not bound in such circumstances; God has called us to live in peace. How do you know, wife, whether you will save your husband? Or, how do you know, husband, whether you will save your wife? [1 Cor. 7:12–16]

A wife must not separate from her husband. But if she does, she must remain unmarried or else be reconciled to her husband. And a husband must not divorce his wife. [1 Cor. 7:10–11]

Note that separation is a valid alternative to divorce, and in many cases should be tried first.

A woman is bound to her husband as long as he lives. But if her husband dies, she is free to marry anyone she wishes, but he must belong to the Lord. [1 Cor. 7:39]

Doctrinal Disputes and Differences

Insight

There are many basic doctrines on which all true Christians agree. These include the Bible's teaching about God as a trinitarian Person, Jesus as God's Son, Jesus' death for sinners and his bodily resurrection, and others. There is historic agreement among Christians about basic doctrines, but there have always been differences about less central issues. The mode of baptism and whether it should be administered to infants has divided the Christian community. The particular gifts given by the Holy Spirit and how they are distributed is another area of difference. We can add disputes about the role of the individual in salvation: the balance that exists between human response to the gospel and God's sovereign superintendence of all things.

Such differences in themselves should not be too upsetting. Devout believers who trust Scripture and seek to base their views on its inspired teaching may reach different conclusions, simply because human beings are by nature finite and fallible. We need to hold our beliefs humbly, aware that however wise or spiritual we may be, we will not be able to understand all things perfectly.

But church history testifies that all too often doctrinal differences have led to bitter disputes that have had Christians acting toward one another like enemies rather than brothers. Such a reaction to differences sets us at odds with Jesus' clear command to love one another and to maintain the "unity of the Spirit through the bond of peace" (Eph. 4:3).

Christians who are committed to the Bible as God's revelation of truth will always take their beliefs seriously. We should. But we should also find ways of expressing our beliefs which allow us to remain in fellowship with Christians with whom we may differ.

Hints

When you are talking with a person who insists that you agree with all of his beliefs, avoid argument. Restate what he or she says so the person knows you have heard accurately. When you talk about your own beliefs, do so graciously. But most importantly, shift your conversation from areas of difference to your mutual love for Jesus. Tell what Jesus is doing in your life, and encourage the other person to do so too. By building a caring Christian relationship you can fulfill Jesus' command to love and at the same time provide a context in which you can talk about your differences without feeling attacked or needing to attack.

Resource Scriptures

We know that we all possess knowledge. Knowledge puffs up, but love builds up. The man who thinks he knows something does not yet know as he ought to know. But the man who loves God is known by God. [1 Cor. 8:1–3]

If I speak in the tongues of men and of angels, but have not love, I am only a resounding gong or a clanging cymbal. If I have the gift of prophecy and can fathom all mysteries and all knowledge, and if I have a faith that can move mountains, but have not love, I am nothing. [1 Cor. 13:1–2]

Be devoted to one another in brotherly love. Honor one another above yourselves. [Rom. 12:10]

You, however, know all about my teaching, my way of life, my purpose, faith, patience, love, endurance, persecutions, sufferings. . . . [2 Tim. 3:10–11]

Warn them before God against quarreling about words; it is of no value, and only ruins those who listen. Do your best to present yourself to God as one approved, a workman who does not need to be ashamed and who correctly handles the word of truth. . . . And the Lord's servant must not quarrel; instead, he must be kind to everyone, able to teach, not resentful. [2 Tim. 2:14–15, 24]

Doubts

Insight

In some people uncertainty is honest. They want to believe, but have questions. They may need the reassurance of answers, the comfort that comes from knowing that Christian faith is rational and worthy of respect.

But the word *doubt* in the New Testament is a technical religious term. The basic idea is of wavering uncertainty or of holding back from full commitment to something set forward in God's Word as an object of our faith. Such doubt can hinder our prayers (James 1:6) and lead us to act against our conscience (Rom. 14:22–23). This doubt is a serious flaw, which can be overcome only by a conscious faith-commitment to God, expressed in a willing obedience to his authoritative Word. Doubt is not something Scripture commends.

Hints

When you are talking with a person who has and expresses doubts, be sure you make appropriate distinctions. Some will have honest doubts about questions that are important to them. Both non-Christians and believers with this kind of doubt may need answers, or at least may need to realize that answers exist. But others will have a wavering lack of trust which causes them to hold back from full commitment to God. Such persons need our prayers and our own example of trust in our living God. And they need those reminders from God's Word that the Lord truly is trustworthy, and thus worth all our trust.

Resource Scriptures

> Trust in the LORD with all your heart
>   and lean not on your own understanding;
> in all your ways acknowledge him,
>   and he will make your paths straight.

> Do not be wise in your own eyes;
> > fear the LORD and shun evil.
> This will bring health to your body
> > and nourishment to your bones. [Prov. 3:5–8]

Without weakening in his faith, [Abraham] faced the fact that his body was as good as dead — since he was about a hundred years old — and that Sarah's womb was also dead. Yet he did not waver through unbelief regarding the promise of God, but was strengthened in his faith and gave glory to God, being fully persuaded that God had power to do what he had promised. [Rom. 4:19–21]

If any of you lacks wisdom, he should ask God, who gives generously to all without finding fault, and it will be given to him. But when he asks, he must believe and not doubt, because he who doubts is like a wave of the sea, blown and tossed by the wind. [James 1:5–6]

> The LORD redeems his servants;
> > no one will be condemned who takes refuge in him. [Ps. 34:22]

> "God is not a man, that he should lie,
> > nor a son of man, that he should change his mind.
> Does he speak and then not act?
> Does he promise and not fulfill?" [Num. 23:19]

> The heavens praise your wonders, O LORD,
> > your faithfulness too, in the assembly of the holy ones.
> For who in the skies above can compare with the LORD?
> Who is like the LORD among the heavenly beings?
> In the council of the holy ones God is greatly feared;
> > he is more awesome than all who surround him.
> O LORD God Almighty, who is like you?
> > You are mighty, O LORD, and your faithfulness surrounds you. [Ps. 89:5–8]

> The LORD is faithful to all his promises
> > and loving toward all he has made.
> The LORD upholds all those who fall
> > and lifts up all who are bowed down.
> The eyes of all look to you,
> > and you give them their food at the proper time.

You open your hand
  and satisfy the desires of every living thing. [Ps. 145:13–16]

To the faithful you show yourself faithful,
  to the blameless you show yourself blameless. . . . [Ps. 18:25]

Failure

Insight

We all fail at times. But for some persons failure is a dev-
astating experience. Failure attacks their sense of personal
value and self-worth. This overreaction to failure may be rooted
in a parent's overemphasis on achievement. If failure as a child
or an adult leads to punishment, ridicule, or a withdrawal of
love, failure is likely to become a fearsome specter.

Some are so afraid of failure that they excel — often at the
expense of personal relationships. Others are so afraid of failure that they are unwilling to risk trying anything which holds
even the possibility of failure.

As Christians we should learn not to fear failures. Because
we are human and live in a society warped by sin, failures are
sure to come. We realize that our worth and value are not
rooted in our accomplishments, but in the fact that God loved
us enough that his Son died for us. We also believe that God's
Spirit will enable us to meet the challenges of the future, so
we can move out with confidence to try again even when we
fail.

The unique perspective that Christian faith brings enables
us to face and to rise above our failures.

Hints

Don't be surprised at how persons react to failure, or at a fear of failure which keeps some from acting. Instead emphasize those truths which bring Christian perspective to failure. Has your friend learned to forgive and accept himself or herself as an imperfect person? Has he or she learned to rejoice in his or her value to God? Has he or she learned to face new challenges with faith?

Resource Scriptures

As a father has compassion on his children,
   so the LORD has compassion on those who fear him;
for he knows how we are formed,
   he remembers that we are dust. [Ps. 103:13–14]

Our people must learn to devote themselves to doing what is good, in order that they may provide for daily necessities and not live unproductive lives. [Titus 3:14]

. . . Make every effort to add to your faith goodness; and to goodness, knowledge; and to knowledge, self-control; and to self-control, perseverance; and to perseverance, godliness; and to godliness, brotherly kindness; and to brotherly kindness, love. For if you possess these qualities in increasing measure, they will keep you from being ineffective and unproductive in your knowledge of our Lord Jesus Christ. [2 Peter 1:5–8]

Forgetting what is behind and straining toward what is ahead, I press on toward the goal to win the prize for which God has called me heavenward in Christ Jesus. [Phil. 3:13–14]

Therefore, strengthen your feeble arms and weak knees. "Make level paths for your feet," so that the lame may not be disabled, but rather healed. [Heb. 12:12]

Therefore, my dear brothers, stand firm. Let nothing move you. Always give yourselves fully to the work of the Lord, be-

cause you know that your labor in the Lord is not in vain.
[1 Cor. 15:58]

You need to persevere so that when you have done the will
of God, you will receive what he has promised. [Heb. 10:36]

"I will strengthen you and help you. . . ." [Isa. 41:10]

Fasting

Insight

Fasting has been promoted both for its supposed spiritual
benefits and as a diet aid. In fasting stored fat is converted
and used to fuel the body. Even hunger is not a problem, as
appetite is lost within two or three days. Many people believe
fasts of a week or so are healthy, if care is taken when one
begins eating again. Typically bodily resources are used up
between thirty and forty days of fasting.

Most biblical fasts lasted only a single day, although a few
seven-day fasts are mentioned. At times a limited diet of basic
foods and water is also called a fast (see Dan. 10:2–3).

In the Old Testament, fasts are generally associated with
repentance, or at times with mourning or prayer. The New
Testament usually links fasting with prayer. Yet there are no
instructions in the New Testament calling on believers to fast
and few suggestions that fasting holds particular spiritual benefits. Although fasting can be a positive experience, it should
not be thought of as a religious duty or as an especially "spiritual" exercise.

Hints

Be sure that anyone who plans on fasting checks first with a doctor. Some persons, especially diabetics, those with low blood sugar, or those with heart disease, should not fast. As the period of fasting lengthens, health should be monitored; fasting can place a strain on the heart.

But do talk with a person who is planning a fast about his motives. Fasting should not be undertaken in spiritual desperation, or with the belief that it will surely bring one closer to God. When one group of Old Testament believers asked a prophet about keeping traditional fasts, they were reminded, "This is what the LORD Almighty says: 'Administer true justice; show mercy and compassion to one another. Do not oppress the widow or the fatherless, the alien or the poor. In your hearts do not think evil of each other' " (Zech. 7:9–10). Spirituality is found in showing God's compassionate love for all in our daily life, not in denying the needs of our flesh.

Resource Scriptures

Then Jesus was led by the Spirit into the desert to be tempted by the devil. After fasting forty days and forty nights, he was hungry. [Matt. 4:1–2]

Then [after losing a battle] the Israelites, all the people, went up to Bethel, and there they sat weeping before the LORD. They fasted that day until evening and presented burnt offerings and fellowship offerings to the LORD. [Judg. 20:26]

Yet when they were ill, I put on sackcloth
and humbled myself with fasting. [Ps. 35:13]

Then [in mourning the deaths of Saul and his sons] they buried their bones under the great tree in Jabesh, and they fasted seven days. [1 Chron. 10:12]

[The prophetess Anna] never left the temple but worshiped night and day, fasting and praying. [Luke 2:37]

[The Lord] has showed you, O man, what is good.
    And what does the LORD require of you?
To act justly and to love mercy
    and to walk humbly with your God. [Mic. 6:8]

Financial Need

Insight

The New Testament models a practical caring for other believers in financial need. New Testament giving provides a pattern that the modern church needs to take more seriously than it has in the past.

At the same time, the New Testament sets down principles of personal responsibility. Each individual is to work to earn his or her own living if this is possible, so that he not only can care for himself but also will have resources to give to others.

Our ministry to people in need then goes beyond giving, although we are encouraged to be generous. Our ministry involves helping individuals and families find work and develop the financial disciplines necessary to live responsibly in contemporary society.

Hints

It takes discernment to know how to best help others in financial need. Surely no one we can help should be permitted to go unfed or unclothed. But we often need to take the additional step of becoming involved enough to help others find work or learn to budget income responsibly. This may be done through a group in your church, such as a board of deacons. But it may be that in some cases you will need to take steps yourself, or with other Christian friends, to provide the kind of support persons in need must have.

Resource Scriptures

Suppose a brother or sister is without clothes and daily food. If one of you says to him, "Go, I wish you well; keep warm and well fed," but does nothing about his physical needs, what good is it? [James 2:15–16]

If anyone has material possessions and sees his brother in need but has no pity on him, how can the love of God be in him? Dear children, let us not love with words or tongue but with actions and in truth. This then is how we know that we belong to the truth, and how we set our hearts at rest in his presence whenever our hearts condemn us. [1 John 3:17–20]

Give proper recognition to those widows who are really in need. But if a widow has children or grandchildren, these should learn first of all to put their religion into practice by caring for their own family and so repaying their parents and grandparents, for this is pleasing to God. [1 Tim. 5:3–4]

For you yourselves know how you ought to follow our example. We were not idle when we were with you, nor did we eat anyone's food without paying for it. On the contrary, we worked night and day, laboring and toiling so that we would not be a burden to any of you. We did this, not because we do not have the right to such help, but in order to make ourselves a model for you to follow. For even when we were with you, we gave you this rule: "If a man will not work, he shall not eat."

We hear that some among you are idle. They are not busy; they are busybodies. Such people we command and urge in the Lord Jesus Christ to settle down and earn the bread they eat. And as for you, brothers, never tire of doing what is right. [2 Thess. 3:7–13]

Our desire is not that others might be relieved while you are hard pressed, but that there might be equality. At the present time your plenty will supply what they need, so that in turn their plenty will supply what you need. Then there will be equality. . . . [2 Cor. 8:13–14]

There were no needy persons among them. For from time to time those who owned lands or houses sold them, brought the money from the sales and put it at the apostles' feet, and it was distributed to anyone as he had need. [Acts 4:34–35]

Forgiving Others

Insight

Forgiveness is one of the most important of the Christian virtues. As James reminds us, "We all stumble in many ways" (3:2). Because of this all our relationships will be marred at times, as what we do hurts others and as their actions hurt us.

The Bible makes it clear that the way to relate to others and to maintain the unity to which we Christians are called in Christ demands the exercise of forgiveness. Only recognizing each other's weaknesses and freely forgiving others when hurts come can restore strained relationships and maintain harmony in our homes and congregations. It is not surprising then to discover that there is much emphasis in the New Testament on forgiving, and that in fact we are commanded to forgive as freely as we have been forgiven in Christ Jesus.

Hints

Failure to forgive has tragic spiritual results. We become bitter, suspicious, and closed to others. When we sense these traits in another person, we're likely to find unforgiven hurts still festering in his or her heart. As these are revealed, we need to pray and to remind this person of those truths and commands about forgiveness which can lead to release from bitterness and to reconciliation with the unforgiven individual.

Resource Scriptures

"Therefore, if you are offering your gift at the altar and there remember that your brother has something against you, leave your gift there in front of the altar. First go and be reconciled to your brother. . . ." [Matt. 5:23–24]

"If your brother sins against you, go and show him his fault, just between the two of you. If he listens to you, you have won your brother over." [Matt. 18:15]

Then Peter came to Jesus and asked, "Lord, how many times shall I forgive my brother when he sins against me? Up to seven times?"
Jesus answered, "I tell you, not seven times, but seventy-seven times.' " [Matt. 18:21–22]

"For if you forgive men when they sin against you, your heavenly Father will also forgive you. But if you do not forgive men their sins, your Father will not forgive your sins." [Matt. 6:14–15]

Bear with each other and forgive whatever grievances you may have against one another. Forgive as the Lord forgave you. [Col. 3:13]

> The LORD is compassionate and gracious,
>   slow to anger, abounding in love.
> He will not always accuse,
>   nor will he harbor his anger forever;

he does not treat us as our sins deserve
    or repay us according to our iniquities.
For as high as the heavens are above the earth,
    so great is his love for those who fear him;
as far as the east is from the west,
    so far has he removed our transgressions from us.
As a father has compassion on his children,
    so the LORD has compassion on those who fear him;
for he knows how we are formed,
    he remembers that we are dust. [Ps. 103:8–14]

Who is a God like you,
    who pardons sin and forgives the transgression
    of the remnant of his inheritance?
You do not stay angry forever
    but delight to show mercy.
You will again have compassion on us;
    you will tread our sins underfoot
    and hurl all our iniquities into the depths of the sea. [Mic.
        7:18–19]

If you, O LORD, kept a record of sins,
    O Lord, who could stand?
But with you there is forgiveness;
    therefore you are feared. [Ps. 130:3–4]

Giving

Insight

The Old Testament established a set proportion of income
to be given as a tithe for the support of the temple and the

priesthood. Additional tithes were required for support of the poor. More offerings were called for as sacrifices for sin, and freewill gifts could be given to the Lord as an additional "thank you."

In New Testament times, giving differed in several significant respects. Those who gave full time to ministry were to be supported by gifts from believers, but most giving was to meet the basic needs of Christian brothers locally or in distant lands. The principle is that of sharing: God charges us with the responsibility of sharing what he has given us, so that the needs of all may be met.

In this era as in Old Testament times, God owns all that the believer possesses. But in this era no set percentage for giving has been established. We may adopt the principle of the tithe set in the Old Testament. Or we may follow the New Testament principle of measuring our possessions against our needs and the needs of others, and giving generously.

Hints

The key teaching on giving in the New Testament is found in 2 Corinthians 8–9. Principles in these chapters can offer a perspective on our giving. Warning and exhortation in other passages will help us realize that money is not only for private use, but also for ministry to others.

Resource Scriptures

. . . see that you also excel in this grace of giving.

I am not commanding you, but I want to test the sincerity of your love. . . . For you know the grace of our Lord Jesus Christ, that though he was rich, yet for your sakes he became poor, so that you through his poverty might become rich. [2 Cor. 8:7–9]

For if the willingness is there, the gift is acceptable according to what one has, not according to what he does not have. [2 Cor. 8:12]

Our desire is not that others might be relieved while you are hard pressed, but that there might be equality. At the present time your plenty will supply what they need, so that in turn their plenty will supply what you need. Then there will be equality.... [2 Cor. 8:13–14]

Remember this: Whoever sows sparingly will also reap sparingly, and whoever sows generously will also reap generously. Each man should give what he has decided in his heart to give, not reluctantly or under compulsion, for God loves a cheerful giver. And God is able to make all grace abound to you, so that in all things at all times, having all that you need, you will abound in every good work. [2 Cor. 9:6–8]

Now he who supplies seed to the sower and bread for food will also supply and increase your store of seed and will enlarge the harvest of your righteousness. You will be made rich in every way so that you can be generous on every occasion, and through us your generosity will result in thanksgiving to God. [2 Cor. 9:10–11]

On the first day of every week, each one of you should set aside a sum of money in keeping with his income, saving it up, so that when I come no collections will have to be made. [1 Cor. 16:2]

For the love of money is a root of all kinds of evil. Some people, eager for money, have wandered from the faith and pierced themselves with many griefs. [1 Tim. 6:10]

Command them to do good, to be rich in good deeds, and to be generous and willing to share. In this way they will lay up treasure for themselves as a firm foundation for the coming age.... [1 Tim. 6:18]

Grief

Insight

Grief is common when a person suffers any great loss. A number of emotions are typically associated with grief: disbelief, anger, guilt, and depression are common. Most of us go through a period of mourning. Intense grief usually lasts about two weeks; more general grief and mourning may extend to months or even years.

This grieving process is normal and is shared by Christians along with the rest of humankind. But our grief, even at the most serious of losses, is "not like [that of] the rest of men" (1 Thess. 4:13). Through it all we have the sustaining conviction that God is with us, that he continues to love us, and that although we may feel hopeless, still the future does contain hope for those who trust in him.

Hints

Ministering to grief calls for great sensitivity. First, simply be there, letting the grieving person know that you care. Talk about the loss, rather than trying to ignore it or pretend nothing has happened. Talking about the situation, and — if a death is involved — remembering the person, does help persons move through the process of grieving.

In it all, while fully accepting the feelings of the grieving person, retain your Christian perspective on the future. God remains close, and tomorrow holds more promise than we can imagine now.

Resource Scriptures

Brothers, we do not want you to be ignorant about those who fall asleep, or to grieve like the rest of men, who have no hope. We believe that Jesus died and rose again and so we believe that God will bring with Jesus those who have fallen asleep in him. [1 Thess. 4:13–14]

> But you, O God, do see trouble and grief;
>   you consider it to take it in hand.
> The victim commits himself to you;
>   you are the helper of the fatherless. [Ps. 10:14]

> Though you have made me see troubles, many and bitter,
>   you will restore my life again;
> from the depths of the earth
>   you will again bring me up.
> You will increase my honor
>   and comfort me once again. [Ps. 71:20–21]

> My soul is weary with sorrow;
>   strengthen me according to your word. [Ps. 119:28]

> May your unfailing love be my comfort,
>   according to your promise to your servant. [Ps. 119:76]

Blessed is the man who perseveres under trial, because when he has stood the test, he will receive the crown of life that God has promised to those who love him. [James 1:12]

> He gives strength to the weary
>   and increases the power of the weak. [Isa. 40:29]

> A righteous man may have many troubles,
>   but the LORD delivers him from them all. . . . [Ps. 34:19]

> Let him who walks in the dark,
>   who has no light,
> trust in the name of the LORD
>   and rely on his God. [Isa. 50:10]

"For I know the plans that I have for you," declares the LORD, "plans to prosper you and not to harm you, plans to give you hope and a future." [Jer. 29:11]

"I will cause all my goodness to pass in front of you, and I will proclaim my name, the LORD, in your presence. I will have mercy on whom I will have mercy, and I will have compassion on whom I will have compassion." [Exod. 33:19]

> Gladness and joy will overtake them,
>   and sorrow and sighing will flee away. [Isa. 35:10]

Guilt

Insight

Usually what moderns mean by "guilt" is an uncomfortable feeling. Some try to be rid of it by visiting a psychiatrist; others try to overcome it by busily doing good deeds. In fact guilt as a biblical concept is not a feeling as much as it is a fact.

In scriptural teaching, guilt always involves three factors: an act which violates the will of God, a guilty condition resulting from the act, and punishment appropriate to the act. When the Bible speaks of guilt any of these three aspects may be stressed. But the biblical concept always incorporates each dimension.

People who are stricken by a sense of guilt without understanding or accepting God's forgiveness are likely to feel shame or worthlessness or to be gripped by anxiety. A person who feels guilty may even try to punish himself, while others may deny their inner conviction by violating moral restraints, in a sense "daring" God to punish.

Hints

Don't try to confront guilt-ridden persons with evidence of their sin. Instead, focus on the forgiveness that God offers. Guilt feelings are a witness within each person to the fact that human beings are morally responsible persons whose wrong choices bring them under the judgment of their conscience and of God. But freedom from guilt and from all that binds us within is ours as the gift of God in Christ Jesus, extended as forgiveness.

Resource Scriptures

"I, even I, am he who blots out
    your transgressions, for my own sake,
    and remembers your sins no more." [Isa. 43:25]

When I kept silent,
    my bones wasted away
    through my groaning all day long.
For day and night
    your hand was heavy upon me;
my strength was sapped
    as in the heat of summer.
Then I acknowledged my sin to you
    and did not cover up my iniquity.
I said, "I will confess
    my transgressions to the LORD" —
and you forgave
    the guilt of my sin.

Therefore let everyone who is godly pray to you
    while you may be found. . . . [Ps. 32:3–6]

Have mercy on me, O God,
    according to your unfailing love;
according to your great compassion
    blot out my transgressions.
Wash away all my iniquity
    and cleanse me from my sin.

For I know my transgressions,
    and my sin is always before me. [Ps. 51:1–3]

You know my folly, O God;
    my guilt is not hidden from you. [Ps. 69:5]

But you are a forgiving God, gracious and compassionate,
slow to anger and abounding in love. [Neh. 9:17]

"But God does not take away life; instead, he devises ways so
that a banished person may not remain estranged from him."
[2 Sam. 14:14]

Let the wicked forsake his way
   and the evil man his thoughts.
Let him turn to the LORD,
   and he will have mercy on him. . . . [Isa. 55:7]

"I will cleanse them from all the sin they have committed against me and will forgive all their sins of rebellion against me." [Jer. 33:8]

   " 'I will not be angry forever.
   Only acknowledge your guilt. . . .' " [Jer. 3:12–13]

In [Jesus] we have redemption through his blood, the forgiveness of sins, in accordance with the riches of God's grace. . . . [Eph. 1:7]

As the Scripture says, "Anyone who trusts in him will never be put to shame." For there is no difference between Jew and Gentile — the same Lord is Lord of all and richly blesses all who call on him, for, "Everyone who calls on the name of the Lord will be saved." [Rom. 10:11–13]

Heaven

Insight

Most often heaven is thought of as the place where believers go when we die. It is also thought of as the place believers will inhabit after the resurrection.

Although the Bible does view the heavens as the realm of God, we need to clarify our understanding of this important term.

First, there is a spiritual realm as well as a material realm.

Human beings are both spiritual and physical, but after death the person continues to exist as a self-conscious individual in the spiritual realm (heaven). Believers are "in heaven," then, in the sense that they are with the Lord in the spiritual realm he inhabits (see 2 Cor. 5:1–6).

Second, resurrection is ahead for believers. Then, with the spiritual and physical rejoined in a resurrected body untainted by sin, we will continue with the Lord in a new heaven and earth he will create (Rev. 21:1–2). We then will be "in heaven" forever, in a new creation of unimaginable expanse.

So there is a heaven to gain, as well as a hell to avoid. In Christ and through faith in him we can be sure that we will go to God when we die, and that we will be with him forever in the resurrection our living Savior guarantees.

Hints

It's not necessary to be technical when answering people's questions about heaven. But we do need to understand and to be able to explain what is ahead for those who trust Jesus. When we understand the good things God has for us, we gain assurance in our hearts and comfort when loved ones pass on before us.

Resource Scriptures

"I am going there to prepare a place for you. And if I go and prepare a place for you, I will come back and take you to be with me that you also may be where I am." [John 14:2–3]

I consider that our present sufferings are not worth comparing with the glory that will be revealed in us. [Rom. 8:18]

So will it be with the resurrection of the dead. The body that is sown is perishable, it is raised imperishable; it is sown in dishonor, it is raised in glory; it is sown in weakness, it is raised in power; it is sown a natural body, it is raised a spiritual body. [1 Cor. 15:42–44]

Now we know that if the earthly tent we live in is destroyed, we have a building from God, an eternal house in heaven, not built by human hands. ... For while we are in this tent, we groan and are burdened, because we do not wish to be unclothed but to be clothed with our heavenly dwelling, so that what is mortal may be swallowed up by life. ...

Therefore we are always confident and know that as long as we are at home in the body we are away from the Lord. ... We are confident, I say, and would prefer to be away from the body and at home with the Lord. [2 Cor. 5:1, 4, 6, 8]

Then I saw a new heaven and a new earth, for the first heaven and the first earth had passed away, and there was no longer any sea. I saw the Holy City, the new Jerusalem, coming down out of heaven from God, prepared as a bride beautifully dressed for her husband. And I heard a loud voice from the throne saying, "Now the dwelling of God is with men, and he will live with them. They will be his people, and God himself will be with them and be their God. He will wipe every tear from their eyes. There will be no more death or mourning or crying or pain, for the old order of things has passed away." [Rev. 21:1–4]

Hell

Insight

Most people think of hell as the place where unbelievers or evil people go when they die. It is also thought of as a place of eternal punishment where the unsaved will be in torment forever.

Although these common notions reflect the Bible's teaching, we need to clarify them.

First, the Bible does teach that each human being born will continue as a self-aware individual beyond death and forever. Those who have not been reconciled to God through faith, on the basis of Jesus' work on the cross, will be forever separated from the Lord.

Second, two main terms are used in speaking of the place where unsaved persons go at death. The noun *gehenna* is used twelve times in the New Testament, and is always translated "hell" in the New International Version. This word was used by rabbis in New Testament times to indicate the place of final punishment. Jesus often warned about gehenna, associating it with fire. The word *hades* is used eleven times, and is sometimes rendered "the grave" or "death." Jesus portrayed a rich sinner who was in hades awaiting final judgment as being "in torment" and in "agony" and "fire" (Luke 16:23, 24).

Hell, then, is a present reality for the unbelieving dead, and a final judgment and ultimate punishment lie ahead.

Hints

Many moderns are disturbed by the idea of hell. They want God to be unconcerned with sin, so loving that justice and holiness are set aside. How do we respond? By pointing out that God does not wish to send anyone to hell, and has actually sacrificed his own Son that whoever believes in him might not perish but have everlasting life. Only those who refuse to accept the forgiveness God offers in Jesus will be condemned to a hell of fire which God created not for humanity, but for "the devil and his angels" (Matt. 25:41).

For descriptions of hell's torments, we can turn to passages like Luke 16 and Revelation 20:14–15. And we can show that Jesus warned of this place (Matt. 5:22; 18:9; Mark 9:43, 48). But it is best to focus on the wonder of God's provision for release from the punishment which, no matter how awful, is fully merited by sin.

Resource Scriptures

The Lord . . . is patient with you, not wanting anyone to perish, but everyone to come to repentance. [2 Peter 3:9]

But because of your stubbornness and your unrepentant heart, you are storing up wrath against yourself for the day of God's wrath, when his righteous judgment will be revealed. [Rom. 2:5]

"For God so loved the world that he gave his one and only Son, that whoever believes in him shall not perish but have eternal life. For God did not send his Son into the world to condemn the world, but to save the world through him. Whoever believes in him is not condemned, but whoever does not believe stands condemned already because he has not believed in the name of God's one and only Son." [John 3:16–18]

Jesus said to [Martha], "I am the resurrection and the life. He who believes in me will live, even though he dies; and whoever lives and believes in me will never die." [John 11:25–26]

Therefore, there is now no condemnation for those who are in Christ Jesus. . . . [Rom. 8:1]

Since we have now been justified by his blood, how much more shall we be saved from God's wrath through him! For if, when we were God's enemies, we were reconciled to him through the death of his Son, how much more, having been reconciled, shall we be saved through his life! [Rom. 5:9–10]

Holiness

Insight

In the Old Testament the word *holy* is a distinctive religious and ritual term. It referred first of all to the nature of God. Second, anything "holy" was set aside for the exclusive use of God. Places, buildings, objects, persons, and even special days that were considered holy could never be used for common or ordinary purposes.

In the New Testament the emphasis shifts. The "holy" is still set aside for God. But the ritual connotation has been replaced by a moral emphasis. The holy is now associated primarily with persons, and what makes a person holy is the presence and work of the Holy Spirit in him or her. The dynamic holiness expressed by the Holy Spirit within us is seen not in our separation from the ordinary affairs of life, but by living according to God's will. In this Jesus provides us with the clearest example. He lived among men, not isolating himself from others, but in every act and relationship expressing the will and the character of the Father.

In Christ we are called to just this kind of holy life. We are to live by the will of God, led and empowered by his Holy Spirit to reveal the loving character and the pure goodness of our God.

Hints

Encourage holiness by your own example. Help others with distorted ideas about holiness to sense that God's people are called to be holy and to live a life of love.

Resource Scriptures

You ought to live holy and godly lives as you look forward to the day of God. . . . [2 Peter 3:11–12]

As obedient children, do not conform to the evil desires you had when you lived in ignorance. But just as he who called you is holy, so be holy in all you do; for it is written: "Be holy, because I am holy." [1 Peter 1:14–16]

You are witnesses, and so is God, of how holy, righteous and blameless we were among you who believed. [1 Thess. 2:10]

It is God's will that you should be sanctified: that you should avoid sexual immorality; that each of you should learn to control his own body in a way that is holy and honorable, not in passionate lust like the heathen, who do not know God. . . . [1 Thess. 4:3–5]

For God did not call us to be impure, but to live a holy life. [1 Thess. 4:7]

Therefore, as God's chosen people, holy and dearly loved, clothe yourselves with compassion, kindness, humility, gentleness and patience. Bear with each other and forgive whatever grievances you may have against one another. Forgive as the Lord forgave you. And over all these virtues put on love, which binds them all together in perfect unity. [Col. 3:12–14]

But among you there must not be even a hint of sexual immorality, or of any kind of impurity, or of greed, because these are improper for God's holy people. [Eph. 5:3]

For [God the Father] chose us in [Jesus] before the creation of the world to be holy and blameless in his sight. [Eph. 1:4]

Do you not know that your body is a temple of the Holy Spirit, who is in you, whom you have received from God? You are not your own; you were bought at a price. Therefore honor God with your body. [1 Cor. 6:19–20]

Therefore, I urge you, brothers, in view of God's mercy, to offer your bodies as living sacrifices, holy and pleasing to God – this is your spiritual act of worship. Do not conform any longer to the pattern of this world, but be transformed by the renewing of your mind. [Rom. 12:1–2]

Homosexuality

Insight

People have been uncertain about how to view homosexuality. It has been treated as a physical problem caused by neurological decay, a genetic problem, a glandular imbalance, an emotional problem caused by a dominant parent or other adult, or a mental illness. In 1973 the American Psychiatric Association stopped classifying homosexuality as a disease. Since then aggressive gay activists have promoted homosexuality as a valid "alternative lifestyle" and have demanded "rights" that amount to recognition by society that there is nothing wrong about a homosexual lifestyle.

The controversy has entered the church, as ministers have been asked to "marry" gay couples, and as homosexuals have insisted on their "right" to be ordained as Christian ministers.

The Bible takes a clear stand on homosexuality, as it does on other sexual activity outside of heterosexual marriage. Christians who recognize the authority of the Word of God will not be moved to accept the notion that homosexual activity or relationships are acceptable. What the Bible identifies as sin *is* sin, and nothing more or less.

Hints

Relating to homosexuals is often difficult. People tend to feel uncomfortable and uncertain. Should a Christian make his or her position plain? How do we respond if a person aggressively announces his or her sexual persuasion? And what if a loved one is drawn into this sinful life orientation?

It is best to remember that God loves sinners and has made provision for all of us in Christ. Coming to know Jesus as personal Savior is the first and paramount issue for anyone. So we need to focus not on judging others for their sins, but on sharing the good news of God's love and forgiveness. However, homosexuals who claim to know Christ as Savior need to be confronted with God's Word and his spoken judgment on their sin. Only repentance and reliance on God's grace for release from their wicked passions offer any hope of fellowship with other believers or with God.

Resource Scriptures

" 'Do not lie with a man as one lies with a woman; that is detestable....

Everyone who does any of these detestable things — such persons must be cut off from their people.' " [Lev. 18:22, 29]

Therefore God gave them over in the sinful desires of their hearts to sexual impurity for the degrading of their bodies with one another. They exchanged the truth of God for a lie, and worshiped and served created things rather than the Creator — who is forever praised. Amen.

Because of this, God gave them over to shameful lusts. Even their women exchanged natural relations for unnatural ones. In the same way the men also abandoned natural relations with women and were inflamed with lust for one another. Men committed indecent acts with other men, and received in themselves the due penalty for their perversion. [Rom. 1:24–27]

I have written you in my letter not to associate with sexually immoral people — not at all meaning the people of this world who are immoral.... But now I am writing you that you must not associate with anyone who calls himself a brother but is sexually immoral.... With such a man do not even eat.

What business is it of mine to judge those outside the church? Are you not to judge those inside? God will judge those outside. "Expel the wicked man from among you." [1 Cor. 5:9–13]

Husband's Role

Insight

Today society is struggling to define appropriate relationships between men and women. Males have dominated in the past; women's rights are increasingly acknowledged. There are also significant economic changes. Women no longer stay home while the husband works: it is estimated that in the 1990s some 75 percent of wives will be employed full or part time. Wives contribute money, not simply the "emotional tone," to the household these days.

As traditional roles change, uncertainty about just what a husband or wife is supposed to "do" has grown. The notion that he makes decisions and she goes along does not quite fit our changing culture. Actually, it does not fit the biblical picture either. The wife is portrayed as an active participant in family and economic affairs in Proverbs 31. Ephesians 5 pictures the husband as one who takes the role of Christ in the home, sacrificing himself as necessary to enable his wife to reach her potential as a Christian and a person. This is a very different attitude from that which we have inherited, which suggests that the husband is significant and the wife exists only to support or help him.

Hints

We all need to reevaluate our family relationships regularly. Here are some verses that provide a basis for thinking about whether a man is taking his biblical role as the true head of a Christian home.

Resource Scriptures

Husbands, in the same way be considerate as you live with your wives, and treat them with respect as the weaker partner and as heirs with you of the gracious gift of life, so that nothing will hinder your prayers. [1 Peter 3:7]

Submit to one another out of reverence for Christ. [Eph. 5:21]

For the husband is the head of the wife as Christ is the head of the church, his body, of which he is the Savior. . . .

Husbands, love your wives, just as Christ loved the church and gave himself up for her to make her holy, cleansing her by the washing with water through the word, and to present her to himself as a radiant church, without stain or wrinkle or any other blemish, but holy and blameless. In this same way, husbands ought to love their wives as their own bodies. He who loves his wife loves himself. After all, no one ever hated his own body, but he feeds and cares for it, just as Christ does the church — for we are members of his body. . . . However, each one of you also must love his wife as he loves himself, and the wife must respect her husband. [Eph. 5:23, 25–30, 33]

The husband should fulfill his marital duty to his wife, and likewise the wife to her husband. The wife's body does not belong to her alone but also to her husband. In the same way, the husband's body does not belong to him alone but also to his wife. [1 Cor. 7:3–4]

If you have any encouragement from being united with Christ, if any comfort from his love, if any fellowship with the Spirit, if any tenderness and compassion, then make my joy complete by being like-minded, having the same love, being one in spirit and purpose. Do nothing out of selfish ambition or vain conceit, but in humility consider others better than yourselves. Each of you should look not only to your own interests, but also to the interests of others. [Phil. 2:1–4]

Judging

Insight

Many Christians are confused about judging. On the one hand we feel no one should have a judgmental attitude toward others. On the other hand, we are convinced that certain things are clearly wrong and that Christians should take a stand concerning them. But how can we judge wrongs without judging people?

In fact the Bible makes a number of distinctions that clarify the issue for us. As to viewing certain things to be sin — and even acting in our congregations to discipline those who practice them — judging is not really involved. Instead we realize that God has already made a judgment about the things that he identifies as sin. We Christians simply agree with God, accept his judgment as to the nature of sinful acts, and then act as his Word directs. This is *not* judging others; rather it is affirming a divine judgment. When fellow believers adopt sinful lifestyles we are called to confront them and to seek repentance and change.

The judging we are not to be involved in has to do with questionable areas. We are not to judge another person's motives or to condemn him for actions which are not specifically identified as sin in Scripture. If we extend freedom to our brothers and sisters to be personally responsible to Jesus in matters of conviction, and if we steadfastly agree with God in his judgment on sinful acts, we will be able to minister graciously and effectively to others.

Hints

The distinctions drawn in the preceeding section can help you apply the appropriate Scriptures to help those who have a judgmental attitude or who are confused about judging.

Resource Scriptures

Brothers, do not slander one another. Anyone who speaks against his brother or judges him speaks against the law and judges it. When you judge the law, you are not keeping it, but sitting in judgment on it. There is only one Lawgiver and Judge, the one who is able to save and destroy. But you — who are you to judge your neighbor? [James 4:11–12]

"Do not judge, or you too will be judged. For in the same way you judge others, you will be judged, and with the measure you use, it will be measured to you." [Matt. 7:1–2]

You must not associate with anyone who calls himself a brother but is sexually immoral or greedy, an idolater or a slanderer, a drunkard or a swindler. With such a man do not even eat.

What business is it of mine to judge those outside the church? Are you not to judge those inside? God will judge those outside. "Expel the wicked man from among you." [1 Cor. 5:11–13]

God does not judge by external appearance. . . . [Gal. 2:6]

I care very little if I am judged by you or by any human court; indeed, I do not even judge myself. My conscience is clear, but that does not make me innocent. It is the Lord who judges me. Therefore judge nothing before the appointed time; wait till the Lord comes. He will bring to light what is hidden in darkness and will expose the motives of men's hearts. At that time each will receive his praise from God. [1 Cor. 4:3–5]

Who are you to judge someone else's servant? To his own master he stands or falls. And he will stand, for the Lord is able to make him stand. [Rom. 14:4]

For this very reason, Christ died and returned to life so that he might be the Lord of both the dead and the living. You, then, why do you judge your brother? Or why do you look down on your brothers? For we will all stand before God's judgment seat. [Rom. 14:9–10]

Marriage

Insight

Marriage is intended by God to be the lifetime bonding of one man and one woman. The Old Testament affirms that in marriage the pair shall be "one flesh." The Hebrew word suggests more than sexual union. To become "one flesh" means that husband and wife are intended to share the experiences of life on earth, growing close to each other as they face life's joys and sorrows together.

Marriage was intended by God to meet a number of basic human needs. There is the need for procreation, and the necessity that children have an emotionally and physically secure environment in which to grow. This is provided by a stable family, with husband and wife committed fully to each other. There is the need for companionship and sharing. The Old Testament notes that "it is not good for the man to be alone." So God acted to provide Adam with Eve, a "helper suitable for him" (Gen. 2:18). Finally, God created human beings with sexual needs. Marriage is his provision for those needs to be met in a context of joyous, mutual self-giving.

Marriage is the first institution established by God, and remains basic in every society. Only in the context of that total, lifelong commitment intended by God can his good purposes in human sexuality and life be achieved.

Hints

Some moderns question the commitment of marriage and opt for "living together." But by its nature marriage demands commitment. Only with full commitment, and the intention of a lifetime union, can the full benefits of life's most intimate relationship be ours.

Resource Scriptures

But for Adam no suitable helper was found. So the LORD God caused the man to fall into a deep sleep; and while he was sleeping, he took one of the man's ribs and closed up the place with flesh. Then the LORD God made a woman from the rib he had taken out of the man, and he brought her to the man.

The man said,

> "This is now bone of my bones
> and flesh of my flesh;
> she shall be called 'woman,'
> for she was taken out of man."

For this reason a man will leave his father and mother and be united to his wife, and they will become one flesh. [Gen. 2:20–24]

> May you rejoice in the wife of your youth.
> A loving doe, a graceful deer —
> may her breasts satisfy you always,
> may you ever be captivated by her love. [Prov. 5:18–19]

"Haven't you read," [Jesus] replied, "that at the beginning the Creator 'made them male and female,' and said, 'For this reason a man will leave his father and mother and be united to his wife, and the two will become one flesh'? So they are no longer two, but one. Therefore what God has joined together, let man not separate." [Matt. 19:4–6]

But since there is so much immorality, each man should have his own wife, and each woman her own husband. The husband should fulfill his marital duty to his wife, and likewise the wife to her husband. The wife's body does not belong to her alone but also to her husband. In the same way, the husband's body does not belong to him alone but also to his wife. [1 Cor. 7:2–4]

Husbands, in the same way be considerate as you live with your wives, and treat them with respect as the weaker partner and as heirs with you of the gracious gift of life. . . . [1 Peter 3:7]

Materialism

Insight

The materialist operates on a simple assumption. All that exists, and all that can make life worthwhile or enjoyable, is to be found in this present universe. Materialism discounts the spiritual and sets aside the Christian's conviction that God is able to act in our world of space and time.

Christians too may develop materialistic attitudes. Such attitudes are evidenced by seeking after money or things; by priorities that are fixed on what can be gained in the here and now.

The Bible criticizes this attitude on several bases. The person who focuses all his attention on material things will ignore relationship with God and thus find himself in eternal peril. Material things are temporary at best: wealth gained can be lost, and when we pass from this life nothing we have accumulated can be brought with us. Only God and his kingdom are truly lasting, and the true riches are those to be gained in loving and serving God. In addition, material possessions, no matter how great, cannot satisfy. Human beings were created with a spiritual as well as a physical dimension, and only relationship with God can bring us wholeness and fulfillment. How much wiser to be content with what we possess, to trust God to meet our continuing needs, and to focus our lives on pleasing our Lord.

Hints

The person whose life is focused on material possessions will lack real satisfaction and peace. Show your own joy in Jesus and the contentment you find in the blessings he has given you. And mention Scriptures which point up the fallacies of the materialistic view.

Resource Scriptures

"Watch out! Be on your guard against all kinds of greed; a man's life does not consist in the abundance of his possessions." [Luke 12:15]

"And do not set your heart on what you will eat or drink; do not worry about it. For the pagan world runs after all such things, and your Father knows that you need them. But seek his kingdom, and these things will be given to you as well." [Luke 12:29–31]

"Do not store up for yourselves treasures on earth, where moth and rust destroy, and where thieves break in and steal. But store up for yourselves treasures in heaven, where moth and rust do not destroy, and where thieves do not break in and steal. For where your treasure is, there your heart will be also." [Matt. 6:19–21]

[A certain rich man thought to himself,] " 'You have plenty of good things laid up for many years. Take life easy; eat, drink and be merry.'
But God said to him, 'You fool! This very night your life will be demanded from you. Then who will get what you have prepared for yourself?' " [Luke 12:19–20]

Whoever loves money never has money enough;
    whoever loves wealth is never satisfied with his income.
    This too is meaningless.
As goods increase,
    so do those who consume them.
And what benefit are they to the owner
    except to feast his eyes on them? [Eccles. 5:10–11]

But godliness with contentment is great gain. For we brought nothing into the world, and we can take nothing out of it. But if we have food and clothing, we will be content with that. [1 Tim. 6:6–8]

I know what it is to be in need, and I know what it is to have plenty. I have learned the secret of being content in any and every situation, whether well fed or hungry, whether living in plenty or in want. I can do everything through him who gives me strength. [Phil. 4:12–13]

Mental Illness

Insight

Mental illness can be organic (linked with changes in the brain caused by a chemical imbalance, tumor, or vitamin deficiency) or functional (not traceable to changes in the brain). Organic mental illnesses may be medically treated. Although some functional disorders can also be treated with drugs, counseling and therapy are also used.

Anyone can become mentally ill (just as anyone can break a leg). Mental illness places unusual strains on a person, his family, and his friends. Few know how to respond to "strange" behavior. Because a mentally ill person's behavior is often erratic, others may fear because they cannot tell what to expect from him.

The Bible does report cases of mental illness. Nebuchadnezzar was stricken with such an illness (Dan. 4:28–34). David pretended to be insane at one time when he was in the land of his Philistine enemies (1 Sam. 41:13–14). Some stories in the Gospels suggest that mental as well as physical illnesses may be associated with demonic activity, but not necessarily so. Jesus' actions demonstrate that mental illness, like other sicknesses, can be cured.

Although God's people may suffer from mental illness (just as we experience other tragedies), we continue to possess God's promises that he will be with us in our times of trial and that his love will undergird us.

Hints

When God brings you in contact with a person who is mentally ill, or who has a family member who is ill, be supportive and remind him of promises from God's Word. If a sick person is not obtaining professional treatment, urge it.

Resource Scriptures

> The LORD Almighty is with us;
> the God of Jacob is our fortress. [Ps. 46:7]

But from everlasting to everlasting
the LORD's love is with those who fear him. . . . [Ps. 103:17]

For I am convinced that neither death nor life, neither angels nor demons, neither the present nor the future, nor any powers, neither height nor depth, nor anything else in all creation, will be able to separate us from the love of God that is in Christ Jesus our Lord. [Rom. 8:38–39]

> Though my father and mother forsake me,
> the LORD will receive me. [Ps. 27:10]

> Yet I am always with you;
> you hold me by my right hand. [Ps. 73:23]

"I, the God of Israel, will not forsake them." [Isa. 41:17]

> My hand will sustain him;
> surely my arm will strengthen him. [Ps. 89:21]

> "Surely God is my salvation;
> I will trust and not be afraid.
> The LORD, the LORD, is my strength and my song;
> he has become my salvation." [Isa. 12:2]

> The LORD helps them and delivers them;
> he delivers them from the wicked and saves them,
> because they take refuge in him. [Ps. 37:40]

"Because he loves me," says the LORD, "I will rescue him;
I will protect him, for he acknowledges my name." [Ps. 91:14]

He will cover you with his feathers,
and under his wings you will find refuge;
his faithfulness will be your shield and rampart. [Ps. 91:4]

. . . I know whom I have believed, and am convinced that he is able to guard what I have entrusted to him for that day. [2 Tim. 1:12]

The LORD is my shepherd, I shall not be in want. [Ps. 23:1]

> For he is our God
> and we are the people of his pasture,
> the flock under his care. [Ps. 95:7]

Parenting

Insight

Families are the context in which the personalities of children are nurtured. Scripture gives us guidance by helping us to set goals for nurturing and by showing us how to nurture effectively.

Hints

Much research has shown that the best way to help parents be more effective in nurturing their children is to form groups of parents who can talk about their experiences with their children and look together at child-rearing practices. Here are some Scriptures which such groups — or any couple — will find helpful.

Resource Scriptures

Love the LORD your God with all your heart and with all your soul and with all your strength. These commandments that I give you today are to be upon your hearts. Impress them on your children. Talk about them when you sit at home and when you walk along the road, when you lie down and when you get up. [Deut. 6:5–7]

Only be careful, and watch yourselves closely so that you do not forget the things your eyes have seen or let them slip from your heart as long as you live. Teach them to your children and to their children after them. [Deut. 4:9]

In everything set them an example by doing what is good. In your teaching show integrity. . . . [Titus 2:7]

For you know that we dealt with each of you as a father deals with his own children, encouraging, comforting and urging you to live lives worthy of God, who calls you into his kingdom and glory. [1 Thess. 2:11–12]

. . . from infancy you have known the holy Scriptures, which are able to make you wise for salvation through faith in Christ Jesus. [2 Tim. 3:15]

. . . God disciplines us for our good, that we may share in his holiness. No discipline seems pleasant at the time, but painful. Later on, however, it produces a harvest of right-eousness and peace for those who have been trained by it. [Heb. 12:10–11]

Do not withhold discipline from a child;
    if you punish him with the rod, he will not die.
Punish him with the rod
    and save his soul from death. [Prov. 23:13–14]

All Scripture is God-breathed and is useful for teaching, re-buking, correcting and training in righteousness, so that the man of God may be thoroughly equipped for every good work. [2 Tim. 3:16–17]

. . . correct, rebuke and encourage — with great patience and careful instruction. [2 Tim. 4:2]

Train a child in the way he should go,
    and when he is old he will not turn from it. [Prov. 22:6]

Let love and faithfulness never leave you;
    bind them around your neck,
    write them on the tablet of your heart.
Then you will win favor and a good name
    in the sight of God and man. [Prov. 3:3–4]

And let us consider how we may spur one another on toward love and good deeds. Let us not give up meeting together, as some are in the habit of doing, but let us encourage one another — and all the more as you see the Day approaching. [Heb. 10:24–25]

". . . tell your children and grandchildren how I dealt harshly with the Egyptians and how I performed my signs among them, . . . that you may know that I am the LORD." [Exod. 10:2]

"Lord, how many times shall I forgive my brother when he sins against me? Up to seven times?"

Jesus answered, "I tell you, not seven times, but seventy-seven times." [Matt. 18:21–22]

Peace

Insight

Although Scripture foretells a time when there will be peace on earth, it is just as clear in asserting that now peace must not be sought in circumstances. There will continue to be wars and rumors of wars. And each of us will experience stress in our life.

What the Bible does promise us is an inner peace that can be found through personal relationship with God. This peace is independent of circumstances and rooted in the conviction that our faithful God is committed to love and to care for his people.

Peace with God is linked initially with salvation, which brings us into personal relationship with God. But peace is to be a growing reality for Christians as we experience within the deepening of commitment to and trust in him.

Hints

The peace that Jesus gives is better shown than talked about. As we demonstrate quiet confidence in the midst of stressful circumstances, others will ask us to explain. It is then, as peace shines through our lives, that the words we have to share about one of Jesus' most wonderful gifts will have the greatest authority.

Resource Scriptures

Therefore, since we have been justified through faith, we have peace with God through our Lord Jesus Christ, through whom we have gained access by faith into this grace in which we now stand. [Rom. 5:1–2]

He promises peace to his people, his saints. ... [Ps. 85:8]

"Take my yoke upon you and learn from me, for I am gentle and humble in heart, and you will find rest for your souls." [Matt. 11:29]

"Do not let your hearts be troubled. Trust in God; trust also in me." [John 14:1]

"Peace I leave with you; my peace I give you. I do not give to you as the world gives. Do not let your hearts be troubled and do not be afraid." [John 14:27]

Great peace have they who love your law,
  and nothing can make them stumble. [Ps. 119:165]

A heart at peace gives life to the body. ... [Prov. 14:30]

You will keep in perfect peace
  him whose mind is steadfast,
  because he trusts in you.
Trust in the LORD forever,
  for the LORD, the LORD, is the Rock eternal. [Isa. 26:3–4]

But the fruit of the Spirit is love, joy, peace, patience, kindness, goodness, faithfulness, gentleness and self-control. [Gal. 5:22–23]

But he was pierced for our transgressions,
  he was crushed for our iniquities;
the punishment that brought us peace was upon him,
  and by his wounds we are healed. [Isa. 53:5]

... live in peace. And the God of love and peace will be with you. [2 Cor. 13:11]

Whatever you have learned or received or heard from me, or seen in me — put it into practice. And the God of peace will be with you. [Phil 4:9]

Grace and peace be yours in abundance through the knowledge of God and of Jesus our Lord. [2 Peter 1:2]

"Peace, peace, to those far and near,"
   says the LORD. "And I will heal them."
But the wicked are like the tossing sea,
   which cannot rest,
   whose waves cast up mire and mud.
"There is no peace," says my God, "for the wicked." [Isa. 57:19–21]

Now may the Lord of peace himself give you peace at all times and in every way. [2 Thess. 3:16]

Praise

Insight

Praise is adoration of God. When we praise God we address him directly, worshiping him and expressing those things about him which we admire. Praise can be individual, offered by us in private prayer, or can be offered by a gathered congregation.

Praise is important to God, who seeks persons to worship him, and to us as well. As we praise God we are reminded of who he is, and our hearts are filled with his love.

Hints

People who are discouraged, have lost hope, or whose faith seems to be weakening should be encouraged to praise God. As we praise God our faith is strengthened, and he becomes more and more real to us. Build the habit of regular praise in your own life. And draw others into the practice of praise. There may be no greater contribution you can make to the spiritual life of those to whom you minister.

Resource Scriptures

> Glory in his holy name;
>> let the hearts of those who seek the LORD rejoice.
> Look to the LORD and his strength;
>> seek his face always. [1 Chron. 16:10–11]

"Yours, O LORD, is the greatness and the power
and the glory and the majesty and the splendor,
for everything in heaven and earth is yours. [1 Chron. 29:11]

I will praise you, O LORD, with all my heart;
I will tell of all your wonders.
I will be glad and rejoice in you;
I will sing praise to your name, O Most High. [Ps. 9:1–2]

Ascribe to the LORD, O mighty ones,
ascribe to the LORD glory and strength.
Ascribe to the LORD the glory due his name;
worship the LORD in the splendor of his holiness. [Ps. 29:1–2]

> It is fitting for the upright to praise him.
> Praise the LORD with the harp;
>> make music to him on the ten-stringed lyre.
> Sing to him a new song;
>> play skillfully, and shout for joy. [Ps. 33:1–3]

> I will extol the LORD at all times;
>> his praise will always be on my lips.
> My soul will boast in the LORD;
>> let the afflicted hear and rejoice.

Glorify the LORD with me;
  let us exalt his name together. [Ps. 34:1–3]

"You are worthy, our Lord and God,
  to receive glory and honor and power,
for you created all things,
  and by your will they were created
  and have their being." [Rev. 4:11]

Through Jesus, therefore, let us continually offer to God a sacrifice of praise — the fruit of lips that confess his name. [Heb. 13:15]

"Give thanks to the LORD, call on his name;
  make known among the nations what he has done,
  and proclaim that his name is exalted.
Sing to the LORD, for he has done glorious things;
  let this be known to all the world.
Shout aloud and sing for joy, people of Zion,
  for great is the Holy One of Israel among you." [Isa. 12:4–6]

"Worthy is the Lamb, who was slain,
  to receive power and wealth and wisdom and strength
  and honor and glory and praise!" [Rev. 5:12]

Praise the LORD.

How good it is to sing praises to our God,
  how pleasant and fitting to praise him! [Ps. 147:1]

Enter his gates with thanksgiving
  and his courts with praise;
  give thanks to him and praise his name.
For the LORD is good and his love endures forever;
  his faithfulness continues through all generations. [Ps. 100:4–5]

Prayer

Insight

Prayer is one of the richest blessings God has given us in Christ. In essence, prayer is an expression of our relationship with God as Father. We come to him, sure of our welcome because of Jesus, and confident that as a Father God cares for us, his children.

Some people have emphasized conditions to be fulfilled if we are to expect our prayers to be answered. But God has not set up a spiritual obstacle course. What God has done is to invite us to come freely to his throne of grace, sure of our welcome and sure that he will help us. As we pray in Jesus' name and in God's will, we gain increasing assurance that we will receive the things we ask him for.

Others are concerned that their prayers do not seem to be answered. But no is as much an answer as yes. Because we realize how wise God our Father is, our prayers are uttered in the conviction that his answer may not be what we think we want, but will be what is best.

Hints

Encourage others to focus on who God is as they pray. Our confidence comes from the assurance that God loves us and that we have access to the Father through Jesus Christ.

Resource Scriptures

Let us then approach the throne of grace with confidence, so that we may receive mercy and find grace to help us in our time of need. [Heb. 4:16]

"Ask and it will be given you; seek and you will find; knock and the door will be opened to you. For everyone who asks receives; he who seeks finds; and to him who knocks, the door will be opened." [Matt. 7:7–8]

For you did not receive a spirit that makes you a slave again to fear, but you received the Spirit of sonship. And by him we cry, "Abba [literally, Daddy], Father." The Spirit himself testifies with our spirit that we are God's children. [Rom. 8:15–16]

"I tell you the truth, my Father will give you whatever you ask in my name. Until now you have not asked for anything in my name. Ask and you will receive, and your joy will be complete." [John 16:23–24]

Do not be anxious about anything, but in everything, by prayer and petition, with thanksgiving, present your requests to God. And the peace of God, which transcends all understanding, will guard your hearts and your minds in Christ Jesus. [Phil. 4:6–7]

Therefore, brothers, since we have confidence to enter the Most Holy Place by the blood of Jesus, by a new and living way opened for us through the curtain, that is, his body, and since we have a great priest over the house of God, let us draw near to God with a sincere heart in full assurance of faith, having our hearts sprinkled to cleanse us from a guilty conscience. . . . [Heb. 10:19–22]

O you who hear prayer,
    to you all men will come. . . .
You answer us with awesome deeds of righteousness,
    O God our Savior. . . . [Ps. 65:2, 5]

You do not have, because you do not ask God. When you ask, you do not receive, because you ask with wrong motives, that you may spend what you get on your pleasures. [James 4:2–3]

"Come to me, all you who are weary and burdened, and I will give you rest." [Matt. 11:28]

"Which of you, if his son asks for bread, will give him a stone? Or if he asks for a fish, will give him a snake? If you, then, though you are evil, know how to give good gifts to your children, how much more will your Father in heaven give good gifts to those who ask him!" [Matt. 7:9–11]

Every good and perfect gift is from above, coming down from the Father. . . . [James 1:17]

Rape

Insight

Rape is not an act motivated by mere sexual desire. Thus the idea that the victim somehow caused her rape by suggestive actions is irresponsible and wrong. Rape is assault, and research has shown that most rapes are motivated by anger and aggression, not sexual desire.

Many cities have set up rape-crisis centers designed to help women deal with this experience. Victims often have feelings of guilt, rejection, anger, helplessness, and uncleanness. The following guidelines for helping rape victims have been developed:

The victim needs a supportive relationship where she can sense that others sympathize and care.

The victim needs an immediate medical examination.

The victim needs to report the rape to the police.

The victim needs time to work through the sense of shame that typically accompanies rape.

Christian friends can provide the needed support. Christians may also consider setting up a rape-crisis center in communities where none exist.

Hints

Be particularly sensitive to the depth of the feelings of a rape victim. Encourage her to talk. Be ready to touch or hold the victim's hand if she is willing. Some women feel too stained to accept another's touch initially. Don't ask questions about the experience that seem to suggest the rape may have been the victim's fault, or that she may have "led him on" by her behavior. Use Scriptures that emphasize God's cleansing and his continuing loving presence.

Resource Scriptures

And by that will, we have been made holy through the sacrifice of the body of Jesus Christ once for all. [Heb. 10:10]

... let us draw near to God with a sincere heart in full assurance of faith, having our hearts sprinkled to cleanse us from a guilty conscience and having our bodies washed with pure water. [Heb. 10:22]

In his great mercy [God] has given us new birth into a living hope through the resurrection of Jesus Christ from the dead, and into an inheritance that can never perish, spoil or fade — kept in heaven for you, who through faith are shielded by God's power until the coming of the salvation that is ready to be revealed in the last time. In this you greatly rejoice, though now for a little while you may have had to suffer grief in all kinds of trials. These have come so that your faith — of greater worth than gold, which perishes even though refined by fire — may be proved genuine and may result in praise, glory and honor when Jesus Christ is revealed. [1 Peter 1:3–7]

For [God] has rescued us from the dominion of darkness and brought us into the kingdom of the Son he loves, in whom we have redemption. ... [Col. 1:13–14]

And the God of all grace, who called you to his eternal glory in Christ, after you have suffered a little while, will himself restore you and make you strong, firm and steadfast. [1 Peter 5:10]

Let him who walks in the dark,
    who has no light,
trust in the name of the LORD
    and rely on his God. [Isa. 50:10]

A little while, and the wicked will be no more;
    though you look for them, they will not be found.
But the meek will inherit the land
    and enjoy great peace. [Ps. 37:10–11]

"My grace is sufficient for you, for my power is made perfect
in weakness." [2 Cor. 12:9]

Salvation (Assurance of)

Insight

Assurance of salvation is not based on the depth or the
strength of our faith. The basis on which we are saved is not
our sincerity or any subjective factor. The basis of salvation is
what Jesus has done. All that we can do is to accept his gift
of life, taking God at his word. Assurance of salvation is based
on our conviction that God is faithful to his Word.

Once a person has received Christ as Savior it is important
to help him or her understand that salvation is a present
possession.

Hints

Use Scriptures that contain God's statements and promises
about salvation. Ask, "Did you receive Jesus as your Savior?"

Show an appropriate verse and let the other person read it. Follow up by asking, "What does God say you now have, then?" Continue the process with other verses to build an awareness that salvation truly is his or her present possession. And be sure to write out the reference for each verse, so that the person can return to Scripture for reassurance should doubt arise.

Resource Scriptures

Yet to all who received him, to those who believed in his name, he gave the right to become children of God — children born not of natural descent, nor of human decision or a husband's will, but born of God. [John 1:12–13]

"Whoever believes in [Jesus] is not condemned. . . ." [John 3:18]

"I tell you the truth, whoever hears my word and believes him who sent me has eternal life and will not be condemned; he has crossed over from death to life." [John 5:24]

"For my Father's will is that everyone who looks to the Son and believes in him shall have eternal life, and I will raise him up at the last day." [John 6:40]

For if, when we were God's enemies, we were reconciled to him through the death of his Son, how much more, having been reconciled, shall we be saved through his life! [Rom. 5:10]

You are all sons of God through faith in Christ Jesus, for all of you who were baptized into Christ have clothed yourselves with Christ. [Gal. 3:26–27]

. . . God, who is rich in mercy, made us alive with Christ even when we were dead in transgressions — it is by grace you have been saved. . . . For it is by grace you have been saved, through faith — and this not from yourselves, it is the gift of God — not by works, so that no one can boast. [Eph. 2:4, 8–9]

Because God wanted to make the unchanging nature of his purpose very clear to the heirs of what was promised, he confirmed it with an oath. God did this so that, by two unchangeable things in which it is impossible for God to lie, we who have fled to take hold of the hope offered to us may be greatly encouraged. We have this hope as an anchor for the soul, firm and secure. [Heb. 6:17–19]

Therefore [Jesus] is able to save completely those who come to God through him, because he always lives to intercede for them. [Heb. 7:25]

Dear friends, now we are children of God. . . . [1 John 3:2]

Everyone who believes that Jesus is the Christ is born of God. . . . [1 John 5:1]

Anyone who believes in the Son of God has this testimony in his heart. . . . And this is the testimony: God has given us eternal life, and this life is in his Son. He who has the Son has life; he who does not have the Son of God does not have life. [1 John 5:10–12]

Salvation (Way of)

Insight

Other religions portray human beings finding a way of salvation. Christianity alone portrays God as acting to bring salvation to a lost and helpless humanity.

Two elements in Christian soteriology (the theology of salvation) must be kept in clear view. First, the basis of salvation is the death of Jesus Christ, who offered himself as a substitutionary sacrifice and so paid the penalty of human sin. It is on the basis of Jesus' death that God has offered mankind forgiveness in every era: Old Testament salvation promises look forward to Calvary and New Testament promises look backward to Calvary. Second, a faith response to God's Word of promise is the one and only way that personal relationship with God can be established. Nothing human beings can do can merit the forgiveness God offers us. So in grace God has chosen to accept faith — trust in his Word of promise — and to give those who so believe a righteousness we do not possess.

We need to be careful never to confuse the basis of salvation and the faith by which God's offer of new life is received. Thus we present Jesus Christ to others as the object of faith, the one in whom we trust. And we ask God to work in the hearts of those who hear the good news about Jesus to enable a faith response to God's promise.

Hints

In presenting the gospel to others, keep the focus on Jesus and what he has done for us. Remember that when a person responds with trust in God's Son, that person passes from death to life. It is after trust has been placed in Jesus that we need to go on and lead the new believer to assurance of salvation.

Resource Scriptures

In [Jesus] we have redemption through his blood, the forgiveness of sins, in accordance with the riches of God's grace. . . . [Eph. 1:7]

. . . all have sinned and fall short of the glory of God, and are justified freely by his grace through the redemption that came by Christ Jesus. God presented him as a sacrifice of atonement, through faith in his blood. [Rom. 3:23–25]

You see, at just the right time, when we were still powerless, Christ died for the ungodly. Very rarely will anyone die for a righteous man, though for a good man someone might possibly dare to die. But God demonstrates his own love for us in this: While we were still sinners, Christ died for us.

Since we have now been justified by his blood, how much more shall we be saved from God's wrath through him! [Rom. 5:6–9]

For God was pleased to have all his fullness dwell in [Jesus], and through him to reconcile to himself all things, whether things on earth or things in heaven, by making peace through his blood, shed on the cross.

Once you were alienated from God and were enemies in your minds because of your evil behavior. But now he has reconciled you by Christ's physical body through death to present you holy in his sight, without blemish and free from accusation. . . . [Col. 1:19–22]

. . . Christ was sacrificed once to take away the sins of many people; and he will appear a second time, not to bear sin, but to bring salvation to those who are waiting for him. [Heb. 9:28]

How much more, then, will the blood of Christ, who through the eternal Spirit offered himself unblemished to God, cleanse our consciences from acts that lead to death, so that we may serve the living God! [Heb. 9:14]

And by that will, we have been made holy through the sacrifice of the body of Jesus Christ once for all. [Heb. 10:10]

To him who loves us and has freed us from our sins by his blood, and has made us to be a kingdom and priests to serve his God and Father — to him be glory and power for ever and ever! Amen. [Rev. 1:5–6]

Sex

Insight

Our society places great emphasis on sex. Sex is confused with love, and many view sex simply as a source of casual pleasure. A healthy attitude toward sex does affirm sexual intercourse as a good and pleasurable thing. But sex is not for casual affairs.

God invented sex when he made human beings male and female. He intended the intimacy of sex not only to be pleasurable, but also to bond a husband and wife closer together. Sex is the sign and seal of total, lifetime commitment between a man and a woman. Outside of this context of lifetime commitment, God's good purposes in sexuality cannot be achieved. Outside of this context, sex becomes increasingly meaningless and empty.

Some Christians, however, feel that sex is somehow "wrong" or "unclean" in itself. This is not at all the Bible's view. In marriage the enjoyment of our sexuality and our partner is intended as one of God's richest and most comforting gifts.

Hints

Sexual sins are always wrong, and include any sexual activity outside of marriage. Many Scriptures make this clear. But the positive view of sex is also presented in the Bible. Be familiar with both sets of verses if you discover a friend has developed an unhealthy attitude toward his or her own sexuality.

Resource Scriptures

So God created man in his own image,
in the image of God he created him,
male and female he created them. [Gen. 1:27]

For this reason a man will leave his father and mother and be united to his wife, and they will become one flesh. [Gen. 2:24]

For everything God created is good, and nothing is to be rejected if it is received with thanksgiving, because it is consecrated by the word of God and prayer. [1 Tim. 4:4–5]

The husband should fulfill his marital duty to his wife, and likewise the wife to her husband. The wife's body does not belong to her alone but also to her husband. In the same way, the husband's body does not belong to him alone but also to his wife. Do not deprive each other except by mutual consent and for a time, so that you may devote yourselves to prayer. [1 Cor. 7:3–5]

Marriage should be honored by all, and the marriage bed kept pure. . . . [Heb. 13:4]

How delightful is your love, my sister, my bride!
    How much more pleasing is your love than wine,
    and the fragrance of your perfume than any spice!
Your lips drop sweetness as the honeycomb, my bride;
    milk and honey are under your tongue. [Song of Songs
        4:10–11]

My lover is radiant and ruddy,
    outstanding among ten thousand. . . .
His body is like polished ivory
    decorated with sapphires.
His legs are pillars of marble
    set on bases of pure gold.
His appearance is like Lebanon,
    choice as its cedars.
His mouth is sweetness itself;
    he is altogether lovely.
This is my lover, this my friend. . . . [Song of Songs 5:10, 14–16]

May you rejoice in the wife of your youth.
A loving doe, a graceful deer —
    may her breasts satisfy you always,
    may you ever be captivated by her love. [Prov. 5:18–19]

Sickness

Insight

In this world all of us are subject to sickness and to death. At times, friends will find themselves in the grip of terminal illness. Others will have chronic illnesses that drastically affect the quality of life. People in this situation may understandably become depressed and discouraged. How can we minister to such a friend?

We need to be aware that some may insist the illness could be cured if only the sick person had enough faith. This approach, if taken seriously, is likely to generate even greater guilt and discouragement. Even the apostle Paul, whose faith no one can question, was subject to a serious chronic illness (2 Cor. 12), as was young Timothy (1 Tim. 5:23). Although God can and does heal, we have no guarantee that health is God's best will for you and me.

Hints

How can we support and minister to the sick? Let's help our friends continue to trust and to hope in God. We should visit often. When we do, we can read Scriptures that will nurture trust in the Lord despite the difficult times that sickness always involves.

Resource Scriptures

> My flesh and my heart may fail,
> but God is the strength of my heart
> and my portion forever. [Ps. 73:26]

Though you have made me see troubles, many and bitter,
   you will restore my life again;
from the depths of the earth
   you will again bring me up.
You will increase my honor
   and comfort me once again. [Ps. 71:20–21]

May your unfailing love be my comfort,
   according to your promise to your servant. [Ps. 119:76]

Is any one of you sick? He should call the elders of the church to pray over him and anoint him with oil in the name of the Lord. And the prayer offered in faith will make the sick person well; the Lord will raise him up. If he has sinned, he will be forgiven. Therefore confess your sins to each other and pray for each other so that you may be healed. The prayer of a righteous man is powerful and effective. [James 5:14–16]

[Paul writes of a sickness he experienced,] Three times I pleaded with the Lord to take it away from me. But he said to me, "My grace is sufficient for you, for my power is made perfect in weakness." Therefore I will boast all the more gladly about my weaknesses, so that Christ's power may rest on me. . . . For when I am weak, then I am strong. [2 Cor. 12:8–10]

Even though I walk
   through the valley of the shadow of death,
I will fear no evil,
   for you are with me;
your rod and your staff,
   they comfort me. [Ps. 23:4]

The LORD will sustain him on his sickbed. . . . [Ps. 41:3]

"Worship the LORD your God, and his blessing will be on your food and water. I will take away sickness from among you, and none will miscarry or be barren in your land. I will give you a full life span." [Exod. 23:25–26]

Heal me, O LORD, and I will be healed;
   save me and I will be saved,
   for you are the one I praise. [Jer. 17:14]

And the God of all grace, who called you to his eternal glory in Christ, after you have suffered a little while, will himself restore you and make you strong, firm and steadfast. [1 Peter 5:10]

> Let him who walks in the dark,
>   who has no light,
> trust in the name of the LORD
>   and rely on his God. [Isa. 50:10]

"I will turn the darkness into light. . . ." [Isa. 42:16]

Singleness

Insight

An increasing number of young adults are choosing to remain single rather than to marry. This can be traced in part to cultural change. Women today have career opportunities that did not exist in earlier eras. Although traditional values (e.g., family, patriotism) are again popular, there are still many who believe that they can have a more meaningful and significant life as a single person rather than as a husband or a wife.

Christians may be a little slow to accept this notion. But there are firm biblical grounds for supporting such a choice. The apostle Paul advances a number of arguments for remaining single as an expresson of full commitment. Christians who are considering singleness should carefully evaluate and test their own motives.

It is particularly important to help those who plan on a single life to resist a tendency toward emotional isolation. The intimacy of marriage will not be possible for the single. But there is still a great need for close, loving relationships. The Christian community is designed by God to be a family. Only when the single person invests the time and effort necessary to build loving and caring relationships with others can some of his or her most basic needs be met. And only in the context of such relationships can full growth as a Christian and a person take place.

Hints

If a person considering singleness wants to talk about the choice with you, help him think about his motives. Compare Paul's view (see 1 Cor. 7). And encourage him to build close relationships with other Christians.

Resource Scriptures

Now to the unmarried and the widows I say: It is good for them to stay unmarried, as I am. But if they cannot control themselves, they should marry, for it is better to marry than to burn with passion. [1 Cor. 7:8–9]

. . . I give a judgment as one who by the Lord's mercy is trustworthy. Because of the present crisis, I think that it is good for you to remain as you are. . . . But those who marry will face many troubles in this life, and I want to spare you this.
What I mean, brothers, is that the time is short. . . .
I would like you to be free from concern. An unmarried man is concerned about the Lord's affairs — how he can please the Lord. But a married man is concerned about the affairs of this world — how he can please his wife — and his interests are divided. An unmarried woman or virgin is concerned about the Lord's affairs: Her aim is to be devoted to the Lord in both body and spirit. But a married woman is concerned

about the affairs of this world — how she can please her husband. I am saying this for your good, not to restrict you. . . .

If anyone thinks he is acting improperly toward the virgin he is engaged to, and if she is getting along in years and he feels he ought to marry, he should do as he wants. He is not sinning. They should get married. But the man who has settled the matter in his own mind, who is under no compulsion but has control over his own will, and who has made up his mind not to marry the virgin — this man also does the right thing. So then, he who marries the virgin does right, but he who does not marry her does even better. [1 Cor. 7:25–29, 32–38]

Let us not give up meeting together, as some are in the habit of doing, but let us encourage one another. . . . [Heb. 10:25]

But God has combined the members of the body . . . so that there should be no division in the body, but that its parts should have equal concern for each other. If one part suffers, every part suffers with it; if one part is honored, every part rejoices with it. [1 Cor. 12:24–26]

Spouse Abuse

Insight

Spouse abuse, particularly of wives by husbands, has become more visible in this decade. People formerly suffered in silence. Many wives, with no way to earn their own living, were literally trapped in brutal marriages.

Abusive spouses typically can be described as angry, resentful, suspicious, or moody. Alcohol and drug abuse are frequently associated with spouse abuse. The abused partner tends to be dependent and to respond to violence by trying harder to please. Such a response is likely to stimulate even more abuse.

The victim of spouse abuse also tends to feel guilty, as if somehow he or she caused the partner to act abusively. In fact, no individual's actions can justify physically or mentally abusive behavior.

It's difficult to know how to counsel the abused. But we do need to recognize that at least three options exist:

Stay in the situation and determine to endure it.

Try to get help for your spouse. The problem is that abusing spouses seldom *want* help, and in fact may be angered at the notion they need help.

Leave, for your own safety and the safety of the children.

It is essential in serious abuse cases *not* to try to impose your opinion of what a person should do. Each individual needs to be responsible to make his or her own decision. You can help most by helping the individual explore each option. In cases of serious abuse, separation is almost always indicated. You can check social agencies and also Family Court in your area to find out what legal protection may be available.

Being a friend, listening, and talking about options and what they may mean, along with sharing biblical promises, is an important ministry to the abused.

Hints

When abuse has just taken place, provide a place where the abused spouse can recover. Show warmth and love. Contact authorities. If the abuse is chronic, some time after an occurrence encourage the person to talk about what is happening. List options on a sheet of paper and think about what taking each might involve. Take the initiative and gather information

from social agencies, Family Court, and other sources to help
the person make his or her decision wisely.

Resource Scriptures

If any of you lacks wisdom, he should ask God, who gives
generously to all without finding fault, and it will be given to
him. [James 1:5]

> Teach me your way, O LORD,
>   and I will walk in your truth. . . . [Ps. 86:11]

The spiritual man makes judgments about all things, but
he himself is not subject to any man's judgment:

> "For who has known the mind of the Lord
>   that he may instruct him?"
> But we have the mind of Christ. [1 Cor. 2:15–16]

. . . "the Holy Spirit will teach you at that time what you
should say." [Luke 12:12]

> I am still confident of this:
>   I will see the goodness of the LORD
>   in the land of the living.
> Wait for the LORD;
>   be strong and take heart
>   and wait for the LORD. [Ps. 27:13–14]

But you, O God, do see trouble and grief;
     you consider it to take it in hand.
The victim commits himself to you;
     you are the helper of the fatherless. [Ps. 10:14]

The oppressor will come to an end. . . . [Isa. 16:4]

Suicide Prevention

Insight

Suicide is a major cause of death among teen-agers. Older adults too may find themselves in the grip of despair and seriously consider suicide. But few suicides take this final action without giving others clues. Most suicides are uncertain about the act. If they are helped over a critical time, their suicidal intentions will often change. If we are sensitive to clues others give, we may be used by God to help them choose life.

What clues should be taken seriously? Any mention of suicide or a suggestion that the person would be "better off dead" should be taken seriously. Withdrawal, loss of appetite, or giving away treasured possessions all may suggest that a person is thinking of suicide.

Hints

Take the initiative by befriending the person whose actions suggest he or she is considering suicide. Invite him or her over. Give the person your phone number and have him or her promise to call you before taking action. If the person is willing, talk openly about suicide plans and point out the difficulties and pain that might be involved. Find time to spend with the person to help him or her deal with depression. Show empathy, but do not express pity. Call often just to talk. Regular contact, evidence that you do care, is important. Your continuing concern and friendship can help a friend over this time and past the crisis to a new perspective on life.

Resource Scriptures

Therefore, if anyone is in Christ, he is a new creation; the old has gone, the new has come! [2 Cor. 5:17]

"Then maidens will dance and be glad,
   young men and old as well.
I will turn their mourning into gladness;
   I will give them comfort and joy instead of sorrow." [Jer. 31:13]

"For I know the plans I have for you," declares the LORD, "plans to prosper you and not to harm you, plans to give you hope and a future." [Jer. 29:11]

And the God of all grace, who called you to his eternal glory in Christ, after you have suffered a little while, will himself restore you and make you strong, firm and steadfast. [1 Peter 5:10]

So do not throw away your confidence; it will be richly rewarded. You need to persevere so that when you have done the will of God, you will receive what he has promised. [Heb. 10:35–36]

. . . "I will cause all my goodness to pass in front of you, and I will proclaim my name, the LORD, in your presence. I will have mercy on whom I will have mercy, and I will have compassion on whom I will have compassion." [Exod. 33:19]

May the God of hope fill you with all joy and peace as you trust in him, so that you may overflow with hope by the power of the Holy Spirit. [Rom. 15:13]

   Weeping may remain for a night,
      but rejoicing comes in the morning. [Ps. 30:5]

   May your unfailing love be my comfort,
      according to your promise to your servant. [Ps. 119:76]

For we do not have a high priest who is unable to sympathize with our weaknesses, but we have one who has been tempted in every way, just as we are — yet was without sin. Let us then approach the throne of grace with confidence, so that we may receive mercy and find grace to help us in our time of need. [Heb. 4:15–16]

Come near to God and he will come near to you. [James 4:8]

Blessed is the man who perseveres under trial, because when he has stood the test, he will receive the crown of life that God has promised to those who love him. [James 1:12]

Temptations

Insight

Temptation is not a bad thing — until we surrender to it. In fact, resisting temptations can help us develop as Christians. Only as we learn to make choices according to the known will of God can we move on to Christian maturity.

But we need to understand the nature of temptations. They do not come from God. Temptations occur as our sin nature responds to pull us toward something that is wrong rather than move us toward what is right. How good to know that God always makes a way for us to meet the temptations of our life successfully, so we can escape. And how good to know that every time we overcome a temptation we are strengthened within.

The Bible also gives us a model to help us meet and overcome temptation. When Jesus was tempted (see Matt. 4:1–11), he responded by quoting the Word of God. Each quote expressed a principle which Jesus then put into practice. Knowing and acting on what the Word of God teaches is the true secret of overcoming temptation.

Hints

Some people believe that it is sin just to experience temptation. Help them to see that Jesus too was tempted. What is important is how we respond to the temptations that draw us toward evil. As you learn how a person thinks about his or her temptations, you can select Scriptures which will correct, strengthen, and encourage.

Resource Scriptures

So I say, live by the Spirit, and you will not gratify the desires of the sinful nature. [Gal. 5:16]

And God is faithful; he will not let you be tempted beyond what you can bear. But when you are tempted, he will also provide a way out so that you can stand up under it. [1 Cor. 10:13]

For we do not have a high priest who is unable to sympathize with our weaknesses, but we have one who has been tempted in every way, just as we are — yet was without sin. Let us then approach the throne of grace with confidence, so that we may receive mercy and find grace to help us in our time of need. [Heb. 4:15–16]

Blessed is the man who perseveres under trial, because when he has stood the test, he will receive the crown of life that God has promised to those who love him.

When tempted, no one should say, "God is tempting me." For God cannot be tempted by evil, nor does he tempt anyone; but each one is tempted when, by his own evil desire, he is dragged away and enticed. Then, after desire has conceived, it gives birth to sin; and sin, when it is full-grown, gives birth to death.

Don't be deceived, my dear brothers. Every good and perfect gift is from above, coming down from the Father. . . . [James 1:12–17]

" 'And lead us not into temptation,
but deliver us from the evil one.' " [Matt. 6:13]

Let not my heart be drawn to what is evil,
to take part in wicked deeds. . . . [Ps. 141:4]

"I am the LORD your God,
who teaches you what is best for you,
who directs you in the way you should go." [Isa. 48:17]

Keep his decrees and commands, which I am giving you today, so that it may go well with you and your children after you. . . . [Deut. 4:40]

Commit your way to the LORD;
   trust in him and he will do this:
He will make your righteousness shine like the dawn,
   the justice of your cause like the noonday sun. [Ps. 37:5–6]

   Trust in the LORD with all your heart
    and lean not on your own understanding;
   in all your ways acknowledge him,
    and he will make your paths straight. [Prov. 3:5–6]

Thought Life

Insight

Christians are called to develop a new and different perspective on life. We are to learn to see things from God's point of view. This troubles some who find their thoughts straying to old or sinful ways of life.

Thinking of a wrong act is not necessarily sin in itself. Luther once said, "I can't stop the birds from flying around my head." But he added, "I can stop them from building a nest in my hair." Random thoughts are sure to come into our minds. What would be wrong would be to dwell on them: to welcome them into our imaginations.

There is another implication of dwelling on wrong actions. The more we imagine or rehearse wrong, the easier it will be to choose wrong. When we mentally practice sin we are far more likely to actually perform those sinful acts in the future.

So we shouldn't underestimate the danger from an undisciplined thought life. Nor should we fail to remember what God is committed to doing in our lives. He is at work in us to make us more like Jesus, so that even thoughts of sins that we're sure we'd never commit are no longer attractive to us.

Hints

The way to overcome an unhealthy thought life is by renewing the mind. We do this by selecting what goes into our minds and by learning to see things and people from God's perspective. Help a troubled friend evaluate. What does he or she watch on television? What kinds of things does he or she read? What places and activities tend to stimulate the troubling thoughts? Avoid these and choose to replace the activities with others that are pure.

Resource Scriptures

Brothers, stop thinking like children. In regard to evil be infants, but in your thinking be adults. [1 Cor. 14:20]

All of us also lived among them at one time, gratifying the cravings of our sinful nature and following its desires and thoughts. Like the rest, we were by nature objects of wrath. But because of his great love for us, God, who is rich in mercy, made us alive with Christ even when we were dead in transgressions. . . . [Eph. 2:3–5]

Therefore, holy brothers, who share in the heavenly calling, fix your thoughts on Jesus, the apostle and high priest whom we confess. [Heb. 3:1]

. . . we take captive every thought to make it obedient to Christ. [2 Cor. 10:5]

Do not conform any longer to the pattern of this world, but be transformed by the renewing of your mind. Then you will be able to test and approve what God's will is — his good, pleasing and perfect will. [Rom. 12:2]

Finally, brothers, whatever is true, whatever is noble, whatever is right, whatever is pure, whatever is lovely, whatever is admirable — if anything is excellent or praiseworthy — think about such things. [Phil. 4:8]

> I have hidden your word in my heart
>   that I might not sin against you. [Ps. 119:11]

May the words of my mouth and the meditation of my heart
   be pleasing in your sight,
O LORD, my Rock and my Redeemer. [Ps. 19:14]

Let the wicked forsake his way
   and the evil man his thoughts.
Let him turn to the LORD, and he will have mercy on him,
   and to our God, for he will freely pardon. [Isa. 55:7]

Turn my eyes away from worthless things;
   preserve my life according to your word. [Ps. 119:37]

Wife's Role

Insight

People in today's society are less certain than in the past of men's and women's roles. The same uncertainty spills over into the realm of marriage. This is in part because today women have opportunities for employment that were not available then. It is estimated that by the 1990s 75 percent of married women will be working outside the home. The wife's role no longer will be simply to stay home and care for children and the house. Wives are expected to contribute cash, not just emotional stability.

At the same time there is a growing awareness that women are persons with abilities and talents which merit development. The older notion that women went along with whatever their husbands decided and always subordinated their needs to his is seriously challenged. The biblical call for "submission," long misunderstood as subjection, has been (rightly) challenged. But Christians are uncertain what pattern of relationship in marriage can replace the older "chain-of-command" view.

In fact, the Scripture presents husband and wife as partners, heirs together of God's grace. Each is subject to the other in that each cares deeply that the other's needs are met and potentials are achieved (Eph. 5:21). Rightly understood, the concept that husbands are the head of the home means that the husband has the obligation to sacrifice himself, as Jesus did for the church, to nurture his wife's growth. To complete the pattern, the wife submits: that is, she takes the lead in cooperating with him rather than struggling against him. When husbands love as Jesus loves, and wives respond as we are called to respond to Jesus, our marriages will be healthy and strong. And the wife's role as a partner in all things will be fulfilled.

Hints

Help wives work on their relationship with their husbands. Career and marriage need not conflict, but call for mutual self-giving and self-sacrifice.

Resource Scriptures

Submit to one another out of reverence for Christ.
Wives, submit to your husbands as to the Lord. [Eph. 5:21–22]

The husband should fulfill his marital duty to his wife, and likewise the wife to her husband. The wife's body does not belong to her alone but also to her husband. In the same way, the husband's body does not belong to him alone but also to his wife. [1 Cor. 7:3–4]

Then [older women] can train the younger women to love their husbands and children, to be self-controlled and pure, to be busy at home, to be kind, and to be subject to their husbands, so that no one will malign the word of God. [Titus 2:4–5]

> She considers a field and buys it;
> out of her earnings she plants a vineyard.
> She sets about her work vigorously;
> her arms are strong for her tasks.
> She sees that her trading is profitable,
> and her lamp does not go out at night. . . .
> She makes linen garments and sells them,
> and supplies the merchants with sashes.
> She is clothed with strength and dignity;
> she can laugh at the days to come.
> She speaks with wisdom,
> and faithful instruction is on her tongue.
> [Prov. 31:16–18, 24–26]

This is the Bible's description of the "wife of noble character."

However, each one of you also must love his wife as he loves himself, and the wife must respect her husband. [Eph. 5:33]

Work

Insight

Biblical words about work contain a dual message. Work in our sin-cursed world can be "painful toil," a frustrating drudgery that brings neither profit nor satisfaction. On the other hand, work can be service that is both productive and fulfilling. God worked when he created the world, and evaluated all he had made as "good." Just as God took satisfaction in his work, so we too can find satisfaction in doing our work well.

Work is viewed positively in other ways as well. Work is service: what we do is useful, for it benefits others. Work also produces income which enables us to help others, providing us with something to share with those in need. We can be givers and not simply receivers in the community of faith.

Although work may be hard and involve toil, if we maintain the attitude of Scripture we will value our work and see it as significant, whatever that work may be.

Hints

Many people who have "ordinary" jobs do not think of themselves or their work as significant. Scripture encourages us to see all work as glorifying to God. Our work serves other persons. Our work enables us to be self-supporting. Our work enables us to earn money with which to meet not only our own needs but also to help others. In every way, all honest work is meaningful and is a calling from the Lord.

Resource Scriptures

Make it your ambition to lead a quiet life, to mind your own business and to work with your hands, just as we told you, so that your daily life may win the respect of outsiders and so that you will not be dependent on anybody. [1 Thess. 4:11–12]

In the name of the Lord Jesus Christ, we command you, brothers, to keep away from every brother who is idle and does not live according to the teaching you received from us. For you yourselves know how you ought to follow our example. We were not idle when we were with you, nor did we eat anyone's food without paying for it. On the contrary, we worked night and day, laboring and toiling so that we would not be a burden to any of you. We did this, not because we do not have the right to such help, but in order to make ourselves a model for you to follow. For even when we were with you, we gave you this rule: "If a man will not work, he shall not eat." [2 Thess. 3:6–10]

He who works his land will have abundant food,
but the one who chases fantasies will have his fill of poverty. [Prov. 28:19]

All hard work brings a profit,
but mere talk leads only to poverty. [Prov. 14:23]

Our people must learn to devote themselves to doing what is good, in order that they may provide for daily necessities and not live unproductive lives. [Titus 3:14]

He who has been stealing must steal no longer, but must work, doing something useful with his own hands, that he may have something to share with those in need. [Eph. 4:28]

Serve wholeheartedly, as if you were serving the Lord, not men, because you know that the Lord will reward everyone for whatever good he does, whether he is slave or free. [Eph. 6:7–8]

Whatever you do, work at it with all your heart, as working for the Lord, not for men, since you know that you will receive an inheritance from the Lord as a reward. It is the Lord Christ you are serving. [Col. 3:23–24]

The sluggard craves and gets nothing,
but the desires of the diligent are fully satisfied. [Prov. 13:4]

Appendix A

Training Guide
for Personal Ministry

Personal ministry is the calling of every Christian. But church leaders need to help men and women in our churches discover and grow in their capacity for personal ministry.

This training guide is intended to help leaders draw together small groups for experiences which will help to motivate the members for ministry and to reduce some of the fears associated with the idea of ministry. Sessions are designed for one and one-quarter to one and one-half hours and may be held in someone's home or in a small, informal room at church.

Members of personal-ministry training groups will each need a copy of this text and the encouragement of others to help them step out in faith to serve others in simple yet intimate personal ministry.

SESSION 1
Ministry Is Personal

Goal: To help group members discover from their own experience that God does work through personal relationships.

Preparation: Place chairs in a circle to encourage conversation. A group of eight to twelve members is ideal. As group members arrive, be sure they meet each other and chat informally. A chalkboard is also necessary.

Launch: Divide into pairs. Give the person on the left in each pair three minutes to "tell your friend all he or she needs to know to understand you as a person." Then reverse, and give the other person the same amount of time.

After the six minutes are up, put each pair with another to form groups of four. Now give each individual exactly one and a half minutes to introduce his or her partner, telling the others "everything they need to know to understand him or her as a person."

Learn: In the groups of four, ask each person to think of an individual who has helped him or her grow as a Christian or as a person. This may be any person at all. But it needs to be a person who had an impact on his or her growth in Christ or as a person.

When each individual has thought of such a person, ask each to take one and a half minutes to introduce that person to the other members of his or her group. The goal is to try to help the others feel that they *know* the person who meant so much in each individual's development.

Now go to the chalkboard and reproduce Figure 1 on it.

Ask each person to mentally place a check mark along the line wherever that check will best describe the relationship that existed between him or her and the person he or she has just introduced to the group as spiritually influential.

FIGURE 1

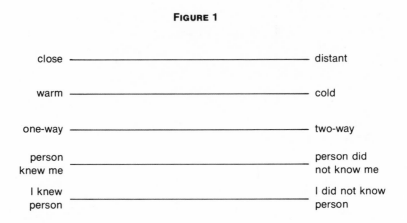

After members of the group have done this, divide each continuum line into quarters. Then poll the group and record where on each line the members placed their check marks.

close ——————————|——————————|——————————|—————— distant

Your group members will discover that the people most influential in their spiritual or personal lives had a two-way, warm, close relationship with them in which there was the feeling that each did know and understand the other. Each talked and listened to the other.

Explain: The results previously mentioned will be consistent in any group. Explain them by pointing out that the New Testament emphasizes love as the catalyst for ministry. Ministry is a personal thing. This principle is demonstrated by the group members' own experience: they were most influenced by someone with whom they had a personal relationship.

Your sessions together will focus on understanding the dynamics of ministering relationships. The goal is that each person will feel confident to encourage, comfort, or tell others about Christ when the opportunity comes.

Close by reading aloud Paul's description of his ministry with others (1 Thess. 2:7–12). Pray that God will give you the same love for and sensitivity to others.

SESSION 2
The Wonder of Our God

Goal: To help your group sense the wonder and awe of knowing God and to express appreciation of him in worship.

Preparation: Have hymnals, paper and pens or pencils, and a chalkboard. Also have a copy of this text for each participant. Again, chat with group members as they come in to establish and maintain a warm, informal atmosphere.

Launch: Write these words on the chalkboard: Grace. Love. Help. Forgiveness. Goodness.

Ask each group member to think of God in these terms for a moment.

Then ask each to let his or her thoughts drift to an experience in which he or she has experienced God's grace, love, help, forgiveness, or goodness. Each person should take a few moments to review that experience and to thank God for touching his or her life at that time.

Then form groups of four, maintaining the same foursomes that worked together during the previous session. In these groups each person is to tell about the experience he or she has just thanked God for. Each person should also explain what that experience taught him or her about God.

Learn: Give each group member his or her own copy of the *Personal Ministry Handbook.* Ask each to look through chapter 1 to find verses or passages which express a vision of God that is relevant to his or her experience.

After ten or fifteen minutes seat the whole group in a circle. Let each member read one or more of the passages selected and tell why the passage was chosen.

Explain: Personal ministry is something like a bridge (see Figure 2). What God has communicated about himself to us in the Scriptures is truth that we can experience. Our experience then becomes a bridge between God and others. As we talk to others about our experiences and explain the truths of Scripture which they illustrate, others are enabled to sense the reality of our God.

FIGURE 2

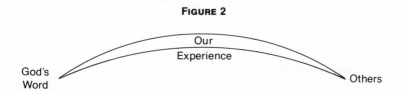

Read Deuteronomy 6:4–7. Focus on our call to acknowledge God in our own lives and to love him. It is as we take his words into our own heart and experience their reality that we are enabled to share with others and help them to develop a deeper, more personal relationship with God.

Worship: Ask your group members to use the verses which they selected and talked about as a stimulus to worship. The worship might involve selecting a hymn or a song that expresses the thought of the passage, writing a call to worship or liturgy, or composing a personal psalm of praise.

Then let your group members use whatever time remains to lead in worship, thanking God for those things about himself which they have experienced and which they now are able to share with others.

Session 3
Me, in Ministry?

Goal: To help your group members appreciate how God has been working in their lives. This is the basis for confidence in their ability to help others.

Preparation: Be sure your group members bring their copies of the *Personal Ministry Handbook*. Each person will also need a large sheet of paper and a pen or pencil.

Launch: When it is time to begin, pass out the paper and pens or pencils. Ask each person to draw a time line which will map the ups and downs of his or her life. Each peak and valley should be labeled. (The time line may include only the span of time between his or her conversion and the present.)

When this process is completed, meet again in the groups of four. Each person should show and explain his or her time line.

When each person has had the chance to talk about the time line, ask the foursomes to discuss these questions:

How have our experiences been similar and how have they differed?

What is the general direction of our lives — up, down, stationary?

Which times, the "down" periods or the "up" periods, were most significant for us spiritually?

What in our experience may qualify us to minister to others?

Learn: God *is* at work in the lives of his people. Join together as a group and ask each group member to read the verses in chapter 2 of the *Personal Ministry Handbook*. Each is to place a check mark beside any verse which is or has been true in his or her life. Your purpose is to help group members realize that God *is* at work in them, and that God's work within them is what qualifies them for personal ministry.

After group members have individually scanned the chapter and checked verses which apply to them, return again to the groups of four. Have group members page through the chapter, reading the verses each has checked and explaining how that verse has or does apply to him or her.

Explain: Come together as a whole group. Read together 2 Corinthians 1:3–10, working through the passage verse by verse. Let group members comment on what they see in each verse. Be sure that these points are brought out:

v. 3 God is one who cares for us and has compassion on us. He is aware of our weaknesses and our needs.

v. 4 God is present in our troubles, in our defeats as well as in our victories. He comforts and helps us, so that by experiencing his help we will be able to comfort and help others. We need to know both God and trouble to qualify as ministers.

v. 5 Suffering was part of Jesus' life, and we will suffer too. But God is able to comfort and strengthen us.

v. 6 We need to look at our suffering and our weakness as gifts. Because we have had troubles, we can understand and sympathize with the troubles and the weaknesses of others. God has worked in our lives so that we can share what he has done with others.

v. 7 Paul is confident about the people he ministers to. He knows that God will work in their lives and in their sufferings, as God has worked in his own.

v. 8 Paul does not hide his weaknesses or the pressures he lives under. He wants others to know the reality of his life, even though he has been close to despair.

v. 9 Paul's great hardships taught him his need to rely more fully on God. There was a good purpose in his sufferings, as there is in ours.

v. 10 God in the past has delivered Paul, no matter how deep the "down" times were. And God will continue to deliver his people.

In short, Paul's personal experience with God, especially the "down" times, had uniquely qualified him for personal ministry. We too are qualified, not because we've achieved perfection, but because in our weakness we have experienced God's strength and comfort.

When you have explored this together, pray and thank God for his goodness in qualifying you, even through your weaknesses, to minister Christ to others.

SESSION 4
Ministering Relationships

Goal: To help your group focus on the personal relationships the members have developed and to pray with and for each other and those whose lives they touch.

Preparation: You'll need a chalkboard, and paper and pens or pencils for each person.

Launch: Draw Figure 3 on the chalkboard. Each circle represents a different level of personal relationship. The outer circle represents those a person does not know and will probably never come in

FIGURE 3

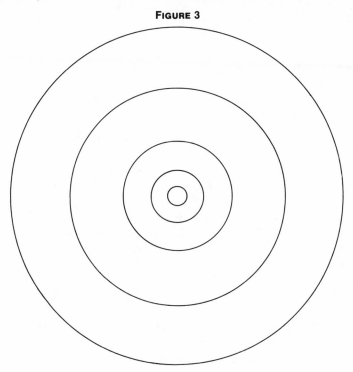

contact with, such as the citizens of a European or South American country. The next circle represents people one might come in contact with because they live in the same state or city, but do not presently know. The next circle represents people one sees regularly but casually (a gas-station attendant, a person on a bus). The next circle represents acquaintances: people one talks with or spends some regular kind of time with (a neighbor or co-worker). The next circle represents friends. These are people we know, like, and choose to spend time with. We will be closer to some friends than to others. This circle may also include family members we do not know very well. The final, inner circle represents people we have intimate relationships with. This will include some family members and may include some very close friends.

Have your group members write in the names of persons they know and place them in the appropriate places in the circles.

Learn: In the groups of four, discuss how any person might try to influence spiritually persons on each of the levels depicted in the diagram. For instance, one might seek to influence a person in a foreign country by giving to missions that work there, but little direct influence could be exerted. Let your group members thoroughly explore how influence can be effected on each level. You may want to draw the group together to hear reports from each foursome on these ideas.

Read aloud and discuss the introduction to chapter 4 of this handbook. Talk about how a climate for personal ministry is developed at each level. How many persons do we have family relationships with? With how many persons do most people develop the context for personal ministry?

Explore: The intent of this session has been to show that the people we are most likely to influence for the Lord are those with whom we have the closest personal relationship and with whom we spend the most time.

Ask each group member to look at the names of persons on the chart and to identify one he or she really wants to influence spiritually.

When that person is identified, write down all the problems or difficulties each foresees in influencing this individual.

Then have each person read through the verses in chapter 4 and put a check mark beside verses that may suggest ways to overcome one or more of the difficulties.

Return to the groups of four. Each person is to tell something about the individual he or she identified as one he or she wants to influence. Discuss some of the difficulties or problems listed. Finally, talk about the verses checked and how they provide some practical guidance as to what to do to build a closer, personal, more ministering relationship.

Close in prayer in the foursomes, focusing in each group on the persons the members want to influence and asking the Lord to enrich the relationship and use it as a bridge to him.

SESSION 5
Comfort for the Suffering

Note: This session can be adapted to chapters 6 or 7 in this book. The process is basic for exploring ministry to any special group of persons, although this is written specifically about chapter 5.

Goal: To develop sensitivity to the needs of the suffering and to explore how to offer Christian comfort.

Preparation: You'll need a chalkboard to record your group members' insights and ideas.

Launch: On the chalkboard list these words: Pain. Suffering. Anguish.

Have your group members brainstorm other words that seem to fit with these. For instance, they may suggest "hurt," "loss," "doubt," or "fear."

When you have listed all the words your group members suggest, note that all of us have experiences marked by such feelings. Ask your group members to read the list and to think of one time or experience when he or she was a sufferer.

In foursomes, ask each to tell about his or her experience in such a way that the others can feel what he or she felt.

Learn: Call the entire group together. Discuss how other people have been helpful and comforting to us when we suffered. What have other people done or said that added to our pain rather than helped? Be sure to list the suggestions on the chalkboard.

Still working as a group, see if you can agree on a list of *Rules for the Comforter.* Work carefully on these so that all members under-stand and agree with the phrasing of each rule. Then ask each person to read through the verses listed in chapter 5 of the *Personal Ministry Handbook.* Put check marks beside verses that might be par-ticularly helpful, either in showing how to comfort or for use in comforting.

After each person has worked through the chapter, ask people to meet in their groups of four and discuss their ideas.

Close this session by talking together about persons the group members know who are hurting now. Pray for these persons by name. Pray too that God might use group members as comforters to share God's continuing and faithful love.

Appendix B

World Religions
and Modern Cults

In this appendix we will consider some basic information about the beliefs of those who are members of other religions or cults.

World Religions

Our focus in this section will be on those religions that, along with Christianity, are sometimes described as the five great faiths of mankind. The religions we will consider are those that readers may be familiar with and whose adherents they are likely to encounter. Other religions or traditions are also significant, but the scope of this work precludes their inclusion. More information about the religions we will examine, as well as other traditions, can be found by consulting the list of sources at the end of this appendix.

Hinduism

One of the most striking characteristics of Hinduism (or perhaps more accurately, the Hindu tradition) is its apparent formlessness. As scholars frequently point out, it has no specific founder, no universally prescribed ritual, no uniformly imposed doctrine. A second significant characteristic is the tendency for facets of other belief systems to be incorporated into this tradition.

Hindu tradition is ancient, and emphases within it can to some degree be traced to the beliefs of the varied peoples who lived in the Indian subcontinent. Some of these people, the Dravidians, shared with even earlier inhabitants a belief in the idea of rebirth of individuals. They also believed in a plurality of gods. Later invaders, the Aryans, conquered India and brought with them belief in their own gods, preeminent among them the god of war. It was the Aryans who, about 1000 B.C., imposed on society the caste system. It is composed of four basic levels:

Brahmins — priests and religious teachers

Kshatriyas — rulers and warriors (in modern terms, civil servants)

Vaishyas — merchants, craftsmen, and farmers

Sudras — servants and laborers

Each of these castes is further divided into numerous subcastes. In addition there are the outcastes. These people were originally slaves or criminals; today they perform work that is considered menial and polluting.

Life under the Aryans was harsh enough that many of the conquered peoples sought ways to deal with the difficulties of their lives. Their focus was on escaping the cycle of rebirth through self-denial; often this took the form of practicing austerities (Marshall, 198).

The Aryans, aware of these ideas and rather dissatisfied with the efficacy of their sacrificial rituals, began to study and adapt them. From their study came the idea of escaping rebirth and achieving union with Brahman, the All or the Absolute. At this time there was also renewed interest in the worship of deities that earlier peoples had believed in: Shiva, for example, and Vishnu, particularly his *avatars* (manifestations) as Krishna and Rama (Marshall, 198a).

The texts of the Hindu tradition are the Vedas, the earliest (and Aryan) texts; these were hymns to be used in religious rituals. Also dating from this time are the Brahmanas, which are instructions for priests who performed the rituals. The Upanishads are abstract, philosophical commentaries on the teachings of the tradition. They reflect the interest in finding deliverance from the cycle of rebirth. The Mabharata is in verse and describes the struggle between good and evil in allegorical terms. The best-known section of this is the

Bhagavad Gita. Another popular piece of literature is the Ramayana, an epic poem that tells the story of Rama and how he overcomes evil through virtue. The Mabharata and the Ramayana are sometimes considered to make the ideas of the Upanishads available and understandable to ordinary people (Schipper, 27–28).

To understand the Hindu tradition, it is necessary to understand that it is a way of life and a specific way of looking at life. A central concept is that everything is cyclical and recurrent. The process of life — changes, births, rebirths — is often described in terms of a wheel. One author calls it the "ocean of *samsara*" (Wolf, 37). D*harma* (cosmic law) controls everything and provides for an orderly universe. One's destiny is shaped by *karma*, the principle of cause and effect. What a person does and how he performs his duty in life determines what happens to him in subsequent rebirths. One can be reborn to a higher station in life, at the same level in life, or at a lower level or form. However, everything in life is ultimately illusion (*maya*). One's ultimate goal is *moksha* (release or liberation) from the endless cycle of rebirth. One seeks union with Brahman. This can be achieved through following a specific *marga* (way) or *yoga* (discipline). There are three such ways.

The first of these, available primarily to male brahmins (and with some modification to the men of the other two higher castes), is *karma marga* (the way of action). This consists of doing one's duty according to one's place in life. Within this way are four stages. The first of these is that of the student. During this time the person is given his *mantra* (sacred word) which he will thereafter use in worship; he studies with a *guru* (a spiritual teacher), and learns the "ritual and conduct" (Wolf, 43) that he will follow during his life. The second stage is that of the householder. A marriage is arranged. During this period of his life the man establishes himself in his work or profession. He takes part in community affairs and is expected to give to charity and worship daily. It is also important that he and his wife produce sons. The third stage is that of retirement. Usually this is marked by a ceremony, and the man then is considered to have increased time to devote to study and meditation. The fourth stage may be described as withdrawal; at this point the man may become a "renouncer" (*sannyasi*), a wandering holy man. The way of action is often considered unable to give moksha in this life (Wolf, 45).

Another method is *jnana marga* (the way of knowledge). This is

a philosophical and intellectual approach; the emphasis is on meditation. Followers of this way often withdraw from society and impose ascetic disciplines on themselves. These disciplines are
intended to give the person insight. Followers of this way are considered to achieve *nirvana* (union with Brahman) when they die
(Wolf, 47).

The third and most popular way is *bhakti marga* (the way of devotion). This is available to anyone. The emphasis is on showing
one's dedication to one's chosen god. This may be one of the "high"
gods, such as Brahman, Shiva, or Vishnu; at least as often it is a
local deity, such as a fertility god, who is perceived to be able to
meet one's needs (Wolf, 51). Central to this way is *puja*, or "prayers
and offerings" (Wolf, 48). Sometimes this is viewed as a bargain
between the god and the devotee (the offering in exchange for a
favor), but it can also be an expression of devotion for its own sake.
One of the prime objects of such devotion is the Krishna (referred
to earlier as an avatar of Vishnu).

The Hare Krishna Movement

In the mid-1960s, A. C. Bhaktivedanta Swami Prabhupada
(1896–1977) founded the International Society for Krishna Consciousness (ISKCON) in New York. Prabhupada taught about the
importance of total devotion to Krishna, and urged his followers
to reject materialistic lifestyles.

Prabhupada's teachings are rooted in Hindu tradition, but some
of the emphases go beyond those of traditional Hindu ideas. For
example, Krishna is considered the supreme god and is furthermore
seen as an intensely personal god. Emphasis is placed on developing a loving personal relationship to him.

The group also believes that if one attains Krishna consciousness, he will be liberated from the cycle of rebirth and will be with
Krishna in the spiritual world. Works — following rituals and litan-
ies, as well as public chanting — are emphasized. (The public chanting is perhaps the best-known aspect of the group's activities.) The
rituals of devotion are perceived as freeing the devotee from earthly
concerns that keep him from focusing on Krishna.

The Bhagavad Gita, which portrays Krishna "as a loving, compassionate incarnation of God" (Schipper, 28), is important to the
members of the Hare Krishna movement.

Studies about this group are sometimes included in books about cults. Adherents of the Hare Krishna movement do not claim to be a Christian group, although some of the group's beliefs (notably that of Krishna as a loving personal god) do parallel Christian teachings.

Transcendental Meditation

Transcendental Meditation (TM) is often described as a way to relieve stress and help an individual achieve his potential.

Transcendental Meditation is based in part on the teachings of Maharishi Mahesh Yogi (b. 1918, in India, as Mahesh Prasad Varma). In 1959, after some years of study with a Hindu teacher now known as Guru Dev, he began teaching about TM in the West. He founded the International Meditation Society in London.

People often hear about TM from friends or acquaintances. At times public lectures may be given. Those who wish to learn more about TM are required to participate in an initiation ceremony (puja). They are told to bring flowers, fruit, and a white cloth, all of which have symbolic meanings, with them. Initiates are given a mantra (each is associated with a particular Hindu deity) and are instructed in specific yoga techniques. Those who practice TM expect to achieve as many as five different levels of consciousness in meditation, "with the goal of ultimately reaching 'enlightenment'" (Enroth, 1108). Transcendental Meditation "teaches belief in the essential oneness of all reality and therefore the possibility of man's unity with the divine" (ibid.).

Buddhism

Siddhartha Gautama (563?–483 B.C.), the founder of Buddhism, was born into the kshatriya caste. His father was the ruler of a kingdom in northeastern India (near or in present-day Nepal). He was determined that his son would become a ruler as well, and to that end provided all sorts of luxuries and pleasures for Gautama. The son was also carefully kept from seeing any misery or anything to arouse his social conscience. It had been predicted that Siddhartha would be either a great ruler or a great holy man, and his father sought to ensure the former.

However, on four occasions the young man was able to leave his father's palace, and these four times he saw what would later be called the Four Sights: an old man, a diseased man, a corpse, and a wandering holy man. For the first time in his life Gautama became aware of a reality outside of his own sheltered experience — that life is full of pain and suffering. The four sights so affected him that he decided to renounce his royal lifestyle and himself become a holy man. On his twenty-ninth birthday he set out to achieve this goal. This later became known as the Great Departure.

For the next six years Gautama studied the Hindu scriptures, meditated, and for a time lived with five ascetics, practicing rigorous austerities. But these disciplines failed to provide him with insight or release. Instead, he decided that a middle way — neither indulgence nor self-denial — and solitary study and meditation were the means through which he would seek enlightenment.

Eventually Gautama was informed in a dream that he was about to receive an "awakening," so he seated himself under a sacred tree and began to meditate. As he meditated, he received insight; by the end of the night he had become freed of ignorance. He had become the Buddha, the Enlightened One. The insights he received consisted of four principles, called the Four Noble Truths.

For seven weeks the Buddha continued to meditate and develop his insights. He was hesitant to proclaim them, but felt called to do so. Therefore he set out for Benares, and at a deer park near that city met the five men with whom he had lived. They became his first converts. After he gained more converts, he established an order of monks, and later an order of nuns, for those who chose to follow the entire discipline. Lay disciples followed only the ethical principles of his teaching.

The four principles, or Four Noble Truths, that the Buddha formulated are these:

All life is suffering (*dukkha*, pain); suffering is unavoidable.

Suffering is caused by ignorance (*avidya*) and attachment (*tanha*) or craving.

Suffering can be eliminated.

Suffering is eliminated by following the Eightfold Path.

A specific discipline and practical guidelines for life are set forth in the Eightfold Path:

Right view or knowledge — one must understand and accept the Four Noble Truths.

Right thought or intentions — one's thoughts must be free of "lust, ill-will, cruelty, and untruthfulness" (Hamilton, 665).

Right speech — one must not slander, gossip, or speak harshly.

Right conduct or action — one must not kill, steal, lie, engage in illicit sex, or drink alcohol.

Right livelihood — one must not do work that violates the rules for right conduct.

Right effort — one must have the will power and the strength to do what is right.

Right mindfulness — one must examine one's thoughts and behavior.

Right concentration — one meditates so that he may gain insight.

The Eightfold Path can be divided into three categories: insight or wisdom (*prajna*), or right views and intentions; morality (*shila*), which consists of right speech, conduct, and livelihood; and mental discipline (*samadhi*), which includes right effort, mindfulness, and concentration (Saunders, 691). These eight steps lead to the individual's purification.

It is worth noting that Buddhism shares some ideas with the Hindu tradition, but in some significant ways Buddhism broke with that tradition. In fact, Buddhism is occasionally described as a reform or "Protestant" movement within Hindu tradition.

The Buddha lived during the time when the Upanishads were being written; part of the religious climate of the times was a questioning or even rejection of the emphasis within the Hindu tradition on complicated rituals of sacrifice. The Upanishads themselves reflect the interest in finding an alternative; at this same time other procedures and teachings also were developed.

Although the Buddha accepted the traditional Hindu ideas about rebirth and karma, he modified the latter slightly. An act had to be intentional before it produced karma (Saunders, 691).

A vital difference between Hindu and Buddhist teaching is that the Buddha rejected the idea of the self (*atman*) as changeless and eternal. Instead, he taught the concept of *anatman* (no-self), that everything is impermanent and changing. This teaching is often summarized by saying that there is no being, only becoming. However, humans think that impermanent things are important, and they become attached to those things. They crave, and therefore they suffer. Only by accepting the Four Noble Truths and following the Eightfold Path can craving be eliminated. When it is, the person has achieved nirvana — in Buddhist thought, the extinguishing of craving or desire. Thus the cycle of rebirth is halted.

The Buddha also rejected the Hindu emphasis on ritual and prayers, the concept of caste, the Hindu scriptures, and the authority of priests. He did not emphasize the importance of a deity or deities, refusing to speculate on the topic. The effort of the individual in attaining his own salvation is paramount.

Two differing interpretations of the Buddha's teaching emerged after his death. One of these, the Theravada tradition (the Way of the Elders), follows closely the teachings of the Buddha that have already been explained. Theravada Buddhists base their doctrine on texts that are called the Tripitaka (three baskets). The first of these consists primarily of the rules governing monks and nuns; the second is a collection of the discourses of the Buddha to his disciples; the third is composed of commentaries on and interpretations of the discourses.

The Theravada ideal is the *arhat* (saint), one who follows the discipline and achieves his own salvation. The Theravada tradition is followed primarily in Sri Lanka and the countries of Southeast Asia.

The other major tradition in Buddhism is the Mahayana (Great Raft) school. Followers of this school sometimes refer to the Theravada school as Hinayana (Little Raft; this is considered a disparaging term). The terminology points up the two different concepts of salvation. Mahayana teaches that it is possible for everyone to become enlightened. The Buddha is considered a manifestation of an eternal being; faith and trust in him are emphasized.

Within the Mahayana school the ideal is the *bodhisattva*. The bodhisattva is someone who, because of his virtues and good deeds, deserves nirvana, but chooses instead to remain in the world so that he can help others.

The Mahayana canon is much longer than the Theravada canon. It is composed of many *sutras* (discourses), and to these are sometimes attributed magical powers.

The Mahayana tradition is followed primarily in Japan, China, Korea, and Vietnam.

In India, the land of its origin, Buddhism was absorbed into Hindu tradition.

Two other schools of thought within Buddhist tradition may be familiar to Western readers. The first of these is Pure Land Buddhism. It is part of the larger Mahayana tradition and the focus of its devotion is a bodhisattva, Amitabha (Amida, in Japanese), who is thought to rule over a paradise (pure land) somewhere in the west. Amitabha was known for his compassion; according to tradition, he promised salvation to anyone who calls on him.

Another bodhisattva, usually associated with Amitabha, is Avalokitesvara (Kuan Yin, in Chinese; Kannon, in Japanese). Avalokitesvara is worshiped as a deity of compassion.

The second school of thought is Zen Buddhism. The discipline of meditation is central to Zen. This is believed to be the most effective way to attain *satori* (enlightenment, wisdom). One way to achieve insight is to consider a *koan*, a riddle or puzzle that cannot be solved through logic. The emphasis is on gaining insights through flashes of intuition.

Islam

The significance of the teachings of Muhammad, the founder of Islam, can best be understood in light of the historical background of his times.

Life for the nomadic tribes in Arabia was difficult, for the environment was harsh. In order to survive, the members of each tribe had to maintain intratribal unity and work together. Defending individual and tribal honor was a point of pride; often this led to lengthy blood feuds between tribes. Moreover, the uncertainties of life fostered an attitude of enjoying what one could, when one could; as a result, the Arabs had a reputation for drinking and gambling to excess.

The nomadic tribes had no strongly organized religion. They believed in the existence of spirits and nature deities, especially a trio of goddesses. At times they made pilgrimages to sacred places; the most sacred of these was the Kaaba in Mecca. In contrast, a group called the Hanifs was developing some sense of monotheism.

Muhammad (570–632) was born in Mecca. His immediate family was a minor and impoverished part of the Quraysh, a formerly nomadic tribe that had gained possession of Mecca, a center for trade routes, and the surrounding area. The Quraysh had (in general) become wealthy merchants. The transition from nomads to urban dwellers had created stresses and changes in the traditional structure of society. As some people became extremely wealthy, they became correspondingly indifferent to the needs of the poor and the call of religion. Such was the state of the social structure when Muhammad was born.

Early in life, Muhammad was orphaned. He was reared first by his grandfather, and after his grandfather's death by an uncle, Abu Talib. Muhammad, as an adult, was employed by Khadija, a wealthy widow, who owned a caravan business. When Muhammad was twenty-five and Khadija forty, they were married. They had four daughters and two sons, but the sons did not survive childhood.

The breakdown of traditional ways disturbed Muhammad, especially as he grew older. His marriage had freed him from economic worries and had also given him the opportunity to spend time in meditation. Often he went to a cave outside of Mecca to meditate. When Muhammad was about forty (c. 610), he received a visitation from the angel Gabriel, who ordered him to proclaim the word of God.

At first Muhammad was troubled; he feared that he was possessed or losing his sanity. He confided in Khadija, who consulted one of her cousins (described variously as a Hanif or a Christian). Muhammad became convinced that he was indeed a prophet of God, and began to proclaim the revelations that he received.

This message, however, was not widely accepted. A few people, among them some prominent residents of Mecca, became converts; for the most part people reacted with hostility, for they perceived the message to be a threat to their beliefs and lifestyle. Moreover, acceptance as a prophet implied that Muhammad "would become ruler also, and this threat the rich merchants could not tolerate" (Adams, 493). Opposition eventually was fierce enough to cause Muhammad and his followers to flee to Yathrib (modern-day Medina) in 622. This flight, called the Hegira, marks the beginning of Muslim chronology.

In Medina Muhammad met with the success he had been denied in Mecca. He mediated a blood feud between two tribes in the area and as a consequence they accepted him as leader. In addition, the tribesmen accepted his message. The only exceptions were the Jews in the area; Muhammad expelled them when they refused to believe. During the years at Medina Muhammad developed regulations about religious observances and social matters (e.g., marriage, divorce, inheritance). This was a time of unifying and consolidating gains.

In 624 Muhammad undertook forays against Meccan caravans. For the next six years there were other encounters and battles, most of them indecisive, but in 630, by a combination of diplomacy and military action, Muhammad was able to conquer Mecca. Thereafter the spread of Islam in Arabia was rapid. Even after Muhammad's death in 632, his message continued to spread. Eventually, often by means of military conquests, it was known even in the Far East.

The revelations that Muhammad received during twenty-two years were gathered into their present form after his death. This written record, the Quran (reading, recitation), is regarded as the final and authoritative word of God to mankind. As such it is considered the basis of faith and practice for all Muslims. The Quran is always treated with great reverence; it is never placed on the ground, for instance. Only the Arabic version is considered the actual word of God; any rendering into another language is merely a "translation" or an "explanation." It is a mark of spirituality to memorize the Quran. To this end, children in Islamic countries are sent to Quran schools so they may learn to recite the Arabic text. The Quran is composed of 114 chapters, each called a *sura*. They are arranged from longest to shortest, in nearly inverse chronological order.

Another influence on the practice of Muslims is the *sunna*, or tradition. (One may distinguish *sunna*, or custom, from *Sunna*, the traditions of Muhammad.) Muslims desire to follow the traditional, orthodox way of behaving and solving problems. These traditional ways of Muhammad were handed down through the *hadith* (oral tradition or history). Also important is *sharia*, the code of Islamic civil and criminal law.

Within the teaching of Muhammad are four emphases. The first of these is on the nature of God. Muhammad maintained that there is only one God (Allah), and that he is one. (The doctrine of the Trinity is offensive to Muslims, for they perceive this to mean that there are three gods.) The second point is that God has spoken to mankind through prophets. Muslims recognize Noah, Abraham,

Moses, Joseph, Mary, and Jesus, for example, as prophets. However, they say that Muhammad was the final and most important of these — the "seal" of the prophets. (In this connection it is important to note that Muhammad insisted he was a prophet only; he never claimed to be divine or to be a manifestation of the divine.) A third point is the importance of moral behavior. The fourth point is the importance of *ummah* (community). The sense of community is based on a common faith; it is expressed, for instance, in the attention a judge pays to community consensus when he makes a decision, or the refusal to make a distinction between church and state. (This sense of community can be a formidable barrier to evangelization, for no one wants to feel that he is isolated from the community.)

The duties of Muslims are summarized in what are called the five pillars of Islam.

The first pillar is confession of faith or witness. The Muslim creed, the *Shahada*, is, "There is no god but God, and Muhammad is the prophet of God." One is considered a Muslim if he can repeat this creed publicly and correctly, with full understanding and no reservations.

The second pillar is prayer or worship. Ritual prayer (*salat*) is to be offered five times daily (at sunrise, noon, midafternoon, evening, and night) and can be done publicly or privately. It is preferable, whenever possible, to attend public services in a mosque. In addition, services on Fridays at noon are considered obligatory. A *muezzin* (cantor) issues the call to worship from the minaret of the mosque. Muslims are expected to ritually purify themselves and then remove their shoes before entering the mosque. An *imam* (prayer leader; *mullah*, in Iran) guides the faithful through the ritual. This service also includes a sermon.

Almsgiving is the third pillar of Islam. This is often called *zakat* and in some countries is essentially a tax, whereas in others it is voluntary (Fry and King, 78).

The fourth pillar is fasting. During the month of Ramadan (according to tradition, the month when Muhammad began to receive revelations) devout Muslims are expected to fast in the daylight hours. No liquids or solid food is consumed during those hours. After dark it is permissible to eat and drink; the lavishness (or lack thereof) of the food is left to the believer's discretion. *'Id al-Fitr*, "the breaking of the fast," marks the end of Ramadan. It is a time of widespread rejoicing.

The final pillar of Islam is pilgrimage to Mecca. Pilgrims wear special robes, walk seven times around the Kaaba, and kiss the Black Stone that is kept in the shrine. They recall that Muhammad destroyed the idols that were once kept there. Pilgrims also spend an entire afternoon standing in a valley outside Mecca. This " 'standing ceremony' creates in the minds of the devout a profound sense of the presence of God in their lives and of divine forgiveness of their sins" (Fry and King, 84). After the rituals at Mecca are completed, many pilgrims also visit the tomb of Muhammad at Medina.

Some scholars cite a sixth pillar, *jihad*, loosely translated "holy war." The term can be used to mean specifically military action, but can also mean " 'struggle for the faith' " (Fry and King, 86) in a broader sense. It is sometimes considered part of the first pillar (ibid., 87).

Within Islam there are two major groups. The larger of these is the Sunnites; the minority group is the Shiites. The break between the two centered on the question of who was to succeed Muhammad. The Sunnites considered the first four successors, the so-called rightly-guided caliphs, the legitimate successors to Muhammad. They emphasize the importance of the Quran, the hadith, and the law. "The Sunnites were constitutionalists, men who stressed the importance of written documents and rational processes; the Shiites insisted that Islam be based on the words of the Prophet as passed down in the *hadith*, or traditional utterances" (Fry and King, 114). In contrast, the Shiites teach the concept of the imamate, imams in Shiite terminology being "divinely appointed and divinely guided leaders ... in a direct line of succession from Muhammad" (Fry and King, 116). They also believe that the imamate continues to exist "in a state of occultation" (ibid.) — that is, even if there is no visible, identifiable imam on earth. The Shiites are further divided into two groups: the "Twelvers," who believe that there were twelve imams after Muhammad, and the "Seveners" or Ismailis, who believe that there were seven. The Twelvers are the larger of the two groups, and are dominant in Iran.

Another influence within Islam is Sufism, usually described as a form of Islamic mysticism. Sufis emphasize developing a loving, intensely personal relationship to God, and seek to achieve a sense of oneness with God.

Judaism

In a sense it is difficult to define Judaism. In simplest terms, there is a concept of the Jews as a religious group. However, Jews are also often described as being a cultural group, an economic group, a social group, or a nation (either in a narrow sense or in the wider sense of being a people; Duker, 119–20). Some religious leaders furthermore make a threefold distinction: a religious Jew "accepts the faith of Judaism"; a cultural Jew has no religious connection but "accepts the ethics, customs, and literature of Judaism"; and a practical Jew is considered "a Jew by the Jewish community" (Schipper, 87–88). What is plain is that a person who converts to another religion is not accounted a Jew by other Jews.

Judaism is rooted in the teachings of the Old Testament, although one may distinguish the "religion of the Jews" from the religion of the Old Testament (Harrison, 727). The emphasis shifted from sacrifice to "ideals and spirituality" (ibid.).

However, one fact is unchanged and unquestioned: Judaism is a monotheistic faith with God at its center. This is reflected in the *Shema*: "Hear, O Israel: The LORD our God, the LORD is one" (Deut. 6:4).

The basic beliefs of Judaism were summarized by Moses Maimonides (1135–1204), a Jewish philosopher and physician. They are included in the Daily Prayer Book (although not all Jews accept all of these statements). These thirteen statements, each beginning with the affirmation "I believe, with a perfect faith," follow:

God is the creator of all things, and works and will work forever.

God, the Creator, is one; no other being exhibits the unity found in him; and he alone was, is, and always will be.

God does not have a body; no "bodily essence" can be compared to him.

God is eternal; nothing existed before him, and he will remain forever.

God alone is to be worshiped.

"All the words of the prophets are true."

All the prophecies of Moses were true; he was premier among all wise men.

The law was given by God to Moses.

The law is not to be changed, and no other law will be given by God.

God understands the deeds and thoughts of all men.

God will give good to those who obey his laws and will punish those who disobey them.

The Messiah will come; even if he delays, "yet I will wait for him till he come."

The dead will be brought to life when God sees fit to do so. (For the full text, see Isaacs, 1057.)

As is evident, these statements of belief focus on the nature of God. It is also evident that the Word of God is esteemed. That Word is divided into three categories: the Torah, or law (the Pentateuch); the Prophets (including the historical books); and the Writings. Of these the Torah, or the written law, is considered the most important. A companion to the Torah is the Talmud, a compilation of traditions and commentaries on the law. The Talmud is made up of two types of materials: the oral law (Mishnah) and the rabbinic comments on the law (the Gemara).

In a broad sense, Torah is defined as a way of life. Jews emphasize keeping the law, it is true; they consider that by doing so they comply with a divine command and also serve as an example to others. The law is to be kept voluntarily and even joyfully (Baron, 66). Jews consider that the specific requirements of the law apply to them, but "the ethical ideals are universal in scope" (Eisenstein, 124).

Intertwined with this is the concept of the Jews as a chosen people. Man is seen as an instrument of God; again, the Jews serve as an example of how man may overcome "external nature and undisciplined human nature" (Baron, 66). This in turn leads to an emphasis on the survival of the group, the chosen people, who can be an instrument God will use in working out his purposes in history.

From a concern with the survival as a group or nation comes the importance Jews attach to the family (a way of ensuring survival) and to social justice (e.g., concern and care for the poor and sick). One author states that support is "owed" to the poor; he points out that the word that is usually translated "charity" actually implies obligation or responsibility (Eisenstein, 124).

Most Jews accept the idea that a messiah is to come, but the messiah is seen in nationalistic terms (Harrison, 730). He will usher in a time of peace, prevent the destruction of the world, and restore the Jewish people. However, the messiah is not perceived to be a divine being or a sacrifice for sin (Isaacs, 1058). Jews deny that Jesus was the Messiah.

Keeping the law entails observance of numerous regulations. Some of these rules apply specifically to Jewish males. For example, all Jewish males are circumcised (see Gen. 17:10). After the ceremony is completed the child is named. And at age thirteen Jewish boys observe their *bar mitzvah*. This indicates that a boy is legally considered an adult, responsible for keeping the commandments and participating in the life of the community.

Education — particularly study of the Scriptures and the Talmud — has always been prized. Jewish boys are expected to study the Talmud in depth.

Prayer is also important. Traditional Jewish men pray three times daily, in the morning, afternoon, and evening. Blessings are offered at meals. In addition, prayers or blessings may be offered on many other occasions (e.g., seeing a friend after a long absence may be cause for reciting a blessing).

The Sabbath, which begins at sunset on Friday and ends at sunset on Saturday, is observed in part by attending services at the synagogue. Services are conducted by a rabbi and a cantor (*hazan*, reader). Work is forbidden on the Sabbath.

A related aspect of Judaism is the celebration of holidays, major and minor. The major holidays are Passover (to commemorate the flight from Egypt; the Seder meal, or "family service," at which the story of the exodus is retold, is part of this celebration); Pentecost (to recall the giving of the law to Moses); Rosh Hashanah (New Year's Day, a time for soul searching and self-examination); Yom Kippur (the Day of Atonement, a day of fasting and penitence that falls ten days after Rosh Hashanah); and Sukkot (the Feast of Tabernacles, a reminder of the time that the Israelites spent in the desert). Minor festivals that may be familiar to readers are Purim (this recalls how the Persian Jews were spared from the destruction Haman planned for them) and Hanukkah, the "festival of lights" (this commemorates the purification of the temple after the Maccabees defeated the Syrian Greeks).

Another example of keeping the law involves following dietary regulations. Some foods are prohibited (*trefah*). Others are *kosher*, or permitted. In some instances the way in which food is to be prepared is covered by the dietary laws. A Jewish wife is responsible for ensuring that the dietary regulations are met in her household.

Thus far everything that has been written applies most precisely to the majority group within Judaism, the Orthodox Jews. One of three major groups, the Orthodox Jews are the strictest in obeying the Torah and the dietary laws and observing the Sabbath (in their synagogues, they segregate the sexes). Orthodox Jews offer prayers and conduct services in Hebrew. They accept the concept of the messiah.

Another group, the Reform Jews, are sometimes called Liberal Jews. They do not observe dietary laws. Their services are conducted in the vernacular; men and women are equal in the synagogue (Schipper, 90). They reject the Talmud (Wise, 1059) and emphasize ethical concepts rather than strict observance of the law. They reject the concepts of the messiah, resurrection, and final judgment, and the gathering of the Jews in Palestine (ibid.).

The third major group is the Conservative Jews. They are less strict than the Orthodox, observing the dietary laws and keeping the Sabbath, but not rigidly. They pray and conduct services in the vernacular.

Hasidism, a term with which readers may be familiar, is a long standing tradition in Judaism. It is a form of mysticism, emphasizing "piety, worship, and contemplation rather than learning, dogma, and ritual" (Minkin, 87). Hasidic communities are led by *saddikim* (or *zaddikim*, holy men). This tradition had its roots in eastern Europe, especially Poland. Critics said it fostered ignorance and superstition, and in some instances this was true, but it also inspired enthusiasm and creativity (ibid., 88).

A survey of Judaism would be incomplete without mention of those who call themselves "completed Jews." These are Jews who have accepted Jesus as the Messiah. Completed Jews often retain many of their Jewish practices and seek to maintain ties with their community. The organization Jews for Jesus does outreach along these lines, particularly among Jewish young people.

Modern Cults

In the broadest sense, a cult may be defined as "a minority religious group holding beliefs regarded as unorthodox or spurious" (Webster's *Third International Dictionary*). Beyond this, it is possible to point out characteristics common to the cults: missionary zeal, charismatic leadership, a claim to have exclusive truth, a sense of group superiority, strict discipline, or repression of individuality (Burrell, 9–20). Other distinguishing features are "an abrupt break with historic Christianity, . . ." "a tendency to major in minors," and "a tendency to perfectionism" (Hoekema, 374–76).

However, a group is not designated a cult solely on these bases. The crucial point that scholars make is that the cults deviate doctrinally from the accepted points of orthodox Christianity. We will concentrate on four specific points:

Views about God. A cult rejects the idea of God as Trinity. This denial takes one of two forms: denying that there are three persons within the Trinity, or seeing God as one of many gods.

Views about Christ. A cult denies the deity of Christ. Cults may recognize Christ as an exemplary man, or teach that he is an incarnation of the divine, but not that he is eternal God.

Views about salvation. A cult denies that salvation is based on faith in Christ. Cults stress that human effort is required for salvation; that is, works are more important than faith. Cults may also teach that the value of Christ's atonement is limited — not always in the sense that it is extended only to a select group, but sometimes that it provides only for a certain aspect of salvation (for example, redemption only from physical death).

Views about authority. A cult does not recognize the Bible as the sole source of authority. Cults emphasize other sources of revelation, accepting these either in place of the Bible or in addition to the Bible.

Our focus is on the doctrines of these groups, rather than practices or behavior. For more information about the practices of the cults, the reader should refer to the sources given at the end of this appendix.

This brief survey considers those groups that readers may be familiar with and would be likely to encounter.

One caution is in order: At some points, these groups are referred to as churches. This terminology reflects common usage and is not intended to give credence to the claims or teachings of these groups. It is also worth noting that some of these groups, notably Christian Scientists, Jehovah's Witnesses, and Mormons, are occasionally considered sects. Some authors use the terms *sect* and *cult* interchangeably; in common usage the word *sect* may be applied to groups that are perceived to be part of "organized religion" — as distinct from "unusual" groups like the "Moonies" or the members of the Hare Krishna movement.

Christian Scientists

The teachings of the Church of Christ, Scientist, are based on the ideas and writings of Mary Baker Eddy (1821–1910), whom Christian Scientists call the "discoverer" of the movement. In part, at least, her ideas represent her striving to come to grips with the sufferings in her life.

Eddy was born to a farm family near Concord, New Hampshire. Her father especially was a strict Calvinist, and as she matured she was increasingly alienated by his rigid beliefs.

Furthermore, she had always been in poor health. As a child she was too frail to attend school, although she read extensively. Also, one of her brothers, a student at Dartmouth, tutored her during the summer.

In her early twenties Eddy married, but she was widowed within the first year of her marriage. Continuing poor health kept her from caring for her only son. A second marriage, about ten years later, was unsuccessful. Eventually she divorced this man on the grounds of desertion. Her third marriage (in 1870) was to a man who had been one of her students and became a Christian Science practitioner. He died in 1877.

In her middle years, increasing invalidism led Eddy to seek relief through a variety of methods that were popular at the time. Finally, under the care of Phineas Quimby, a mental healer, she did find relief from her suffering. In fact, she herself went on to become a practitioner of mental healing. (Critics would later raise the issue of Quimby's influence on Eddy and the extent to which she was indebted to his ideas. Christian Scientists reverse the matter, saying that she influenced Quimby. In any case, their teachings had some common ideas.)

The turning point in Eddy's life came only a few months after

Quimby's death in 1866. Eddy slipped on an icy sidewalk and injured her back. While she was bedridden, she read the account of Jesus healing the paralytic. She recalled that as she read, she, in faith, experienced an urge to get out of bed and walk. This experience convinced her that she had received significant new insights into the means of healing. She spent some years studying the Bible, writing, and expounding her interpretation of Scripture. She first began to lecture about healing in 1870. Her teaching was published in *Science and Health with Key to the Scriptures* (1875).

For the second half of her life Eddy consolidated and systematized her teachings. This included revising *Science and Health*; the standardized version was published in 1907. She also personally supervised the Church of Christ, Scientist, as it increased its membership. During the final two years of her life she specifically concentrated on providing for a church organization and structure that would enable the church to function without her personal supervision.

Central to the teaching of Christian Science is the idea that spirit and matter are incompatible (Burrell and Wright, 84). The importance of spirit is emphasized, whereas matter is considered, in Eddy's words, "a human concept"; it is not real. This concept is most plainly seen in the distinction made between immortal (or divine) Mind and mortal mind. Mortal mind is seen as sending a person false messages, such as that disease is real, or evil is real, or pain is real. In some of Eddy's writings mortal mind is equated with matter (*Science and Health*, p. 591) and is defined as "nothing claiming to be something" (*Science and Health*, p. 591). By contrast, immortal Mind tells people that mortal mind is an illusion. Immortal Mind emphasizes that only what is good actually exists. Anything that is evil (e.g., disease) is an illusion.

Christian Scientists emphasize that God is Spirit; he is impersonal and is a divine Principle. God is further defined as being Love, Truth, Life, and Soul. Eddy's teaching about God, states one author, "adds up to a pantheism which is thoroughgoing and all-embracing: all is God and God is all" (Hoekema, 189). Moreover, she taught that the concept of the Trinity "suggests polytheism" (ibid., 190).

The Holy Spirit is not regarded as a personal being; rather, the Holy Comforter is equated with Christian Science.

The Christian Scientists' view of Jesus Christ is rather confusing. Jesus is considered to have been human, but with something more (often called the Christ spirit) added. Jesus was a man who "presented Christ, the true idea of God" (*Science and Health*, p. 473). Thus he is referred to as the Way-shower. Furthermore, Eddy wrote, "in Science, Christ never died. In material sense Jesus died, and lived. The fleshly Jesus seemed to die, though he did not" (*Unity of God*, p. 62). The resurrection, she taught, was not that of a real body. Moreover, at the time of the ascension "the human, material concept, or Jesus, disappeared, while the spiritual self, or Christ, continues to exist in the eternal order of divine Science" (*Science and Health*, p. 334).

In view of the Christian Science teachings about sin (sin is a message of mortal mind — an illusion), the atonement of Christ is hardly an issue. Eddy wrote that "Christ came to destroy the belief of sin" (*Science and Health*, p. 473). Therefore, Christian Scientists focus on the role of works in salvation, in the sense that people must overcome sin, sickness, or other evils (illusions) by correctly understanding God (Schipper, 114). The necessity is to ignore the messages of mortal mind.

In *Science and Health* Eddy wrote that the Bible is inspired and that it is the "sufficient guide to eternal life" (p. 497). However, Christian Scientists are expected to understand the Bible in a "spiritual" way — literal or symbolic interpretations are not considered correct. Moreover, to help them interpret Scripture, they rely on *Science and Health*, which Eddy said was "divine and unerring." She claimed that it had been dictated to her. In Christian Science worship services, passages from *Science and Health*, as well as passages from Scripture, are read. In Christian Science churches, two lecterns are always provided — one for the Bible and one for *Science and Health*. This practice points up the importance given to *Science and Health*.

Jehovah's Witnesses

The Jehovah's Witnesses (sometimes known as the Watchtower Society) trace their origin to the teachings of Charles Taze Russell (1852–1916). Russell had been reared in the Presbyterian church and later joined a Congregational church (Hoekema, 223). However, even early in his life, Russell was troubled by fears and doubts about teachings on predestination and eternal punishment. Eventually he became an agnostic. At this point in his life he heard a sermon by an Adventist preacher, and later wrote that this rekindled his faith.

As a result, Russell again began to study the Bible. He gathered a small group of followers who accepted his teachings. In at least one significant break with Adventist doctrine, Russell taught that Christ's second coming would be "spiritual or invisible" (Hoekema, 224). Russell expounded his own view in the pamphlet *The Object and Manner of the Lord's Return*.

In 1876 Russell affiliated with N. H. Barbour, whose views about the second coming were similar to his own. They expressed their views in the magazine *The Herald of the Morning* and also in a book, *The Three Worlds or Plan of Redemption*. However, the two later parted company on doctrinal issues, with Russell going on to publish his own magazine. It eventually came to be known as *The Watchtower*. He traveled frequently to preach his doctrines. He also wrote extensively on doctrine, notably *Studies in Scripture*, a multivolume work.

After Russell's death, Joseph Franklin Rutherford succeeded to the presidency of the Jehovah's Witnesses. Since 1907 he had been legal counsel for the society; on his election to the presidency he reorganized the structure of the society and removed those who opposed him. The changes were enough to make several groups break away in protest.

Rutherford, like Russell, was a prolific writer. His writings include *The Harp of God*, *Jehovah*, *Creation*, and *Life*. In effect his writings replaced those of Russell. During his presidency emphasis was given to witnessing and reporting about the contacts one had made. Beginning in 1922, Rutherford wrote specific instructions that members were to use in their witnessing.

Rutherford died in 1942 and was succeeded by Nathan H. Knorr. Prior to his election, Knorr had been a full-time worker at the society's headquarters. His emphasis was on improving the training program of the Jehovah's Witnesses. During his presidency the Witnesses greatly increased their membership through their work in other countries; this was at least in part due to Knorr's emphasis on training methods (Burrell and Wright, 25).

In 1961 the *New World Translation* of the Bible was published. This is the version preferred by the Witnesses, although they are free to read any version. The *New World Translation* reflects the doctrinal concepts of the group. Also during Knorr's presidency, the society published several doctrinal works: *The Truth Shall Make You Free, Let God Be True, Make Sure of All Things,* and *From Paradise Lost to Paradise Regained.* Several textbooks for Witnesses were also published: *Aid to Kingdom Publishers, Equipped for Every Good Work,* and *Qualified to Be Ministers.*

On Knorr's death in 1977, F. W. Franz became president of the society.

Jehovah's Witnesses reject the concept of the Triune God, believing instead that the teaching about the Trinity is a pagan and therefore satanic idea. They believe that there is only one God, Jehovah. He is a spirit who created the world and all other beings, including Jesus Christ.

Christ is regarded as a god, but is not God. The Witnesses believe that Christ existed in three stages. In the first of these he was a spirit creature, Michael, who was made by Jehovah. In this sense he was the first, only begotten son of Jehovah. He was pre-existent but not eternal. He was not immortal (Hoekema, 271). In the second stage he came to earth as Jesus of Nazareth. He was born of the virgin Mary and was a sinless human being, but he was not incarnate God. Furthermore, "Christ was not a spiritual or spirit-begotten Son of God until his baptism" (Hoekema, 274). In the third stage, Christ was resurrected as a spirit and is in heaven as Jehovah's Son. "At the time of his resurrection Christ was given immortality as a reward for his faithful course on earth; he was, in fact, the first creature to receive this gift" (Hoekema, 275).

Christ's death, according to the Witnesses, was a human sacrifice, a ransom for sin, and thus provided redemption only from physical death. The Witnesses teach that there are two levels of salvation. The first of these is promised to the 144,000 (also called the little flock or the anointed class). These people believe and repent; they then dedicate their lives to serving God. Baptism by immersion is a symbol of this dedication. They are "justified" by God and receive his holy spirit. They are to preach faithfully about Jehovah and his kingdom, and if they do so until death, they will receive immortality and will rule in heaven with Christ. In essence, they must earn this reward.

The second level of salvation is available to the other sheep (sometimes referred to as the great crowd). These people also believe, serve God faithfully, and are baptized. Unlike the 144,000, they are to earn "justification" during the millennium.

It is necessary here to briefly consider the Jehovah's Witnesses' teachings about the millennium. The Witnesses believe that in 1918 Jesus began to rule over the kingdom of God and also began the process of judging the nations. The culmination of this activity will be the battle of Armageddon. The Witnesses stress the necessity of doing good works, particularly witnessing, during this time, for they believe that only they will survive the battle of Armageddon. After Armageddon, Jesus will establish the millennial kingdom; the earth will be transformed into a paradise. During this time, those who died before Armageddon will be raised. Some of these people (e.g., Old Testament heroes) will automatically live forever on the perfect earth. Others will be raised and will have the opportunity to accept the teachings about righteousness (i.e., the teachings of the Witnesses). Those who are disobedient or reject these teachings will be judged deserving of eternal death (annihilation). At the end of the thousand years, Satan will be loosed briefly and there will be a final test of one's loyalty. Satan and his followers will be annihilated. The righteous will live forever in the perfect earth; the 144,000 will rule with Jesus in heaven.

Jehovah's Witnesses believe that the Holy Spirit (in their usage, the holy spirit) is an impersonal force that works in the world. They deny that the Spirit is part of the Trinity.

The source of authority for Witnesses is ostensibly the Bible; the preferred version is the *New World Translation*. This version is supposed to be free from any doctrinal bias or presuppositions. However, scholars cite numerous passages in which the *New World Translation* imposes a specifically Jehovah's Witness viewpoint on the text. Also, the Bible is interpreted according to the teachings of the Watchtower Society. In study groups, attention is paid to the society's publications rather than the Bible. Witnesses are expected to believe precisely what is taught in these publications.

Mormons

Joseph Smith (1805–44), the founder of the Church of Jesus Christ of Latter-day Saints, was born in Vermont but spent much of his youth near Palmyra, New York, later described as part of the "burnt-over district." The term refers to the effects of revival meetings in which traveling evangelists, using vivid language, exhorted people to repent or face the prospect of an eternity spent in hell. Such meetings often resulted in emotional excesses.

Another influence on Smith was the proximity of several communes; the leaders of two of these claimed to be the reincarnated Christ (Schipper, 56–57). It is possible, even probable, that Smith had heard of these claims — they were part of the rather eccentric religious climate of the time.

Yet another factor was the folklore and speculation about the origins and practices of the North American Indians. Smith was fascinated by the subject; he spent a great deal of time exploring the burial mounds in the area and developed his own theories about them (Schipper, 58–60). This interest was reflected later in *The Book of Mormon*, which includes information about the supposed origins of the North American Indians.

A final factor that influenced Smith was the number and variety of churches, each claiming to be the one true church. As an adolescent Smith was baffled by these conflicting claims. He later explained that when he was fourteen, he prayed for guidance in resolving his dilemma. He recalled that he had a vision in which two "personages," God and Jesus Christ, appeared to him and told him that he was forbidden to join any of the "sects." They informed him that the churches and their message had been corrupted, but that Smith had been chosen to reveal true Christianity.

When he was about eighteen, Smith said, he received a visitation from the angel Moroni. Moroni, the son of Mormon, an early inhabitant of the North American continent, promised Smith that he would receive instructions for finding a set of golden plates and "spectacles" which would enable him to translate the hieroglyphics on the plates. These plates were to contain information about the North American Indians and the early history of the continent, and would also reveal a new gospel. Smith was also promised a revelation about the priesthood.

Smith went to the spot he had been directed to — the hill Cumorah near Palmyra — but he was unable to actually take the plates from the stone box that contained them. This inability, Moroni told him, sprang from his pride. Smith was to repent and purify himself before he would be allowed to take possession of the plates. He returned once a year thereafter; in 1827 Smith was able to take the plates. (There is some question about Smith's conduct during those four years; court records show that in that time he was found guilty of being a "disorderly person" and an "imposter.")

From that time on, Smith began to translate the plates, which he said were written in Reformed Egyptian. He dictated the text to a scribe. The completed work, *The Book of Mormon*, was published in 1830. After he finished translating the plates, Smith said, he gave them to the angel Moroni, who returned them to heaven.

At this point it is worthwhile to pause and examine some of the controversy that surrounded *The Book of Mormon*. Mormons claim that when Smith was translating the plates, his scribe took a copy of some of the characters and the translation to Charles Anthon, a professor of Greek and Latin, in New York City. They further state that Anthon vouched for the authenticity of the characters and the accuracy of the translation. Anthon, however, denied that claim.

The existence of the plates is supposed to be attested by eleven witnesses, and copies of their sworn statements are still included in each copy of *The Book of Mormon*. Some of these people later left the church; in any case, critics contend that their testimonies are questionable, as there were ties of both blood and marriage among the witnesses.

Other questions about the authenticity of *The Book of Mormon* revolve around the archaeological information in it and the inclusion of large sections of the King James Version of the Bible. Archaeologists have disputed the descriptions of early North American civilizations that are included in *The Book of Mormon*. And the use of material from the King James Version militates against the Mormons' claim that the original book dates from A.D. 400.

In 1830, Smith claimed that he and one of his converts were ordained in the Aaronic priesthood by John the Baptist. Later they were ordained in the Melchizedek priesthood by Peter, James, and John. At this time Smith was given the authority to establish the church. He was to be considered a prophet, and his teaching was the authoritative word of God.

Smith immediately attracted both converts and critics. Mormons were often ridiculed and persecuted; the group moved from New York State to Kirtland, Ohio, then to Missouri, and next to Nauvoo, Illinois. Here some of Smith's followers, disapproving of his practice of polygamy, left the Mormon church. They published a newspaper that criticized Smith and some of his practices (notably polygamy); Smith ordered some of his followers to destroy the printing press.

They did; the result was the arrest and jailing of Smith and his brother Hyrum. They were to be held for trial, but a mob stormed the jail and killed them. Thus the Mormons consider Smith a martyr.

After Smith's death, several groups broke away from the Mormon church. The most important of these is the Reorganized Church of Jesus Christ of Latter-day Saints, which is still led by a descendant of Smith. The original group, led by Brigham Young, eventually moved to what is now Utah.

Perhaps the most significant of the Mormon teachings about God is the concept that God is only one of many gods. He is considered the supreme God, who rules over a council of other gods (including Jesus Christ, some of the Old Testament prophets, and Joseph Smith [Burrell and Wright, 55]). Furthermore, they believe that God was once human; by a series of progressions or exaltations he became God. Related to this teaching is the idea that humans can become gods, for they all pre-existed as spirit-children of God. This is expressed in the maxim "As man is, God once was; as God is, man may become." An additional tenet is that God has a tangible body of flesh and bone.

Mormons do profess to believe in the Holy Spirit, and sometimes state that the Holy Spirit is the "third personage of the Godhead." However, they distinguish between the Holy Spirit and the Spirit of God (or of Christ). The Spirit of God enlightens every person when he or she is born. By contrast, the Holy Spirit functions only in baptized Mormons who have received the laying on of hands by a member of the priesthood. This laying on of hands is the means by which a Mormon receives the Holy Spirit (Burrell and Wright, 56–57).

According to Mormon teaching, Christ is a spirit-child of God; in fact, he is the first spirit-child and the "first-begotten" son of God. He is considered sinless. Like him, all humans are spirit-children of God. "The implications of this are very serious. Either Christ is a creature like us, or we are part of the Godhead like him. In both cases the essential uniqueness of Christ, as upheld in the Scriptures, disappears completely" (Burrell and Wright, 56).

Mormons do not accept the concept of original sin. They believe that men are punished for their own sins. The atonement of Christ, Mormons believe, freed man from physical death; it provides for the resurrection of all people. This is termed general salvation. However, man must earn what is called exaltation (or eternal life).

There are three levels of exaltation: celestial glory (reserved for the most devout Mormons), terrestrial glory (for less devout Mormons and devout Christians), and telestial glory (for those who are considered worthy of immortality but little else). These levels are sometimes referred to as the three kingdoms or heavens. The Mormons also teach that some people will not be saved, but that the majority of humans will be.

This teaching about salvation leads to an emphasis on the necessity of good works; one's degree of exaltation depends on one's acceptance of and adherence to Mormon doctrine and practices. Essential is baptism, for Mormons believe that baptism remits sin and is a way to exaltation. The Mormon practice of baptism for the dead is related also, for only those who have been baptized will have the opportunity to attain salvation.

Mormons recognize the Bible as the Word of God only "insofar as it is translated correctly." This stipulation is not made about their own scriptures and revelations. They further believe that the Bible is God's Word to the old world. The primary authorities for Mormons are *The Book of Mormon*, *Doctrine and Covenants* (formerly the *Book of Commandments*), and *The Pearl of Great Price*. Mormons also believe that the First President of their church is a prophet of God and receives new divine revelations. These revelations are accepted as the word of God.

Scientology

Scientology, based on the ideas and writings of L. Ron Hubbard (1911–1986), incorporates concepts from diverse sources.

Hubbard was born in Tilden, Nebraska. His father was a naval officer and thus his parents moved frequently, so Hubbard lived with his grandfather during his early years. As a youth he rejoined his parents, who lived in the Far East for a time. There Hubbard studied Asian religions. He claimed to have later learned from various shamans and medicine men. Also, he said that he had studied psychology, mysticism, and spiritualism. From these sources Hubbard distilled what he considered to be the ultimate truth. Some of the teachings of Scientology can be traced to one of Hubbard's early works, *Dianetics: The Modern Science of Mental Health* (1950).

Scientologists define dianetics as an anatomy of the mind,

whereas Scientology is a study of what "animates" the mind. Hubbard made a distinction between the analytical mind and the reactive mind. In Hubbard's terms, the analytical (or "optimum" or "unaberrated") mind is approximately equivalent to a computer. It is concerned with providing for the individual's survival; it is what distinguishes humans from animals. Hubbard also says that the analytical mind is one's basic personality and is in itself good. The reactive (or "stimulus-response") mind is that part of the mind in which are stored memories of painful events (engrams, in Hubbard's terminology). Evil — that is, irrational behavior — stems from the reactive mind when an incident or circumstance triggers an engram.

The other aspect of humans, what Hubbard termed the thetan, is man's "spirit or essential being." The thetan, Hubbard taught, cannot die; it is always reincarnated.

Hubbard postulated a series of eight dynamics (drives or impulses) and saw them not as a ladder up which one advances, but rather as a series of concentric circles across which one grows. In fact, Scientology is supposed to lead a person to total freedom. This is reflected in the group's terminology; those who have achieved total freedom are called "clears"; those who have not are "pre-clears."

As the first step to achieving total freedom, enquirers are encouraged to attend an auditor's course. The enquirer is seated before a device called an E-meter. He holds an electrode in either hand as an auditor asks a series of questions. The responses registered by the E-meter are supposed to indicate engrams in his reactive mind. As he is able to be released from these, he is able to proceed to the next level of courses and eventually to total freedom.

Scientology presumably is a religion (the group was registered in 1954 as the Church of Scientology of California), but its teachings do not focus on or mention the traditional doctrinal concepts that are basic to Christianity. Therefore, unlike the summaries of other groups' teachings, the summary of how Scientology differs from orthodox Christianity is primarily a comment on what Scientologists do not teach.

Scientology says almost nothing about God. Hubbard defined the eighth dynamic as "the urge towards survival as God or infinity" and expressed a personal belief in a Supreme Being. But Scientologists are not urged to think of God in specific ways or terms (e.g., that he is personal, eternal, etc.). Some Scientologists started with and retain a belief in God; others do not.

In a similar fashion, Hubbard recognized Jesus as a teacher, but said nothing about him as the Son of God or the Savior.

Nor does Scientology address the question of salvation. The group's creed does state that "man is basically good," that "he is seeking to survive," that "his survival depends upon himself and his fellows, and his attainment of brotherhood with the Universe," and that "the spirit can be saved and that the spirit alone may save or heal the body" (quoted in Burrell, 141).

Scientologists consider the Bible to be a holy book but not the authoritative Scripture. They would give the same credence to the Quran or other scriptures. As has already been pointed out, Hubbard drew on varied sources for his ideas, and those ideas are the basis for the tenets of Scientology.

Unification Church

Yong Myung Moon was born in 1920 to a Presbyterian family in what is now North Korea. Information about Moon's early years, especially, is scanty, but it is known that he attended high school in Seoul; later he studied electrical engineering at Waseda University in Tokyo. He returned to Korea when he was twenty-four. He then became a businessman.

What is more significant is that at the age of sixteen, Moon later claimed, Jesus gave him a revelation: he would complete the work that Jesus had started. For the next several years, he prayed, meditated, and read and studied the Bible. When he was twenty-six, Moon studied under Park Moon Kim, who claimed to be a new messiah. At this time Moon changed his name to Sun Myung Moon. He seemed to consider Kim his forerunner and himself the new messiah. It was also at this time that he founded the Broad Sea Church. "He seems to have been closely associated with an extreme branch of Pentecostalism which believed that Korea was to be the site of the New Jerusalem and the birthplace of a new Messiah" (Burrell, 54). In 1948 the Presbyterian church excommunicated him for his unusual views.

It is difficult to account for Moon's activities during the next six years. It is known that the Communists imprisoned him for a time.

There are indications that he was later jailed for draft-dodging and "immorality."

What is clear is that Moon founded the Unification Church in 1954. His first marriage also ended that year. In 1957 the *Divine Principle*, an exposition of the movement's teaching, was first published. A book of Moon's speeches, *Master Speaks*, has also been published.

In 1960 Moon married his current wife (there is a question whether she is his second or fourth wife). Moon's followers refer to them as "Father" and "Mother" and the "True Parents."

Moon moved to New York in 1972. His rather opulent lifestyle has drawn criticism. At one point he was convicted on charges of tax evasion and served time in prison.

Moon proclaims that the 1980s are the time when the new messiah will be revealed.

Moon's teachings about the nature of God are sketchy. He does recognize that God is a Creator, but also teaches that Satan thwarted God's plans. Moon further defines God as Father and the Holy Spirit as Mother. He does not teach that Jesus is the Son.

To understand Moon's ideas about Christ and his work, it is necessary first to briefly consider his views about sin and the fall. Moon teaches that Adam and Eve were to have been the True (i.e., perfect) Parents who started a perfect family on earth. Instead, Satan seduced Eve and had intercourse with her; this resulted in man's spiritual fall. The physical fall occurred when Eve had intercourse with Adam.

According to Moon, Jesus was a perfect, obedient man with God incarnate in him, but he is not God. He is also seen as the second Adam. Jesus' crucifixion accomplished the spiritual salvation of mankind. Physical salvation would have resulted if Jesus had found a perfect mate and fathered God's family, but he died before he could do this. He did not rise from the dead, Moon says; his appearances after his death were those of a spirit being.

Physical salvation, then, will be attained by the Lord of the Second Advent (the Messiah). Moon's writings are unclear on this point — at some places he implies this will be Jesus Christ. However, *Divine Principle* indicates that the Lord of the Second Advent will be a man of flesh who is born on earth, in the East — in short, Moon. The designations *Father*, *Mother*, and *True Parents* that are applied to Moon and his wife would also seem to indicate this. His followers believe that he is the new messiah. Physical salvation, then, comes by becoming a member of his "family."

In Moon's theology, the Bible is considered to be obscure in places and thus needs interpretation. This is supplied by *Divine Principle*, considered the authoritative source of interpretation.

The Way International

The Way International, which calls itself a Bible research organization rather than a church, was established in the 1950s by Victor Paul Wierwille (b. 1917). Wierwille was reared as a strict fundamentalist and went on to become an ordained minister in the Evangelical and Reformed Church. After several years in the ministry, he was plagued by doubts and confusion. He prayed about this; later he claimed that God spoke to him, telling him that he would be given the true meaning of the Bible, on the condition that he must then teach others about this new meaning. At first Wierwille said nothing about this experience.

When Wierwille was in his early thirties, he destroyed his theological reference books. He began to study the Bible only and formed his own interpretation of it. This interpretation was the basis for his series of lectures, called Power for Abundant Living (PFAL), which he first taught in 1953. (The lectures have been videotaped; the series is thirty-six hours long and is shown to prospective members of The Way in three-hour sessions.) In the late 1950s Wierwille resigned his pastorate so he could spend all of his time lecturing about PFAL.

Wierwille does teach that God is eternal, personal, a Spirit, and the Creator. However, he maintains that only the Father is eternal God; the Holy Spirit is also God, but is not a distinct person. Christians do not receive the Holy Spirit (i.e., a distinct person); they receive a human holy spirit.

Furthermore, Wierwille distinguishes God and the Word (or Idea) of God. Only God, he teaches, is eternal; the Word of God is not, although it existed in the mind of God prior to creation. After creation the Word was given orally (e.g., to the patriarchs) and later in writing (the Old Testament). The Word was enfleshed in Jesus of Nazareth, who was an expression of the Word (although Jesus was independent of God and was not God). After the resurrection, the

Word was given by God living in the believer, and is given to the believer who is baptized by the Holy Spirit.

Wierwille says that God exists to please and help members of The Way.

In a similar fashion, Wierwille holds to some orthodox teachings about Jesus: his death, resurrection, ascension, and second advent. Jesus is the son of God, Wierwille says, but he was not and is not God the Son. Jesus was not pre-existent; he was only the Word (or Idea) of God. The Word was implanted in Jesus; by virtue of his miraculous birth he was a sinless human being. As such, he cannot be worshiped. His obedience was the basis for his becoming the son of God.

Because Jesus was not divine, he needed to receive power to work miracles and become Savior; thus, at his baptism he received a human holy spirit. His authority came from his baptism, not because he was God. After his ascension, he gave the gift of a human holy spirit to the disciples. Therefore they were able to do the things he did.

In view of Wierwille's teaching about the person of Christ, it is not surprising that little attention is given to the importance of Christ's work.

Wierwille maintains that as a result of the fall, humans lost the image of God and their spiritual dimension. Therefore, all people are merely flesh unless and until they receive a human holy spirit. This they do by believing in Christ. Only then are they made of both flesh and spirit.

Receiving a human holy spirit is equivalent to what happened to Jesus at his baptism. The sign of receiving this spirit is the ability to speak in tongues. Also, receiving the spirit gives a person power to do the same works that Jesus did. The ability to do these things depends on the extent to which a person practices speaking in tongues. Moreover, Wierwille holds that when persons receive a human holy spirit, they become sinless and can do anything they want.

Wierwille considers that Pentecost is the most important event in the history of the church, and that most of the Bible, especially those sections that are pre-Pentecost, are basically irrelevant for today. The only pertinent portions of Scripture are the epistles of Paul and, to some extent, Acts. Members of The Way believe that

Wierwille's insights and interpretations are necessary for correctly understanding the Bible. In essence he is a second source of authority.

Worldwide Church of God

Herbert W. Armstrong (1892–1986) had been reared in a Protestant family, but for many years his faith was more intellectual than active. As a young man, he was preoccupied with his business, a successful advertising agency in Iowa. However, in the 1920s his business failed (through no fault of his) and this provided impetus to become more interested and involved in religion.

About this time, Armstrong's wife had been influenced by a Seventh-day Adventist neighbor, who emphasized the importance of obedience to the Ten Commandments and a turning from sin as prerequisites for salvation. At first Armstrong angrily rejected these ideas. He was so perturbed that, in order to refute these teachings, he began his own study of the Bible. But his study instead convinced him that these concepts were correct.

In 1931 Armstrong was ordained as a minister in the Church of God. He disagreed with his colleagues, however, and in 1934 made the first broadcast of his own teachings. He also began to publish a magazine (*The Plain Truth*) to expound his views. This eventually led to the formation of the Worldwide Church of God. The headquarters for its activities is Ambassador College in Pasadena, California. The organization sponsors a television broadcast.

Armstrong rejected the idea of God as Triune. He also believed that the concept of the Holy Spirit as a person of the Trinity was a pagan one. Instead, he taught that the Hebrew word *Elohim* (usually translated "God") is a plural and should be translated "family of God." The Father and the Son are the first two persons in the Godhead, but the Godhead is not limited to only two persons. Rather, Armstrong said, at the resurrection believers will become part of God.

Christ, according to Armstrong, is divine and eternal. However, he tended to emphasize Christ's human nature, coming close to saying that he was merely a perfect human being. Furthermore, he wrote that Christ's death only paid the penalty of sin. And he taught that the resurrection body was not human; instead, Christ was "converted into immortality."

When he wrote about salvation, Armstrong made a distinction between being "begotten of God" and being "born of God." According to Armstrong, one is begotten of God upon conversion. One is born of God when he receives immortality. Being born of God depends on whether one obeys the laws of God as they are summarized in the Ten Commandments.

The Worldwide Church of God claims to accept the Bible as its source of authority, although some of Armstrong's ideas do not coincide with the orthodox interpretations.

Ministry to a Member of a Cult or Another Religion

In your contacts with those who are adherents of a cult or another religion, a few points are basic.

One of these, perhaps too obvious to be mentioned, is to be courteous and controlled. It is helpful to listen carefully and to clarify the terms and definitions that you and the other person are using. This promotes effective communication.

It is also important to show "genuine love" and "humility" (Hoekema, 412–13). We need to know as well what "lessons we can learn" from those with whom we are talking and "know the teachings" of the group (ibid., 413).

Vital to this ministry is a thorough, correct understanding of what the other person believes; the prerequisite to this is a thorough understanding of what you believe. To understand what another person believes, you need to study the teachings of his group. The publications of the group will help you. You will also want to read books or articles by Christian authors who analyze these teachings. (One note: The summaries in this appendix are necessarily short; there are nuances to each group's teachings that can best be explored through intensive personal study.) At all points it is useful to ask yourself what you believe and what Scripture passages you base your beliefs on.

Perhaps the most effective witness you can offer is your personal testimony about your faith.

Specific instructions for dealing with the members of cults are found in Hoekema, chapter 7; Burrell, pages 157–60; and Burrell and Wright, pages 38, 61–62.

A Note About Sources

World Religions

Basic information about world religions can be found in Earl Schipper's *Religions of the World* (Grand Rapids: Baker, 1982). For additional perspectives — including information about religions or traditions not surveyed in this appendix — consult C. George Fry, James R. King, Eugene R. Swanger, and Herbert C. Wolf, *Great Asian Religions* (Grand Rapids: Baker, 1984). These two sources are particularly helpful in clarifying aspects of the Hindu and Buddhist traditions. Other sources are Maurice C. Burrell, *The Challenge of the Cults* (Leicester: InterVarsity; Grand Rapids: Baker, 1982; on the Hare Krishna movement and Transcendental Meditation); R. M. Enroth, "Transcendental Meditation," *Evangelical Dictionary of Theology*, edited by Walter A. Elwell (Grand Rapids: Baker, 1984); Roderick Marshall, "Hinduism," *Encyclopedia Americana* (1970); Clarence H. Hamilton, "Buddha and Buddhism," *Collier's Encyclopedia* (1964); and E. Dale Saunders, "Buddha and Buddhism," *Encyclopedia Americana* (1970).

C. George Fry and James R. King provide in-depth information in *Islam: A Survey of the Muslim Faith*, rev. ed. (Grand Rapids: Baker, 1980). This work offers insights into aspects of Islam that could not be surveyed here; it also has "models for contact" between Christianity and Islam (chap. 9). The bibliography gives suggestions for further reading. Another perspective can be found in the books of Phil Parshall: *New Paths in Muslim Evangelism* (Grand Rapids: Baker, 1980), *Bridges to Islam* (Baker, 1983), and *Beyond the Mosque* (Baker, 1985). For more than twenty years Parshall was a missionary to Muslims, and although his books deal with evangelism specifically in Muslim countries, his experience and perspectives may prove useful for personal ministry. *Bridges to Islam* concentrates on Sufism, to the benefit of those who want more information about that aspect of Islam. A minor source for the section about Islam is Charles J. Adams, "Islam," *Encyclopedia Americana* (1970).

In addition to Schipper, sources for the section about Judaism are Salo Wittmayer Baron (an overview of Judaism), Jacob S. Minkin (Hasidism), Abraham G. Duker (on the "ethnic status" of Jews), and Ira Eisenstein (traditions and customs) in "Jewish History and Society," *Encyclopedia Americana* (1970). Also helpful are the comments of M. S. Isaacs (on Judaism) and I. M. Wise (on Reform Judaism) in the *Cyclopedia of Biblical, Theological, and Ecclesiastical Literature*, edited by John McClintock and James Strong (1867–87; reprint ed., Grand Rapids: Baker, 1981), and R. K. Harrison, "Judaism," *Zondervan Pictorial Encyclopedia of the Bible*, edited by Merrill C. Tenney (Grand Rapids: Zondervan, 1975). For those whose tastes run to fiction, Chaim Potok's *The Chosen* (1967; New York: Fawcett, 1978) offers insights into Orthodox and Hasidic beliefs and practices.

Modern Cults

For a detailed exposition of the teachings of Christian Scientists, Jehovah's Witnesses, Mormons, and Seventh-day Adventists, Anthony A. Hoekema's *Four Major Cults* is an outstanding source. The book also includes an extensive bibliography.

Other helpful works are Maurice C. Burrell, *The Challenge of the Cults* (Leicester: InterVarsity; Grand Rapids: Baker, 1982); Maurice C. Burrell and J. Stafford Wright, *Today's Sects*, 2d ed. (reprint; Grand Rapids: Baker, 1984); Walter A. Elwell, ed., *Evangelical Dictionary of Theology* (Grand Rapids: Baker, 1984); and Earl Schipper, *Cults in North America* (Grand Rapids: Baker, 1982). The author is particularly indebted to Schipper for information about The Way International and to Burrell for information about Scientology and the Worldwide Church of God.